PAPERS RELATING TO THE

ABORIGINAL TRIBES OF THE CENTRAL PROVINCES

PAPERS RELATING TO THE

ABORIGINAL TRIBES OF THE CENTRAL PROVINCES

BY THE LATE REVD. STEPHEN HISLOP,

MISSIONARY OF THE FREE CHURCH OF SCOTLAND

AT NAGPORE

EDITED,

WITH NOTES AND PREFACE,

R. TEMPLE, C.S.I.

GYAN

Published by

Gyan Publishing House
5, Ansari Road
Daryaganj, New Delhi-110002
Phone: 011-47034999, 9811692060
E-mail: books@gyanbooks.com

Distribution Network
gyanbooks.com
India, USA, Canada, UK, Australia, France

ISBN : 978-81-212-9470-6 (PB)
First Published, 1866

2nd Impression 2023

Printed at: Gyan Press, Delhi.

PAPERS RELATING TO THE ABORIGINAL TRIBES OF THE CENTRAL PROVINCES
Author: Revd. Stephen Hislop, Editor: R.Temple

PAPERS RELATING TO THE

ABORIGINAL TRIBES OF THE CENTRAL PROVINCES,

LEFT IN MSS

BY THE LATE REVD. STEPHEN HISLOP,

MISSIONARY OF THE FREE CHURCH OF SCOTLAND

AT NAGPORE:

EDITED,

WITH NOTES AND PREFACE,

BY

R. TEMPLE, C.S.I.,

CHIEF COMMISSIONER OF THE CENTRAL PROVINCES.

1866.

INDEX.

PREFACE.

PART I.—Essay by Mr. Hislop; with note by Editor.

PART II.—Vocabulary by Mr. Hislop; with note by Editor.
Supplement to the Vocabulary as respects the Gondi dialect only; with note by Editor.
Comparative Vocabulary of the Muási or Kuri dialect; with note by Editor.

PART III.—Songs:
Note and Abstract English version by the Editor.
The Songs reduced to writing with English equivalents by Mr. Hislop and examined or supplemented by Mr. Pandurang.

PART IV.—Appendices, consisting of miscellaneous memoranda; with note by the Editor.

PREFACE.

It is but too well known to all persons interested in the Nagpore Country that the Rev. Stephen Hislop, Missionary of the Free Church of Scotland at Nagpore,—a gentleman distinguished for all the virtues and qualities becoming his sacred profession, and for attainments in scholarship and in practical science,—died by accidental drowning on the 4th September 1863. During nineteen years of labour in the service of the Mission, he had diligently and perseveringly enquired, not only into the physical resources of the country, but also into the languages, the manners, the religions, the histories, and the antiquities of the people. In the pursuit of these enquiries, he investigated much regarding the aboriginal tribes inhabiting the territories now known as the Central Provinces, and especially regarding the Gond people. The results of this investigation were embodied in several elaborate papers, which were intended for publication ultimately in a complete form, but which were inevitably left scattered and incomplete at the time of his sudden and lamented death.

It was naturally considered by the late Mr. Hislop's relations and friends, that these valuable and important papers should not be lost to the public, but should be examined, collated, and prepared for publication, in a manner which (though falling far short of what the author himself would have produced had he lived) might yet present the work in a sufficiently intelligible shape. At first there was hope that some gentlemen possessing more or less of literary leisure might be found to fulfil the task of editing these papers. But it is difficult to secure such assistance in these Provinces. And at length, at the request of Mr. Hislop's friends, I undertook to have the papers brought out under my own supervision and direction. The work is now done, imperfectly no doubt, but as well as time and means permitted; and if not actually good, it is perhaps better than nothing at all.

Mr. Hislop had considerable opportunities and facilities for obtaining reliable and detailed information regarding, what are commonly called, the aboriginal tribes of this part of India. In the cold season of each year, he made tours by marching in the interior of the districts, and thus saw much of, and heard much from, the pepole in their homes, their villages, their fields and their forests. He was generally accompanied by educated natives connected with the Mission, who helped him in securing full and correct answers to all queries. These were native catechists and preachers, either stationed in, or moving about, the country— and especially in Chindwara, the heart of the Gond region,—who recorded and transmitted facts to him. He was acquainted with various European officers and gentlemen who resided among, or otherwise came in contact with, these tribes, and who supplied him with information. He made use of all these several advantages with patience, assiduity, and research. He tested and verified the information thus accumulated, by extensive study of the works of other authors on the aboriginal races of India and of other countries.

These tribes will, from their numbers, their position, and their antecedents, be found worthy of the erudition and study which Mr. Hislop bestowed on all that belonged to them.

Though much imbued with Hinduism, they are yet quite distinct in race and language from the Hindus. Again, they are not all of one tribe, perhaps not even of one nationality, for some of their dialects differ altogether from others. By themselves, in the aggregate, they form an important section of the population. They are spread, thinly perhaps, but broadly, all over the large territories now known as the Central Provinces— from our extreme limits in one direction to our furthest frontier in another; from Bundlecund in the north to the Teloogoo coast districts in the south; from Malwa and Candeish in the west to the confines of Orissa in the east; and right through the very centre of the country, among the Vindhya Mountains which overlook the valley of the Nerbudda and the Sautpoora Ranges which bound the plains of Nagpore and the cotton-fields of the Wurda.

Among these tribes one, namely the Gonds, have formed political annals of their own, have wielded dynastic power in most parts of these Provinces, and have left architectural remains in attestation of former greatness. On this subject it may be well to transcribe some brief passages from my first Administration Report (for the year 1862):—

"The earliest dynasties in this part of India of which anything is now either recorded or remembered are those of the Gond-Rajpoots. But prior to these, and superior to them in civilization, there must have been several Hindu dynasties, which are only now known by architectural remains: some at

Jubbulpore on the banks of the Nerbudda; some in the hilly part of Chutteesgurh; and some at Bustar in the heart of the wilderness.

" The ancient Gondwána, or country of the Gonds, comprises most of the countries now included in the Central Provinces, both below and above the Sautpoora Range. The earliest settlers in the woods and hills and the oldest dynasties were Gond. The Gonds seem, without doubt, to have been one of the most powerful and important of the aboriginal races of India. Existing prior to the advent of the Hindus, they possessed their own forms of heathenism, which often are preserved entire and intact to this day, and which have always, and under all changes, impressed their mark on the character of the tribe. But some Gonds, while retaining their external and distinctive characteristics, adopted the Hindu, and some few the Mahomedan, religion. Thus there are seen in the present age, as respects faith and custom, three kinds of Gonds, namely the aboriginal Gonds, the Hindu Gonds, and the few Mussulman Gonds. In physique and morale all three seem much alike. The Hindu conquerors of the Gonds were principally Rajpoots. These intermarried with the conquered, and their descendents are called Rajpoots, and pride themselves on their descent. Most of the indigenous Rajpoots so called are really Gond Rajpoots. These mixed races, becoming acclimatised to countries that would have proved deadly to many civilized nations, spread themselves over wide domains, and in arms and policy emulated the achievements of superior tribes. Their original boundary in the south may perhaps have been the Godavery If it was, they must have crossed that river, and extended far into the Dakhan.

" They formed from first to last four kingdoms within the present limits of these provinces. The northern kingdom had its capital at Mundla, and at Gurra (near the modern city of Jubbulpore) and dominated the greater part of the Nerbudda Valley. Of the two midland kingdoms, one had its capital at Deogurh on the southern face or slopes of the Sautpoora Range, over-looking and commanding the plains which now belong to Nagpore. Deogurh is now ruined and utterly desolate; but it was a city before Nagpore was even a village. The other midland kingdom has its capital at Kherla, a hill commanding the rich valley of Baitool, in the heart of the Sautpoora Hills. To this also belonged the celebrated forts of Gawilgurh and Nurnalla, both in the same range. The southern kingdom had its capital at Chanda on the Wurda, and comprised a vast, but wild, territory: it streached far up to to the north-east, and again, commanding the Godavery, stretched far down to the south. These four dynasties existed at least some time before the formation of the Moghul Empire. They were brave and independent, but they could never have been rich or powerful. Still, each of them must have possessed an annual revenue of some lakhs of rupees. They were quite inferior in art and civilization to the Hindu and Mahomedan dynasties known in other parts of India; but still they each left architectural remains and monuments of great interest; at Mundla, at Gurra near Jubbulpore, at Chouragurh near Nursingpore, at Deogurh near Chindwara, at Kherla near Baitool, and at Chanda. These ruins, surrounded by, or adjacent to, the waste, or the rocks, or the forest, fill the modern enquirer with surprise, and attest the former energies of half-civilized races contending with the wildness of Nature. As the Mahomedan rule absorbed the different parts of Central India, it attacked these Gond Kingdoms in turn. The northern kingdom, however, in some struggles well known to local tradition, maintained something of its independence, though it may have lost many of its richer provinces. The southern kingdom also does not appear to have been entirely subdued, though it was rendered tributary; but its branches across the Godavery were carried away and added to the Mahomedan kingdoms in the Dakhan. That dominion indeed spread over both banks of the Godavery; and up to a recent period the strip of territory on the left, or Nagpore side of the river, belonged to the Nizam. The midland kingdom was at all events rendered tributary, and its Princes were, by force or influence, converted to Islam.

"Besides these four kingdoms there was a Gond Rajpoot dynasty at Wurungal in the Dakhan. When that place fell to the Mahomedan, the Raja fled northward across the Godavery, and established himself in wild independence among the inaccessible forests."

But besides forts, palaces, and tombs, they have in some parts of the country left traces of works wisely designed for material improvement. On this point, it may be proper to insert the following passages from my official report on the river Wynguriga :—

"This tract, as already seen, lies between a low range of hills and a river, having an average breadth of thirty miles. Though partly champaign, it is yet much broken up and diversified by hills and jungles. Advantage has been taken of the undulations in the ground and the streams permeating it, to construct a regular tank system. These are not so large as the lakes mentioned in the upper basin of the Wyngunga; but are second to them alone. This tract belonged to the Gond dynasty of Chanda, who, probably established at a later period, were comparatively more civilized; and these have left behind them a noble mark on the land. In 1865, after visiting these tanks, I caused a letter to be written to the local authorities, which, as it conveyed impressions on the spot, may furnish a few extracts to make up the description, as follows:—

'The number and size of these tanks is certainly remarkable. In some parts they even cluster thick round the feet of the hills. From the summit of the hill, called "Pêrzagurh" by the Gonds, and "The Seven Sisters" by the Hindus, no less than thirty-seven tanks were counted as distinctly visible.

'These tanks are indeed the pride and ornament of the district. They are, as the people themselves told the Chief Commissioner, the very life of the place. They are the object to which much of the industry and capital of the people are devoted; and are the main source of agricultural wealth. The two staples are rice and sugarcane—and both are entirely dependent on the water supply for irrigation from the tanks. Not only have large, indeed sometimes very extensive, sheets of water been formed by damming up streams by heavy earthwork dykes, but masonry escapes and sluices and channels have been constructed. Some of the sluices, as head works for irrigation channels, present an almost elaborate apparatus, creditable to the skill and ingenuity of the people.

'With many, perhaps with most, of the largest tanks, the works were in good, even capital repair.' "

Thus it is that some knowledge of these tribes must be useful, indeed almost essential, to the various Officers engaged in the Civil Administration of these Provinces.

Though these people have in bygone ages lorded it over the plains cultivated with regular husbandry, they live in recent times, for the most part, in the hilly and wooded tracts. These are the tracts which yield those vast supplies of timber wood and fuel; those extensive seams of coal; those iron ores; those mineral riches; that lac dye, and many other jungle products, which constitute in the mass so large a part of the resources of these Provinces. In all efforts that are being, or may yet be made to utilize these resources, an acquaintance with the people who dwell in these often desolate and inaccessible tracts, is really requisite.

It behoves especially those who are employed in the conservation and management of the forests—a department of fast-growing importance—to learn all about the hill tribes whose co-operation is necessary to departmental success, and over whom influence can be won only by conciliation. Regarding the important position occupied by these people in the hill districts, the following pssage may be extracted from my second Administration Report, for 1863:—

"One great cause of wastage and destruction of the forests is what is called "Dhya" cultivation. This "Dhya" cultivation is practically a substitute for ploughing, and a device for saving the trouble of that operation. It is resorted to by hill people, who are averse to labor, and have little or no agricultural capital. The method is in this wise: A piece of ground on a moderate slope is selected, clothed with trees, brushwood, and grass; the trees are cut down in November, the brushwood and grass are set fire to in May, the charred ground is left covered with ashes; in the beginning of June quantities of seed are placed at the upper end of the slope; the rains descending wash the seed over and into the prepared ground; no ploughing or any other operation is resorted to. There springs up a plentiful crop, which has to be watched all day and night, till it is cut. If not so watched, it would be eaten up by wild animals. In this manner all the pulses are raised. Besides this culture, there will be a few fields around the homesteads, regularly ploughed, and growing superior products. The pulses, however, form the staple food of the hill people in four districts,* and in many parts of districts adjacent to them. The population dependent mainly on Dhya cultivation may be a million or more. Unfortunately the best ground for this peculiar cultivation is precisely that where the finest timber trees like to grow. It may be hoped that by degrees these hill people will learn a better mode of cultivation. But to prohibit the Dhya cultivation, would be to drive this widely-scattered population to despair. Though rude and ignorant, they are not destitute of spirit and endurance. They have clans and Chiefs; they are always predatory; and they have on occasions shown themselves capable of armed resistance. If by a prohibition of their favorite culture they were reduced to any distress, they would resort to plunder, and especially to cattle-stealing. And it is to be remembered that the great pasturage whither the cattle from the plain districts resort, is situated in their country. And if they were not in the country, the last state of the forests would be worse than the first. For then the traces of human habitation, settlement, and clearance, would disappear. The foresters and the woodmen could no longer live in, or even enter into, the wilderness, rank and malarious with uncleared jungle, and overrun with wild beasts. These animals are already so destructive as to constitute a real difficulty. The only check upon their becoming masters of the forests is the presence of the hill tribes."

*Mundla.
Seonee.
Chindwara.
Baitool.

There is much in the character of these tribes to attract

British sympathies. They are honest and truth-telling; they are simple-minded; though superstitious, they are yet free from fanaticism; they have great physical endurance. Their courage is remarkable: the instance is freshly remembered in the Chindwara District, where an English officer was saved from instant death in the grip of a panther by the bravery of a Gond hunter: and still more recently, a wounded officer on the Godavery was rescued from the wild beasts by his native hunter.

In former days, the bane of all these tribes has been the drinking of ardent spirits, and even wilful and deliberate drunkenness. But of late years radical changes in the management of the excise have removed many temptations from their way. And it is the concurrent testimony of all persons, European and Native, most competent to judge, that a marked reform in the habits of these people has been setting in of late.

While a knowledge of these aboriginal tribes is thus seen to subserve so many practical uses, it will not be without its scientific and ethnological value. For it is the opinion of the best informed persons, that in their languages and religions, these people have much in common with the wild races of other parts, both of the Indian peninsula and of the Asiatic continent; and that numerous points of interesting comparison suggest themselves.

Such, then, very briefly, are the tribes for the elucidation of whose character Mr. Hislop devoted so much of his heavily-taxed time and thought. From the inevitably incomplete and fragmentary papers which he left, those which follow have been selected for publication in the order as below:—

I. Essay.
II. Vocabulary.
III. Songs and descriptive *precis*.
IV. Appendixes, consisting of miscellaneous memoranda.

To each paper have been appended such notes or other explanation as seemed to be required.

The words in the Gondi, the Muâsi, and other dialects, are written in the Roman character; all these languages being destitute of any written character of their own. But it is supposed by some well able to judge, that the Oriental Devanâgri character would afford much better means of conveying the sounds of the words of these dialects as really pronounced by the people. This point may deserve consideration, as a mission to the Gonds has recently been commenced by the Free Church of Scotland at Chindwara; and as hereafter schools for secular instruction in Gondi may be established there.

Though the preparation of these papers may be imperfect, still the labour of several gentlemen has been given to it, whose assistance I have pleasure in acknowledging. They are, Mr. G. Barclay (Superintendent of the Chief Commissioner's Office), the Rev. Mr. Baba Pandurang (of the Free Church of Scotland Mission), and Syud Noor (the Meer Moonshee of the Secretariat).

And though this work must necessarily be altogether inferior to what it would have been had it been completed and brought out by its author himself, yet the publishing of it, even in this broken shape, seems desirable, in justice to the subject, and from regard to Mr. Hislop's memory,—a memory which is revered and beloved by all who knew him; is respected by all scientific persons interested in the practical advancement of these Provinces; and is cherished by the natives, for whose moral and lasting welfare he laboured so long.

NAGPORE:
31*st October* 1866.

R. TEMPLE.

PART I.—ESSAY.

Note by the Editor.

THIS Essay, by Mr. Hislop, on the aboriginal tribes of the Central Provinces was not left by its author in exactly the shape in which it is now presented. It appears from the autograph manuscript that he first composed an Essay on the aboriginal tribes of the Nagpore country before the incorporation of that territory in the present Central Provinces. Afterwards he enlarged his design so as to embrace the whole of these Provinces; and he obtained more specific information regarding the subdivisions of the Gond tribe in particular. This induced him to amplify that portion of the essay which related to the Gonds, and to include among the Gonds proper two tribes (the Mádias and the Kolâms), which he had reckoned among the other aborigines. For these, or for some such reasons, he began to rewrite his essay. But at the time of his death, he had proceeded only so far as the specification of ten out of the twelve sub-divisions of the Gonds. Thus there are two manuscripts—the first, being the original, carried to its conclusion; the second, being the rewritten, or revised essay, carried only a short way into the subject.

It seemed, therefore, desirable, even necessary, to make up one new essay out of these two manuscripts; following the rewritten essay, so far as it goes, and taking the rest from the originaly-prepared manuscript. On examination of the papers, I have found that this adaptation is quite feasible, and is the best means of carrying out the intention of the author, to the utmost that is now possible. Thus, although the essay which follows has something of compilation and re-arrangement, yet it contains nothing that is not to be found in one or other of Mr. Hislop's two manuscripts above described; and it comprises everything essential that is to be gathered from them.

To the essay, as now published, are appended as foot notes various annotations taken from Mr. Hislop's manuscript. Some hesitation was felt in ordering the publication of these notes, for they were incomplete at the time of the author's death; it was often very difficult to decypher them; and sometimes they contain references to authorities not now obtainable at Nagpore, and, therefore, are not always capable of being verified. But so far as verification has been practicable, it has been made. And though the notes are not by any means what they would have been had they been finished, still they have been put into a readable shape: and, even with their unavoidable imperfections, they may be useful, and may, at least, give some idea of Mr. Hislop's minute and extensive research.

R. T.

ESSAY on the Hill Tribes of the Central Provinces.

BESIDES the general population of the Central Provinces, consisting of a great preponderance of Hindus and a small minority of Mahomedans, there are various tribes residing in the hilly and jungly districts, of whom comparatively little is known. Though among these there are diversities of dialect, and in one instance a complete difference in language, yet there are some features which are possessed by all in common.

Physical appearance.—All are a little below the average size of Europeans, and in complexion darker than the generality of Hindus. Their bodies are well proportioned, but their features are rather ugly. They have a roundish head, distended nostrils, wide mouth, thickish lips, straight black hair, and scanty beard and moustache. It has been supposed that some of the aborigines of Central India have woolly hair; but this is a mistake. Among the thousands that I have seen I have not found one with hair like a Negro. A few indeed have curly locks, as a few Britons have: but I have not met with one inhabitant of the forest who exhibited any marked resemblance to the African race. On the contrary, both their hair and their features are decidedly Mangolian.

Dress.—All are scantily attired; but what they want in clothing they make up for by the abundance of their ornaments and beads, of which they are passionately fond.

Character.—All are endowed with an average share of intelligence and a more than ordinary degree of observation. Shy in their intercourse with strangers, they are not wanting in courage, when there is an understood object to call it forth. Truthful in their statements, faithful to their promises, and observant of the rights of property among themselves, they nevertheless do not scruple to plunder those to whom they are under no obligation to fidelity. But the great blot on their moral character is their habitual intemperance. Besides their daily potations, a large quantity of liquor is an essential element in their religous rites. No festival can be held in the forest or village in honour of their deities; no birth, marriage, or death can take place in their families, without an excessive indulgence in ardent spirits. Their acts of worship invariably end in intoxication.

Literature.—Among none of our jungle tribes can the slightest approach to learning be said to exist. All are destitute of any written character of their own; and, with the exception of a very few individuals who have come in contact with Hindus, they are entirely uneducated in any other language.

Tillage.—The system of cultivation, which all prefer, is migratory, like that of the ancient Germans, and many forest tribes in Asia at the present day. Here it is called Dáhi or Dáhyá, and is essentially the same with the practice of the Torus, of the Terai, of the hill Cacháris, the Bodos, the Mikirs, the Kukis, the Rajmahalis, the Kôls, &c. On the Western Ghats, near Sattara, it is known as Dale or Kumari, and in the mountainous districts of Burmah it goes by the name of Toungya. In the hot weather they select some spot on a plateau or declivity of a hill, on which they cut down the brushwood and lop off the boughs of the larger trees, and place them in layers to dry. Before the beginning of the rains in June they set the whole on fire, and spread the ashes over the cleared space. On these, after they have been slightly mingled with the soil by the first showers, they scatter a variety of inferior grains, chiefly millet, along with one or two species of cucurbitaceæ. In sowing the castor-oil plant, and different kinds of pulse, they use a tool in some places somewhat resembling a hoe. The crops are not very productive the first season; but the following year, without any further sowing, they are more abundant. The third year the land is comparatively unremunerative, yielding little but grass; but the houses that had been erected at the place are still allowed to stand there until the cultivators have burnt down the jungle on another spot, when they remove thither with their families and property. They do not return to an old piece of ground till after the lapse of about 12 years, when they find it again covered with jungle, and requiring the same process of burning and cultivation as before. This rude system of farming is doubtless unfavourable to the growth of valuable timber. It is only on superior soil that Teak thrives, and, of course, these are the very soils chosen for Dáhi tillage. As a necessary consequence, Teak falls a sacrifice. This tree, as Captain F. G. Stuart, late Superintendent of Nagpore Forests, suggests, yields a large amount of ash, and our jungle cultivators are specially anxious to secure it for manuring their temporary fields; or, as they themselves allege, its large, broad leaves, catching and retaining the rain, cause a heavy drip, which washes out the grain—and hence they rest not till it is either cut down or deprived of its crown and branches. From such motives many parts of the country have been stripped of the finest forest trees, and in their place has sprung up nothing but a worthless scrub.

Religion.— All introduce figures of the horse in their worship.

Marriage.—Among all, this ceremony does not take place until both bride and bridegroom have reached maturity. A consideration in the shape of money or service is always given to the father of the former. The nuptial rites are performed at the house of the latter. The expenses, which are considerable, are borne by the parents of both. Polygamy is permitted, though, from the straitness of their wordly circumstances, not commonly practised. On the death of either party the survivor may remarry ; but when it is a woman who a second time enters on wedded life, the rites are few and simple.

Death.—Both interment and cremation are observed. The old are often burned, though frequently also buried : the bodies of the young are always committed to the earth.

The above description is intended to apply only to those members of the hill tribes who adhere to their original customs. With respect to those who have conformed to Hinduism, several of the remarks will not hold good. Of the points of resemblance, some may have been produced by similarity of circumstances, and others may have been borrowed by one tribe from another.

Whether any indicate a community of origin, will be considered towards the conclusion of this paper.

THE GOND RACE.

The name of Gond, or Gund, seems to be a form of Kond,* or Kund, the initial gutturals of the two words being interchangeable, as in *gotal ghar*, an empty house: from *Kotal*, a led horse, and *ghar*, a house. Both forms are most probably connected with *Kondá*— the Teloogoo equivalent for a mountain—and therefore will signify "the hill people." And no designation could be more appropriate to the localities which the majority of them inhabit. Though they are also found residing in the villages of the plains along with the more civilized Hindus, yet they chiefly frequent the mountain ranges lying between 18° 40′ and 23° 40′ north latitude, and between 78° and 82½° east longitude. This tract somewhat corresponds with the old Mahomedan division of Gondwána, but differs from it in not reaching so far to the east and in extending considerably further towards the south-east. The

* I believe the above, and not the common aspirated mode, is the correct spelling of the name of the Orissa aborigines.

Moghul geographers seem to have included with the Gonds of Nagpore the Kôls on their east frontier, and to have been ignorant of the relationship between them and the inhabitants of Bustar. In the north, Gonds are met with about Saugor and near the source of the Hasdo ; on the east, they cross that river into Sargujá, where they border on the Kôls, and are found with Konds and Uriyas in Nowagudda, Kareal, and Kharond or Kálahandi ; in the south, they form the mass of the population of Bustar and a portion of the inhabitants of Jeypur (in the Madras Presidency), while they occupy the hills along the left bank of the Godavery, about Nirmul ; and on the west, they are intermingled with the Hindus of Berar for 30 miles from the right bank of the Wurdah, and, along the Kûrs, extend along the hills both north and south of the Narbadda to the meridian of Hindia, where they give place to the Bhils and Nahals.

In such a large extent of country, as might be expected, they are divided into various branches, and distinguished by specific names. The classification adopted by themselves is into twelve and a half castes or classes, in imitation of the Hindus. These are: Ráj Gond, Raghuwál, Dadave, Katulyá, Pádál, Dholi, Ojhyál, Thotyál, Koilábhutál, Koikopál, Koiám, Mádyál, and an inferior sort of Pádál as the half caste. The first four, with the addition, according to some of the Kolám, are comprehended under the name of Koitor—the Gond, *par excellence*. This term, in its radical form of Koi, occurs over a wide area, being the name given to the Meria-sacrificing aborigines of Orissa and to the jungle tribes skirting the east bank of the Godavery, from the apex of the delta as far up nearly as the mouth of the Indrawati. Its meaning is evidently associated with the idea of a hill; the Persian name of which, *Koh*, approaches it more closely than even the Teloogoo, *Kondá*. I need scarcely, therefore, add that it has no connection with the interrogative *Koi*, as some have supposed, nor has Koitor any relation to the Sanskrit *Kshatriya*, as suggested by Sir R. Jenkins. Though there are a few of the more wealthy Koitors who would gladly pass themselves off as Rajputs, yet the great majority of those known by that name resent, with no small vehemence, the imputation of belonging to any portion of the Hindu community. The sacred thread of the twice-born, instead of being an object of ambition, is to them a source of defilement.

The Ráj Gonds are so called because they have furnished from their number most of the families that have attained to royal power. They are widely spread over the plains and mountains of the province of Nagpore, and are found in Berar and the jungles south of the Wurdah, as well as those north of the Narbudda. The Raghuwál and Dadave are more limited in their range, being confined chiefly to the district of Chindwára. These three classes generally devote themselves to agriculture. They eat with each other, but do not intermarry. The Katulyá, though not a very numerous class in regard to individuals, is extensively scattered. It includes all those who, originally belonging to one or other of the preceding Koitor classes, have begun to conform to the Hindu religion and to ape Hindu manners. Professing to be Kshatriyas, they have invested themselves with a sacred thread, and make great efforts to have their claim allowed, by contracting marriage with needy Rajpoot brides. With scrupulous exactitude, they perform the prescribed ablutions of their adopted faith, and carry their passion for purification so far as to have their faggots duly sprinkled with water before they are used for cooking. At the time of dinner, if a stranger or a crow come near them, the whole food is thrown away as poluted. These practices, which other Koitors regard with profound contempt, are gaining ground among the rich. It was only one or two generations ago that the Zemindar, or petty Raja of Kheiragad,—the present bearer of which title still carries in his features unmistakeable traces of his Gond origin,—was received within the pale of Hinduism; and similar transformations, though at a more distant date, seem to have been undergone by the royal dynasties of Bustar, Mundla, and various smaller principalities. This tendency to claim connection with Rajpoots is not peculiar to ambitious Gonds: it prevails among the Bhils of Malwa, and is not unknown to the wandering Keikádis of the Dakhan, both of whom boast of being Yádawas, or Powárs, or some other equally high born section of the Kshatriyas. On the other hand, there was a temptation in the days of Aurangzib, when Mahomedanism was rampant, to adopt that religion. In comparison with the Bhils, however, few of the Gonds actually made the change. The only instance that has come to my knowledge is that of Bakht Buland, the Rajah of Dewagad, who was converted to Islam when on a visit to Aurangzib at Delhi. Still his descendants, though adhering to this change of creed, have not ceased to marry into Gond families; and hence the present representative of that regal house is not only acknowledged by the whole race about Nagpore as their head and judge, but is physically regarded a pure Ráj Gond.

The Pádál, also named Páthádi, Pardhán, and Desái, is a numerous class found in the same localities as the Ráj Gonds, to whom its members act as religious counsellors (Pradhána).

They are, in fact, the *bhats* of the upper classes,—repeating their genealogies and the exploits of their ancestors, explaining their religious system, and assisting at festivals, on which occasions they play on two sorts of stringed instruments, named Kingri and Jantur (yantra). For their services they receive presents of cows or bullocks, cloth, food, and money. The birth or death either of a cat or dog in their family defiles them; and from this uncleanness they cannot be free till they have shaved off their moustache, purchased new household vessels, and regaled their caste fellows with a plentiful allowance of arrack. These have assumed the name of Ráj Pardháns, to distinguish themselves from a subdivision of the same class, which is degraded to the rank of a half-caste; consisting of those who in the vicinity of Nagpore speak Marathi, play on wind instruments of brass, and spin cotton-thread, like the outcast Hindus.

The Dholis are so styled from the kind of drum (dhola) which they are in the habit of beating. They also play on a kind of wooden clarionet, named Surnai ; and at marriages, where they exercise their musical powers, they prompt the women when they hesitate in their songs. The Nagárchis are a subdivision of this class, whose instrument is the kettle-drum (nakara). These are also known by the name of Chherkya in the more jungly districts, where they are employed as goatherds. The wives of both Dholis and Nagárchis act the part of accoucheurs in Hindu as well as Gond families.

The Ojhyál follow two occumaking caps, of bards, as their name implies, and that of fosame bird, which two classes to be next mentioned, they lead a assaults of life; and in the villages which they pass through, they sing from house to house the praises of their heroes, deemed with castanets in their hands, bells at their ankles, and long feathers of jungle birds in their turbans. They sell live quails, the skins of a species of Buceros, named Dhanchidiyá, which are used for making caps, and for hanging up in houses in order to secure wealth (dhan) and good luck, and the thigh bones of the same bird, which fastened around the waists of children, are deemed an infallible preservative against the assaults of devils and other such calamities. Their wives tattoo the arms of Hindu women. Of this class there is a subdivision, who are Naudis, Máná Ojhyál. Laying claim to unusual sanctity, they refuse to eat with any one—Gond, Rajpoot, or even Brahmin, and devote themselves to the manufacture of rings and bells, which are in request among their own race, and even Lingas and Naudis, which they sell to all ranks of the Hindu community. Their wives are distinguished by wearing the cloth of the upper part of the body over their right shoulder, whereas those of the common Ojhyál, and of all the other Gonds, wear it on their left.

The Thotyál, *i. e.* the maimed, or inferior class, are also known by the more honorable appellation of Pendabaryá, or minstrels of God. Their songs are in honor of their deities; but the divinity whose service they find most profitable is the Goddess of small-pox—the power of Mátá being equally dreaded by Hindus and Gonds. Hence they are frequently called Mátyál, though among Hindus they wish rather to be styled Thákurs. They may be seen travelling about with a kawad over their shoulder, from one end of which is suspended a bambu box, containing an image of their favourite goddess, and from the other a basket, designed to be the receptacle of grain and other gifts. A tambourine (daph) is their usual musical instrument. To their sacred occupation they add the trade of basket-making; while their woman acquire a knowledge of simples, and practise the art of physic in rural districts.

The Koilábhutál are the third class of itinerants. Their occupation, however, is neither of a religious nor secular kind, but consists in making a profit of vice. Their women are dancing girls, in both senses of the word. They follow their profession chiefly among the Hindus, it being reckoned disreputable by the people of their own race. The Bhimá, not included in our list, are found in the north-east of the Bundara District. Though they resemble the Koilábhutál in their habit of dancing in the villages through which they pass, they are believed to abstain from their open depravity.

Unlike the three preceding, the Koikopál are a settled class, devoted entirely to the employment of cow-keeping—Kopál being the Gondi corruption of Gopál. They have the epithet of Koi., *i. e.* Gondi, prefixed to distinguish them from other Ahirs living in the province of Nagpore, of whom three subdivisions, the Kánojiyá Gwálwanshi, and Malhá, speak Hindi, while the Dudh Gowars use Maráthi.

Of the remaining two classes on the list, viz. the Mádyas and Koláms, some account shall now be given.

The name of the Mádya subdivision of Gonds* seems to be derived from Mará, the Gondi term for a tree. In Bustar they are also called Jhorias, probably from Jhodi, a brook. Every-

*Inhabitants of Soonchoor Talook generally Gonds, with a few Holiers. Most of the Gonds, *i. e.* Mádias, subsist on roots and flower of Mhowa dried in sun, of which latter

where they are wilder than the Gonds commonly so called; but on the Beilá Dilá Hills, which run south-east parallel to the Godavery, and where they are known by the name of Mádians, they are perfectly savage.

On the east of Chánda District the men wear no covering for their head or for the upper part of their bodies, and constantly go about with a battleaxe in their hands. The women deck themselves with 30 or 40 strings of beads, to which some add a necklace of pendant bells. Bangles of zinc adorn their wrists, and a chain of the same metal is suspended from the hair, and attached to a large boss stuck in the ear. But the greatest peculiarity connected with their costume, is the practice, which prevails in the more remote districts, of the women wearing no clothes at all; instead of which they fasten, with a string passing round their waists, a bunch of leafy twigs to cover them before and behind. The Rev. Mr. De Rodt says that this practice was reported to exist south of the Kôl country,† which he visited about 1840 or 1841. His allusion may refer to said Juangas, who fell under the personal notice of Mr. Mádians in 1854. This custom was observed by Mr. Samuells to years also in Orissa. In his notes on them in the Bengal Asiatic Journal, Volume XXV., page 295, Mr. Samuells states the somewhat interesting fact, that the practice is traced up to the command of one of their deities when reproving the women for their pride. A similar custom is said to obtain among the Chenchawas that inhabit the jungles between the Mádians and Masulipatam; and it did exist till about 30 years ago among the Holiers in the vicinity of Mángalur.

In their villages bothies for bachelors are universal. Everywhere they are extremely shy in their intercourse with stangers: but on the Beilá Dilá Hills they flee at the approach of any native not of their own tribe. Their tribute to the Raja of Bustar, which is paid in kind, is collected once a year by an officer who beats a tom-tom outside the village, and forthwith hides himself, whereupon the inhabitants bring out whatever

---

eat 4 seers for every seer of rice. All armed with bows and arrows, and good marksmen. Gonds and Holiers live long about Soonchoor. Even when old they cut wood, make mats, and build houses.—*Tuke.*

A thief is beaten out, according to Tuke. The Gonds are honest among themselves (see Macpherson). Dr. Walker's fugitives robbed.

In Ruga and Chikhilnada Talook chiefly Gonds.

Dr. Walker's men said: Near Buster town dress of Gonds simply a bit of cloth 1½ cubits long, and 7 or 8 inches broad, called in Hidustani a "langoti;" their heads and bodies bare; food—rice, and dal of green gram. Coarse cloth brought by Mussulman merchants from Madras and Nagpore to Marunkah, where blind Bhopal Deo lived.

† The Bhils have bows with bambu string, like Mádias.—*Tod,* p. 34.

they have to give, and deposit it on an appointed spot.

Religion.—They have one great festival in the jungles, at the beginning of the monsoon, before they sow their crops, for which a priest (Seadi Mánji) goes round and collects contributions. The ceremony consists in setting up stones in a row, to represent their gods, daubing them with vermilion, and presenting the accustomed offerings. On gathering in their crops, they have a day of rejoicing in their respective abodes.

Birth.—The separation of a mother lasts for a month, during which no one touches her, and unless there are grown-up daughters, she is obliged to cook for herself.

Marriage.—On the east of Chánda District the chief part of the nuptial ceremonies is confined to one day. In the morning, about 7, a bower having been erected near the bridegroom's house, the two young people are led into it and made to stand up together, when a vessel of water is dashed upon their heads from above. They then put on dry clothes, and sit down in the midst of their friends, who lay on their heads some grains of rice. The marriage is completed by an exhortation from the parents. On the east of Arpeili Zemindary, which is farther south, the ceremony commences in the morning by setting up at the door of the cow-house a row of carefully washed stones, with one in the middle, to represent the "great god." Round all a thread is passed, and each is honoured with a black mark, made with a mixture of charcoal and oil. A brass drinking vessel is placed in front of the chief deity, into which each married woman drops four cowries, which become the property of the principal man of the village. They then present their offerings, burn incense, and sprinkle water three times before their gods, whereupon they retire to the house for refreshments. At noon the nuptials are solemnized, commencing with the pouring of water on the heads of the young people as before. Their clothes being changed, and the bridegroom having received from the head man a dagger, which he is to hold during the remainder of the ceremony, he and his partner are both seated at the door with the corners of their garments knotted together; and a white mark having been applied to the forehead of each, water in which saffron and lime have been mixed, so as to form a red liquid, is carried round them thrice, as an honorary gift, and thrown away. The elder people are seated near, and music and dancing are kept up for two or three hours among the unmarried youth of both sexes. In the evening, at the sound of the tom-tom, the people again assemble, and similar rites are repeated, as also on three occasions the following day. With the customs in the wildest parts of the country I am not acquainted.

Death.—When a Mádiá dies, the relatives kill and offer before his corpse a fowl. They then place the body on a bambu mat, and four young men lift it on their shoulders. All the neighbours, calling to mind their own deceased fathers, pour out, on the ground, a handful of rice in their honor; then turning to the corpse, they put a little on it, remarking that the recently departed had now become a god, and adjure him, if death had come by God's will to accuse no one, but if it had been caused by sorcery to point out the guilty party. Sometimes, it is said, there is such a pressure exerted on the shoulders of the bearers, that they are pushed forward and guided to a particular house. The inmate is not seized at once; but if three times the corpse, after being taken some distance back, returns in the same direction, and indicates the same individual, he is apprehended and expelled from the village. Frequently, also, his house shares the same fate. The body is then carried to a tree, to which it is tied upright and burned amid the wailing of the spectators. Funeral rites are performed a year or eighteen months after the cremation, when a flag is tied to the tree where it took place. After sacrificing a fowl the friends return and eat, drink, and dance at the expense of the deceased man's family for one or more days, according to their ability. The dancing is performed by men and women in opposite rows, alternately approaching to, and receding from, each other. On occasion of these funeral festivities it is reckoned no sin for a virgin to be guilty of fornication, though such conduct is strictly forbidden at other times; and unfaithfulness in a wife is punished by the husband with death.

Names of men: Bursu, Kutmánji, Máhingu, Newara, Tiyá, and Wárlu. Women: Ledi, Máhingi, Masi, Semi, and Tomi.

The Kolâms extend all along the Kandi Kondá or Pindi Hills, on the south of the Wurda River, and along the table-land stretching east and north of Mánikgad, and thence south to Dántanpalli, running parallel to the western bank of the Pranhitá. The Kolâms and the common Gonds do not intermarry, but they are present at each others nuptials, and eat from each others hands. Their dress is similar; but the Kolâm women wear fewer ornaments, being generally content with a few black beads of glass round their neck. Among their deities, which are the usual objects of Gond adoration, Bhimsen is chiefly honoured. In the celebration of their marriages they follow a custom, which prevails also among the Khonds, as it does among the tribes of the Caucasus, and did among not a few of the ancient European nations.* I mean the practice of carrying off a bride apparently by force. When a young man desires to enter on the connubial state, two or three friends of the family, having heard of a suitable partner in the neighbourhood, and most probably having come to a good understanding with her relations, proceed thither on their errand of abduction. The men in the village, who see what is going on, do not interfere, and the opposition of the matrons is easily overcome. The nuptials are celebrated at the bridegroom's house; after which he and his bride pay a visit to the family of the latter, and the friendship, which had seemingly been interrupted, is formally re-established.

This completes the account of the twelve tribes, as specified in the earlier part of this Essay.

The following are further particulars regarding the Gond nation generally:—

Personal appearance.†—They are about the middle size of natives, with features rather ugly, though among those living in Hindu villages I have seen a considerable approximation to the Hindu type of countenance. They have been said to possess curly hair: but this is a mistake.

Dress.—The men seldom wear more than a piece of cloth around their waists (dhoti) and a small kerchief about their heads. The more civilized, in addition, throw a loose cloth (ángwastra) over the upper part of their body. The women, besides a lower garment, which is tucked up so as to expose their thighs and legs, wear a sádi (cloth), which passes like a broad sash over the back, and is somewhat more spread out in front upon the chest. The men are fond of silver or brass chains round their ears and a narrow bangle at their wrists. The women tie up their hair into a knot behind, which in the Bundara District they adorn with a profusion of red thread. Their ears above and below are decked with a variety of rings and pendants: chains of silver are suspended from their necks; big brass bangles, named sinum, enclose their wrists; and the backs of their thighs and legs are tattooed down to their ancles,‡ on which they wear plated ornaments (kharging).

---

* A dance among the Benuas, during which the bride-elect darts off into the forest, and requires to be captured by the bridegroom.—*Nicol.* Art. Khonds. *Calcutta Review*, p. 31., Vol. V.

† See description of Physique of Khonds—*Calcutta Review*, p. 41, Vol. V; intellectual, p.p. 42—30, Vol. V.

‡ Their cloths can't go with them to heaven; but the marks are the only thing that does. Tho Ojha and Thota women only tattoo when about 20 years of age, before or after marriage. First make the forms with juice of Biwali and lamp black with four needles. The forms of the tattoo are a peacock, an antelope, and a dagger. The mark is done on the back of the thighs and legs: the operation is painful, and the patient requires to be held down. The hair sometimes naturally curls; but so does that of Hindoos, Europeans, &c.

Food.—They make two meals a day: their breakfast, consisting generally of gruel, and their supper of some boiled coarse grain, with pulse and vegetables. Occasionally this routine is varied, when the chase or a religious festival has provided them with the flesh of dear, hog, goat, or fowls.*

Social position.—In the plains, where they are mingled with Hindus, the Gonds take rank above Mahárs and other outcasts. In this honor they are partly indebted to the political influence which some of their race have retained up to the present day. Indignity cannot be heaped on those whose kindred are known to be at no great distance the owners of property on which even respectable Hindus are content to live.† But it must be confessed that the Gonds have acquired their honorable position, in a considerable degree, by yielding to the prejudices of the Hindus. Though their own principles admit of the slaughter of cows, yet, in deference to the feelings of their more powerful neighbours, they abstain from the practice, and, if I mistake not, do not partake of the carrion, which Mahárs are ready to devour. In many cases the wish to stand well with the followers of the dominant faith has led them in a great measure to embrace it and surrender their own; and some of their Thákurs or Zemindars, or, as they are sometimes called, Rajas, have used their utmost endeavours to be recognised as Kshatryas, by contracting marriages with needy Rajput brides.‡ The family at Kheiragad has succeeded in this attempt. On the other hand, there was a temptation in the days of Aurangzib, when Mahomedanism was rampant, to adopt that religion; and we find that this change was actually made by Bakht Buland, the ancestor of the Raja of Dewagad. Still the present representative of that regal house, though adhering to the change of creed, has not ceased to marry into Gond families—and hence is acknowledged by the whole race about Nagpore as their head and judge, and is, physically, a pure Ráj Gond. In their hill retreats the Gonds are left to their own standard of respectability; but when they have there another

---

* At Nagpore women at 9½ a.m. eat millet, bread, and dál. Men eat at noon when released from work, and sup at 9½ p.m. on vegetables. Husband and wife don't dine together. At Kamptee same hours, only early part gruel, made of rice flour boiled in much water. At night they eat rice and pulse.

† INHERITANCE.—After death of father family remain together, or if the sons wish to separate they divide the property equally. They may give their sisters some ornaments or cloth, but the latter have no share.

‡ The tendency of the Gond Rajas to claim connection with Rajputs. Chohan Bhils—*Tod*, p. 34; and even Kooroos—*Dr. Balfour*. In Aurangzib's time we find these Gond Princes in Mundilla, Deoghur, and Chanda; and, according to Kafee Khan, the tribute in cash, jewels, and elephants taken from the two latter was very great.—*Jenkins*, p. 41.

jungle race living among them, as on the range of hills north of Ellichpoor, they generally are the *patêls*, or head men of their villages; and their neighbours occupy an inferior position.

*Houses and Villages.** —When residing in the midst of a Hindu population, the Gonds inhabit mud houses, like the inferior sort common in the Dakhan. But in the jungles the houses are of wattle and daub, with thatched roofs. The internal arrangements are of the simplest kind, comprising two apartments, separated from each other by a row of tall baskets, in which they store up their grain. Adjoining the house is a shed for buffaloes; and both house and shed are protected from wild beasts by a bambu fence. The villages are situated on table-lands, or on slight elevations above the general level of the country, and they seldom number more than 10 houses, and more frequently contain only 3 or 4. But, however small the village may be, one house in it is sure to be the abode of a distiller of arrack.

Occupations.—In the immediate vicinity of the city of Nagpore, and of all British stations throughout the province, the Gonds have entered into the service of Europeans as grass-cutters. In rural districts they are employed as assistants in farm labor by Hindu cultivators, or sometimes plough a few fields for themselves in the usual way. In the jungles, as we have seen, they dispense with the plough, and adopt the nomadic system of tillage. In places of mixed population, some of their women add to their husband's gains by tattooing the forehead and arms of Hindu females. In their own wilds the men increase the means of their family's subsistence by hunting, in which their chief reliance is on their matchlocks, though in some of the more remote parts they kill their game with arrows, which most shoot in the common mode, but others in a sitting posture, their feet bending the bow, and both hands pulling the string. When they go out on such expeditions, and frequently at other times, they carry a small axe and knife for lopping off the branches that might obstruct their path.

Religion.—Though the Gond pantheon includes somewhere

---

* Khond houses are of boards plastered inside; thatched; in two rows.—*Calcutta Review*, Vol. V., p. 46. At Hutta, in the Bundara District, the Gond houses are of bambu tatti, daubed with mud; thatched; with veranda; 2 doors, one front and the other behind; no windows; divided by tatti or by baskets of grain—larger half with door, in which they cook and eat; other dark, in which they keep goods, vessels, &c. Around single houses is a compound. But in the jungle houses are in two rows, with compound behind. They keep cows, sows, buffaloes, fowls, but no horses, except those who are rich. Cows are yoked to the plough, where the plough is used.

about fifteen gods, yet I have never obtained from one individual the names of more than seven deities. These were Bádu Dewa (the great god), who in other districts is called Budhál Pen (the old god), Mátiyá (devil or whirlwind), Sale, Gángará (little bells), or more properly Gágará, Pálo, Gadawá, and Kham; or, as enumerated by another, Badú, Mátiyá, Salei, Gángaro Mal, Pálo, Chawar, and Kank. The above lists were furnished to me by worshippers of seven gods near the Mahadeva Hills. To the "great" god, common to all the sects, the adherents of these deities join Kuriyá and Katharpár. Besides these, I have heard at various times the names of Kodo Pen, Pharsi Pen, and Bangáram; and the Rev. J. Phillips, who visited the Gonds at Amarkantak, mentions Hardál as the principal object of veneration there.*

What are the characters or offices of these deities, whose very names are so imperfectly known by their worshippers, it is vain to inquire from any Native authority. I have been left therefore merely to conjecture, and would wish my remarks on the subject to be received simply as suggestions. It appears to me that Budhál Pen is the same as Burá Pen,† the chief god among the Khonds. Perhaps Hardál may be the synonym near the source of the Narbadda. Mátiyá‡ I would suppose is a name for the god of small-pox, who is also one of the Khond divinities, and may be identical with Bangáram, afterwards to be mentioned. Sale may probably be the god who presides over cattle-pens (Salo). Kuriyá may denote the deity who takes care of the tribe (Kûl), or, as it is frequently mispronounced, (Kûr). Kattarpár may correspond with the Katti Pen of the Khonds, *i. e.* the god of ravines. Kodo Pen is considered by the Rev. J. G. Driberg, in his "Report on the Narbadda Mission, 1849," to preside over a village, and

* Jungoo (war or wild). Royata is also given, to whom they pray on eighth day of the Dusara; make a circle of a pusti, and in middle fill jaggery, and make with their hands rays like the Sun's, and so make a half moon with Bhumuk, and fry both in oil.

† Sun god and Moon god.—*Calcutta Review*, Vol. V., p. 55. The Bhumuk of the Dewalwada said his gods were Bhimsen and Matadewa, who, he said, was same as Sun. Boorapennee, god of light, Supreme in other districts. Bellapennee, Sun god.—*Church Mission Intelligencer*.

According to Lieut. Hill, the great sacrifices among Khonds take place at full moon of Pooshnm and Maghum.

At Dali 3 times: on 8th of Dusara, when new rice comes; 9th of Cheitum, when Mhowa flowers; in Jhiet, before rice sowing.

Among Khonds, to Pattooripennee a hog is sacrificed before sowing.

Boorapennee among ditto is worshipped at rice harvest.

Hill god (Soropennee), *i. e.* Durgudeo.—*Calcutta Review*, Vol. V., p. 57.

Bura Pen is worshipped once a year, at rice harvest; the worship lasts 5 days: a hog sacrificed.

‡ Mátiyá is not known by the three Gond women belonging to Nagpore whom I questioned, but is considered by Pahad Singh and Gadi Rawaji to mean a devil. It is the name given to a whirlwind, against which Hindus lift up their shoe and utter threatenings.

would thus be the counterpart of the Nadzu* Pen of the Khonds. But may it not signify rather the god who is believed to bless crops of grain, of which *Kodo (paspulum frumentaceum)* among Gonds is one of the chief? The name of Pharsi Pen, who is represented by a small iron spear-head, may possibly be formed from Barchi, which in Hindi denotes a spear, on which hypothesis this deity would be the equivalent of the Khond Loha† Pen, the iron god, or god of war.

In the south of Bundara District the traveller frequently meets with squared pieces of wood, each with a rude figure carved in front, set up somewhat close to each other. These represent Bangárám Bungara‡ Bai, or Devi, who is said to have one sister and five brothers—the sister being styled Danteshwari, a name of Káli, and four out of the five brothers being known as Gantárám, Champárám and Náikárám, and Potlinga. These are all deemed to possess the power of sending disease and death upon men, and under these or different names seem to be generally feared in the region east of Nagpore City. I find the name of Bungara to occur among the Kôls of Chybásá, where he is regarded as the god of fever, and is associated with Gohem, Chondu, Negrá, and Dichali, who are considered, respectively, the gods of cholera, the itch, indigestion, and death. It has always appeared to me a question deserving more attention than it has yet received, how far the deities who preside over disease, or are held to be malevolent, are to be looked on as belonging to the Hindus or aborigines. Káli in her terrible aspect is certainly much more worshipped in Gondwána and the forest tracts to the east and south of it, than in any other part of India. As the goddess of small-pox she has attributed to her the characteristics of various aboriginal deities, and it is worthy of remark, that the parties who conduct the worship at her shrines, even on behalf of Hindus, may be either Gonds, fishermen, or members of certain other low castes. The sacrifices, too, in which she delights would well agree with the hypothesis of the aboriginal derivation of the main features of her character. At Chánda and Lánji in the province of Nagpore, there are temples dedicated to her honour, in which human victims have been offered almost within the memory of the present genera-

* In worshipping Pidzu Pen and Bura Pen Khonds call on Bura and Tari and the other gods.

† Loha Pen, a piece of iron or an iron weapon is buried; fowl, rice, and arrack are offered in grove. Village god, Nudzu Pen. Horatin Ko (*Tickell*, p. 800) are spirits of the forefathers of a newly married woman—worshipped on the road, invoked in sickness.

‡ Bungara, or ram, may be a deity named from Sontal and Ho;—generic word for god. V. 12. There is a goddess named Pangara.—See *Tickell*, IX., p.p. 799, 800. Bhungara—a tribe among the Warális.

tion. The victim was taken to the temple after sunset and shut up within its dismal walls. In the morning, when the door was opened, he was found dead, much to the glory of the great goddess, who had shown her power by coming during the night and sucking his blood. No doubt there must have been some of her servants hid in the fane, whose business it was to prepare for her the horrid banquet. At Dantewáda in Bustar, situated about 60 miles south-west of Jagdalpur, near the junction of the Sankani and Dankani, tributaries of the Indrawati in Bustar, there is a famous shrine of Káli, under the name of Danteshwari. Here many a human head has been presented on her altar. About 30 years ago, it is said that upwards of 25 full-grown men were immolated on a single occasion by a late Raja of Bustar. Since then numerous complaints have reached the authorities at Nagpore of the practice having been continued, though it is to be hoped that, with the annexation of the country, it has entirely and for ever ceased. The same bloody rite in the worship of Káli, as we learn from Major MacPherson, prevailed among the immediate predecessors of the present hill Rajas of Orissa, including those of Boad, Gumsur, &c.*

Whether Bhima,† who by Hindus is esteemed one of their greatest heroes, is to be regarded as borrowed from that nation, or lent to them, it is difficult to say. One thing is certain, that, under the name of Bhim Pen, or Bhimsen, his worship is spread over all parts of the country, from Berar to the extreme east of Bustar, and that not merely among the Hinduized aborigines, who have begun to honour Khandobá, Hanumán, Gunpati, &c., but among the rudest and most savage of the tribe. He is generally adored under the form of an unshapely stone covered with vermilion, or of two pieces of wood standing from 3 to 4 feet in length above the ground, like those set up in connection with Bangáràm's worship.

But, in addition to the deities generally acknowledged, there are many others who receive reverence in particular local-

---

* Regarding Manko, compare *Indian Review*; where it is said that in Jeypur there is Maniksoro—god of war; but afterwards it is remarked that Hindu chiefs before any great enterprise used to propitiate goddess Maniksoro.

Tooahmool are Meria-sacrificing Gonds.

The Sontal Marung Bura and his elder brother Maniko may be our Budhál, or Royata, and his consort Manko.

The chief Khond deity, Bura Pen, however, is obviously our Budhál Pen.

† Bhiwasu is admitted to be chiefly a Gond deity, and to be named after Bhim the Pandu. About one coss south-west from Bajar Kurd (north of Parseuni) is a large idol of Bhiwasu, 8 feet high, formed into shape, with a dagger in one hand and a burchie (javelin) in the other. A Bhumuk is the Pujári; and the people repair to worship on Tuesdays and Saturdays, offering hogs, he-goats, cocks, hens, cocoanuts. The Patél of Awareghat, who is a Mussulman, gives Rupees 2; and Hindoo cultivators give rice for an annual feast, which takes place at the commencement of the rains, when the Bhumuk takes a cow by force from the Gowar, and offers it to Bhimsen in the presence of about 25 Gonds.

ities. It is the custom of the Gonds to propitiate, for at least one year, the spirits of their departed friends, even though they have been men of no note. But when an individual has been in any way distinguished,—if, for example, he has founded a village, or been its headman or priest,—then he is treated as a god for years, or it may be generations, and a small shrine of earth (Thápaná, or, more properly, Sthápaná), is erected to his memory, at which sacrifices are annually offered.

It has been stated that the Gonds have no idols. It is true they have no images in their dwellings, but at the scene of their religious ceremonies in the jungle there are for the most part some objects set up, either iron rods, stones, pieces of wood, or little knobs of mud, to represent their deities. Among these, when there is a number together, the representation of the "great god" usually occupies the chief place.

Though one of their deities is styled the "great god," yet, if I may judge of the whole race by what I heard in one of their districts, they hold that this chief of their divinities is to be distinguished from the Invisible Creator and Preserver of the World, of whom my informant stated they had a distinct conception, and to whom, in imitation of the Hindu agricultural population, they give the name of Bhagawán. According to this view their "great god" is only the first of their inferior gods, who are all looked on as a sort of media of communication in various departments between God and man, though, as is the case in every form of polytheism, the near, or visible inferior, receives more attention than the unseen Supreme.

Worship.—The Creator, as I was told by a Gond in the neighbourhood of the Mahadeva Hills, is occasionally adored in their houses by offering prayers, and by burning sugar (gul) and clarified butter in the fire.

The public worship of these forest tribes seems to be connected with their crops. In places, where rice is produced, there are three great days, when they leave their villages, and proceed to worship under the shade of a Saj or Ein tree (*Pentaptera tomentosa*),—1st, the day when rice begins to be sown; 2nd, when the new rice is ready; and 3rd, when the Mhowa tree comes into flower. The great festivals among the Bodos, of which there are four, appear, in like manner, to be associated with their crops.

In the wilder villages, near the Mahadeva Hills, Kodo Pen, as we learn from Mr. Driberg, is worshiped at a small heap of stones by every new comer, through the oldest resident, with fowls, eggs, grain, and a few copper coins, which become the property of the officiating priest. Bhimsen, who is there regarded as the god of rain, has a festival of four or five days' duration held in his honour at the end of the monsoon, when two poles about 20 feet high, and 5 feet apart, are set up with a rope attached to the top, by means of which the boys of the village climb up and then slide down the pole. The same offerings are presented to this god as to Kodo Pen, with the exception of the money.

Ceremonies connected with Births.—A woman remains apart for thirteen days after her delivery. On the fifth day after the occurrence of a birth, the female neighbours are feasted: on the twelth the male friends are similarly entertained: and on the thirteenth the purification is ended by giving a dinner to both parties. The child is named a month or two later.*

Marriage.—The expediency of a marriage is occasionally determined by omens. A vessel is filled with water, into which is gently dropped a grain of rice or wheat, in the name of the respective parties, at opposite sides of the vessel.† If these approach each other the union will be a happy one, and the marriage day is fixed. Another way of settling the question, is to consult some man with a reputation for sanctity, who sits and rolls his head till he appears furious, when, under supposed inspiration, he gives the answer. But frequently the matter is determined by personal negociation between the fathers, who call in some neutral parties to name the sum that should be paid for the bride. This obligation is discharged on the day of the betrothal, along with a present of such things as are necessary for feasting the friends assembled at the bride's father's house on that occasion. On the day fixed for the commencement of the marriage ceremonies the bridegroom and his father go to the father-in-law's house with presents, which contribute again to the entertainment of the guests. Next day an arbour is constructed at the bridegroom's house, to which the bride is taken, and a dinner is provided. The day following, the two young people, after running round the pole seven times, retire to the arbour and have their feet washed. Pice (*i. e.* copper coins) are waved round their heads, and given to the musicians, when the ceremonies are concluded by a feast.

---

* Among Gonds of Kolit the child is named on 9th day; among the Hindus on 12th day.

† This omen is resorted to among the Khonds to determine a child's name—only it is if grain swim at a particular ancestor's name.—*Calcutta Review*, p. 31, Vol. V. A few of every class—1 out of 1,000—become celebites, and are received among Gosains.

They put turmeric and then ghee over whole body, and on a woman they put Kuku (red powder) besides.

*Funeral rites.**—The relatives of a deceased person are unclean for a day. The ceremonial impurity is removed by bathing. Some time after the occurrence of a death a sort of low square mound is raised over the remains† of the deceased, at the corners of which are erected wooden posts, around which thread is wound, and a stone is set up in the centre. Here offerings are presented, as in the jungle worship of their deities, of rice and other grains, eggs, fowls, or sheep. On one occasion, after the establishment of the Bhonsla (or Maratha) government in Gondwána, a cow was sacrificed to the *manes* of a Gond; but this having come to the hearing of the authorities, the relatives were publicly whipped, and all were interdicted from such an act again. To persons of more than usual reputation for sanctity, offerings continue to be presented annually for many years after their decease. In the district of Bundara large collections of rude earthenware, in the shape of horses, may be seen, which have accumulated from year to year at the tombs of such men.

Priesthood.‡—There is scarcely an institution among the Gonds that may properly be called priesthood; marriage, and such like ceremonies being for the most part performed by some aged relative. There are, however, some men, who, from supposed superior powers, or in consequence of their hereditary connection with a sacred spot, are held to be entitled to take the lead in worship. These men are named Bhumuks, Pujáris, &c. About the Mahadeva Hills the higher Pardháns act as Pujáris, and the lower as rude musicians: the Koitars seeming to look down upon both offices as somewhat menial. But in other districts the last mentioned class appear rather to take the lead as holy men, and many of them make use of their supposed sacred character to impose on their simpler neighbours. They profess to be able to call tigers from the jungles, to seize them by the ears, and control their voracity by whispering to them a command not to come near their villages. Or they pretend to know a particular kind of root, by burying which they can prevent the beasts of the forests from devouring men or cattle. With the same view, they lay on the pathway small models of bedsteads, &c., which are believed to act as charms to stop their advance. They are supposed to have the power of detecting

* They are buried at Kolitmárá naked, as unmarried Kooroos are burned naked, with face upwards, and leaf of Rui (*Calotropis gigantea*) or Palas tree in the jungle, the head south, and the feet north. Sometimes they burn house of deceased and desert it.

† At Umret they burn the dead, and after burning ashes erect chubutras; and at corners place tall red stones.

‡ Khond priests possessed of magical arts.—*Calcutta Review*, p. 59, Vol. V.

sorcery,* which is greatly dreaded, and, like the gipsies in this country, they are consulted by their more civilized neighbours on the fortunes of the future, which they read in the lines of their applicant's hand. At Mandanpur, about 100 miles north-west of the city of Nagpore, there is a Gond, named Sonsei, who boasts of the possession of miraculous powers. He and his sons are engaged in quarrying red ochre, the property of a Gond Ráni, who lives at Gandei, still farther to the north-west. Near his quarry he has erected a sacred mound to the *manes* of his father, who was similarly gifted; and he uses the awe which attaches to this spot as a means of extorting money from the deluded Queen. Besides 5-16ths of the proceeds of the quarry, which he receives for the labour of himself and family in working it, he induces his superior to send him Rs. 50 (£5) every two years, on the pretence that his deified ancestor in the neighbourhood is angry, has turned the ochre into material of very indifferent quality, and will not be appeased until the sum named is spent in offerings. The sum is sent: a part of it is expended on fowls, a goat, hog, arrack, &c., which go to the entertainment of the cunning quarryman, and the remaining rupees go into his pocket.

Names of males among the Gonds: Bhádu, Chiná, Dhánu, Gondá, Jilu, Kokarrá, Mahingu, Pándá, Phágá, Ramman, Rigá, Runa, Woja.

Of females: Birjo, Buto, Jámo, Jango, Mahingi, Mirgo, Peto, Renu, Súkaro, Sonaki, Polai, and Tumki.

Tribes connected with the Gonds.—Badiyás and Balwás.

The Badiyás are found in the Chindwára District, scattered from the town of that name to the Mahadeva Hills. They seem to be Gonds, who retain much of their original customs, but have conformed to the Hindus in language and some of their religious observances. They worship the gods of their ancestors under the shadow of the Saj tree; but they have adopted the use of idols of stone and brass, which they keep in their houses, and carry out only on the recurrence of their festivals, which are the same as those of the Gonds. Except in rare cases they burn the bodies of their deceased relatives, and throw the ashes into an adjoining river. They observe

* Sorcery—See also the Beigas of Phillips, though some reckon them simply a distinct race. The Ojhas are bird catchers and exorcists. Goj Raj omens compared with Khonds.—*Calcutta Review*, p. 51, Vol. V. Numbers of unfortunate persons fall victims to belief in witchcraft.—*Tuke*, p.p. 811 and 807. (Ragapar). Diviner.—*Tuke*, p.p. 802 and 803. Sickness believed to come from supernatural course.—*Calcutta Review*, Vol. V., p. 50. In Poudacole magicians are burned: three were so treated at Pipulpanka in 1834-35.—*Calcutta Review*, Vol. V., p. 53.

more of the Hindu feasts than is done by the great majority of the Gonds.

The Halwás* form a pretty numerous body in the districts of Bundara and Raepore and the dependancy of Bustar. In these parts of the country they seem to occupy a position similar to that of the Badiyás to the north-west of them, though they have perhaps still more imitated the manners of the Hindus. They wish to hold a respectable place in their village, and eagerly covet the distinction of wearing a sacred thread over their shoulder. This privilege, till recently, was sold to those in Bustar by the Raja of that principality, and such may have been the beginning of the practice among those in the more civilized parts of the country. But even there they still retain the custom of offering worship to their deceased ancestors, and presenting at their tombs the usual number of earthenware horses.

Admitting the identity of their origin with that of the Gonds, among whom they at present dwell, it is difficult to explain the abandonment by these Badiyás and Halwás of their mother tongue. Their case, however, is not singular, for the Gonds of Amarkantak have also laid it aside, although it is generally spoken in the district to the west of them as far as Jubbulpore. But in this instance we can see the reason of the change. Lying in the highway between the plains of Chutteesgurh and Sohagpore, they have constant intercourse with the Hindu merchants, who pass by that route, and have thus come to be more familiar with their language than their own.

Gáiti Gonds.

These call themselves also Koitars, and are as much Gonds in language and everything else as those who are known by no other name. Their chief peculiarity, which I have not found among common Gonds, though it may exist even among them, is to have in each village a separate tenement set apart for the occupancy of unmarried men during the night. This they call a *gotalghar* (empty bed house) and answers to the *dekha chung* of the hill Cacháris and the Nágás, and to *morang* among Abors or Padans. In some villages there is a like provision made for the unmarried Gáiti women. Mr. Samuells, who has given us some interesting information regarding the Juangas of Orissa, doubts the report he had heard of similar establishments existing among *them*; but I have been assured by my friend Dr. Shortt, that he found them in the villages which he visited

* Halwás won't kill bison or buffalo. In Soonchoor they are mixed with a preponderance of Gonds (Marrees). Halwás are mixed in Jeypur (*Tuke*) with Uriyas and Gonds.

in Keonjur. When the Gáitis have returned in the evening from their work in the jungle, where they are very industrious in cultivation and cutting timber, all the families go to their respective houses for their supper; after which the young men retire to their common dwelling, where, around a blazing fire, they dance for an hour or two, each having a small drum suspended in front from his waist, which he beats as he moves about, while the young women sit at no great distance accompanying the performance with a song.

Religion.—The worshippers of six deities could enumerate Budhál Pen, Saleng, Gágarál, Rayetál, and Purjál: but those, who are devoted to seven, could not mention more than Kodiyá, Supári Dewa, Sakra Bái, and Dewa Dulá, without having recourse to Hindu divinities.

Their great festival seems to be after the ingathering of the rice harvest, when they proceed to a dense part of the jungle, which no woman is permitted to enter, and where, to represent the "great god," a pice has been hung up enclosed in a piece of bambu. Arrived at the spot, they take down the copper Budhál in his case, and selecting a small area about a foot square under a tree, to be cleaned, they lay on it the pice, before which they arrange as many small heaps or handsful of uncooked rice, as there are deities worshipped by them. The chickens brought for sacrifice are loosed and permitted to feed on the rice, after which they are killed and their blood sprinkled between the pice and the rice. Goats are also offered, and their blood presented in the same manner. Until prohibited by the Hindus, sacrifices of cows were also common. On the blood, arrack is poured as a libation to their deities. The pice is now lifted and put in its bambu case, which is shut up with leaves, wrapt in grass, and returned to its place in the tree, to remain there till it is required on the following year.

Names of males: Kanhu, Kokshá, Kopá, Mahávu, Pundi, and Sáu.

Of females: Gursi, Konji, Konsi, Mahári, Mási, Milo, Minkú, Silo, and Tursá.

Moria Gónds.

These are more civilized than the Márias. They form the bulk of the agricultural population in the north and centre of the Bustar dependancy. Beyond the east frontier, however, where they mix with the Khonds in Pátná, Khárond, and Jeypur, they are somewhat wilder, and devoted to the chase. With their long hair tied in a knot behind, and their spare arrows hanging down from it by the barb between their shoulders, they pursue the deer of their forests, and at short distances (according to Lieutenant Hill) seldom miss in their aim. In these districts they are evidently immigrants, having come from the plains on the west, where they are separated from the Khonds by the physical character of the country, which would allow peculiarities of manner and language to spring up between the neighbouring tribes. Even now, however, the two are not much more distinct from each other, than are the Gáitis from the adjacent Márias. In Bustar the Moria villages generally contain individuals of a different race, as we find to be the case among the Khonds. And here we meet with the distillers of the Eastern Ghats, under the identical name of Sundis; and the Gahindás of the same district are represented by the Gándás, who act as Kotwáls and weavers for their villages.

Religion.—I do not possess detailed information regarding the mythology of the Morias; but from the names, Gágaru and Kodál, borne by their males, I would infer that they have somewhat the same gods as are recognised in the vicinity of Nagpore City. Major Charles Elliot states that their most common deities are the earth goddess, the hill god, and Bhim Pen. Of the first two there are no images in use: but a small hut, similar to those erected for the accommodation of the tiger god in the jungly districts of the Dakhan, is set apart for the people offering arrack and sacrifices in their honour. Before the two pieces of wood, representing the third, worship is regularly performed previous to the period of sowing. Of course, in every village, as in the other parts of the province, Bhawáni comes in for her share of superstitious reverence under the two forms of the small-pox goddess, and Máoli or Danteshwari, the counterpart of the great Káli at Dantewádá.

Marriage.—The marriage ceremony combines certain customs that we have already had to notice. As in the north-west of Chindwára, the expediency of a match is decided by what may be called the attraction omen. At the time appointed for the union oil and saffron, which have been employed in the worship of Bhim and the small-pox goddess, are brought from their shrines, and used to anoint the bride and bridegroom; who are then attired in the usual coarse cloth of the country, and have a yellow thread tied round their wrist; water descends on their heads in the bower; their clothes are knotted together; and sometimes they run round the marriage pole.

Names of males: Bádál, Bukál, Boyál, Dhelá, Dhodi, Dorge, Gágaru, Gedi, Higál, Judahál, Kodál, Malál, Mulál, Milol, Musiál, Odhi, Pichke, Samárc, Surka, Suval.

Females: Gágari, Hinge, Judahi, Kodo, Káni, Sukali.

Naikude Gonds.

These have more than any other section of their race conformed to Hinduism. They inhabit the jungles on the north and south banks of the Pain Gangá, but especially abound in the tract between Digaras and Umarkhed. They are found about Apárawa Pet, and as far as Nirmul, from whence, intermingled with Hindus, they are scattered westward nearly to Bidar. Of all the subdivisions of the Gond race, with the exception of the Halwás and, perhaps, the Badiyás, they have the most been influenced by Hinduism. They dress like Hindus, and will not eat beef. Some partly support themselves by the produce of the chase, which provides them with the flesh of the antelope, elk, and wild hog, and partly by collecting honey, wax, and lák for sale. The poorer classes earn a bare subsistence by cutting wood and grass. In the more considerable villages they cultivate land, and are employed by patêls or headmen as sipáhis. None of them have abandoned their aboriginal love for liquor. They are a terror to their neighbourhood by their depredations.

Religion.—Ancestor-worship forms an important part of their religion. They also acknowledge as deities Bhimsen and Rájubá, not to mention those dreaded by the Hindus as well as the forest tribes of their part of India,—Wághobá, the tiger god, and Márai, the cholera goddess. In the month of Cheitra these Gonds go on a pilgrimage to Sasarkund, a pool in the Mahur jungle, in which the Pain Gangá is said to be engulphed. Here in a gorge there is a huge stone rising out of the ground and covered with vermilion, which goes by the name of Bhimsen. In front of this, Naikude Gonds mingle with Ráj Gonds and Kolâms in acts of adoration. The order of the religious service seems to be the following: at 5 p.m., having cooked a little rice, the worshippers place it before the god, and add a little sugar. They then besmear the stone with vermilion, and burn resin as incense in its honour; after which all the parties offer their victims, consisting of sheep, hogs, and fowls, with the usual libations of arrack. The god is now supposed to inspire the Pujári, who rolls about his head, leaps frantically round and round, and finally falls down in a trance, when he declares whether Bhimsen has accepted the service or not. At night all join in drinking, dancing, and beating their tom-toms. Early in the morning they partake of a meal and depart for their own houses. Those who are not able to go to the place of pilgrimage repair to the shade of a Mhowa tree, where they go through similar rites. Rájubá is worshipped in the month of Kártik, with ceremonies somewhat like the above. The tiger god is honoured with a jatra, or gathering, of two days at the village of Pipalgaum, south of Mahur, where Hindus, as well as Gonds, take part. On the 5th day of Shráwun a feast, named Jámbatas, is celebrated by the latter in their own dwellings; but to what god I am unable to say.

The services of a Brahmin are called in to name their children and to celebrate their marriages, which always take place before the parties have come to years of discretion. The influence of Hinduism is also seen in the prohibition against the remarriage of their widows.

The dead are either burned or buried. The relatives are unclean for two days. On the third day, the *manes* are worshipped in the usual Gond manner; and on every Saturday, and feast day thereafter, they are treated to incense and some of the family food.

Names of males: Bheisi, Bhutiyá, Gontiyá, Gunaji, Jhádiyá, Mánáji, Ráji, Sambhu, Satwá, and Wághee.

Females: Bhimi, Chimmi, Eiti, Gadin, Gangi, Housi, Jaggi, Mukhi, Nousi, Rukhma, Satai, and Yemnai.

in another; from Bundlecund in the north to the Teloogoo coast districts in the south; from Malwa and Candeish in the west to the confines of Orissa in the east; and right through the very centre of the country, among the Vindhya Mountains which overlook the valley of the Nerbudda and the Sautpoora Ranges which bound the plains of Nagpore and the cotton-fields of the Wurda.

Among these tribes one, namely the Gonds, have formed political annals of their own, have wielded dynastic power in most parts of these Provinces, and have left architectural remains in attestation of former greatness. On this subject it may be well to transcribe some brief passages from my first Administration Report (for the year 1862):—

"The earliest dynasties in this part of India of which anything is now either recorded or remembered are those of the Gond-Rajpoots. But prior to these, and superior to them in civilization, there must have been several Hindu dynasties, which are only now known by architectural remains: some at

Religion.—The chief objects of their adoration are the sun and moon, rude representations of which they carve on wooden pillars.* After reaping their crops, they sacrifice to Sultan Sakadá, whom they suppose to have been some king among them in former times.

A feast is generally provided on the 4th or 5th day after a birth, and without any further ceremony the father, in the course of a month or two, gives a name to his child.

As among the Bodos, or, to quote a more illustrious example, like Jacob of old, a Kûr bridegroom, in the absence of the money demanded for his bride, comes under an obligation to serve his father-in-law for a certain number of years. The marriage ceremonial, which, like that of the Gonds, includes the tying of garments together and the running round a pole or Mhowa tree, concludes on the third day with a feast and dance; during which the newly married pair are carried about for some time on the backs of two of the company.

In some cases the dead are burned; but, for the most part, they are interred with their head towards the south. Near their villages they have a place appointed for burials, where, after having offered a goat to the *manes* of the deceased, they set up a rude representation of him in wood about 2 feet above the ground. There worship continues to be paid for at least a year.

Names of males: Bendu, Bongá, Dhokol, Naru, Sukáli, Surprái, and Tutá.

Females: Batro, Bádám, Irmá, Jáso, Mánjibakan, Pundiyá, and Rajani.

Conclusion.

In looking over the vocabularies, which I have collected from the dialects of the above tribes, I find that among the words used by the different subdivisions of the Gond race there is the utmost similarity, and that these, with the exception of the vocables of the Kolâm and Naikude Gond dialects, agree more with the distant Tamil than the neighbouring Teloogoo type of Dravidian speech. The dialects excepted, while exhibiting proofs of the modifying influence of Teloogoo, retain enough of their original structure to show that they also were once more closely allied to the Tamil. In the additional list of words derived from a wandering tribe, named Keikádis, whose route

* According to Mr. Bullock, wooden pillars, with horse, sun, and moon, set up before house of married people. Nahals are not allowed music at their weddings. Nahals on north-east of Khandeish.

The Scythian origin of Kûrs and of Gonds might perhaps be inferred from Kodo Pen, and earthen horses, which are offered instead of living sacrifice. Gonds don't use horses or ponies much.

lies more remote from the Tamil country, than from Telingana or Cánadá, I find evidence of the same fact. Thus the Keikádi name for "fire"—*narpu*—agrees exactly with the Tamil term for that element, but differs considerably from the Teloogoo,—*nippu*,—and still more from the Canarese—*benki*.

As the language of the Kûrs is found within the territory assigned to the Gonds, it has been supposed to be another of their dialects. This seems to be the opinion of two such eminent philologists as Dr. Latham, and Mr. Logan of Singapore, who, I fear, have been misled by a list of words furnished by the first and, certainly, one of the ablest geological observers that ever sojourned in India—I mean Dr. Voysey. That list its complier distinguished as Kûr Gond. The vocabulary of the Kûr language, which I have drawn up, demonstrates that there is no relation between it and the Gondi, but that there is a connection, amounting almost to identity, between it and the speech of the Kôls.*

For the affinities of the Kûr and Kôl tongues we must look in another direction than the south of India. They must be sought at the foot of the north-east Himalayas, and still more among the Môns of Pegu, and the Benwas, described by Captain Newbold, inhabiting the mountainous regions of the Malayan peninsula. Thus the word for "*water*" in the language of the Kûrs and Kôls, *dâ;* among the Bodos, Cacháris, and Kukis in the north-east of India, is *doi, di, tui;* among the Karens and Môns in Burmá, is *ti* and *dat;* and among the Benwas of Malacca, *di.* Again, the word for "eye" among the Kûrs and Kôls—*med* or *met*—is among the Kukis and Mikurs in north-eastern India, *met* and *mek;* among the Karens and Môns, *me* and *mot;* and among the Benwas, *med.* Time will not permit me to prosecute this investigation further, than to add that the first three numerals, which among the Kûrs and Kôls are miá bárá, ápiá, are among the Môns, mue, bá, and pâi. May we not conclude then, that while the stream of Dravidian population, as evidenced by the Brahuis in Beluchistan, entered India by the north-west, that of the Kôl family seems to have found admission by the north-east; and as the one flowed south towards Cape Comorin, and the other in the same direction towards Cape Romania, a part of each appears to have met and crossed in Central India.

* Bhumiyas and Kûrs—this becomes Kôls on the east according to Bengali custom, Kooroos on the south. Among rude tribes names for whole tribe are seldom found. It is their neighbours that know them in their collective capacity. Todd in his Travels, page 32, thinks that the name Bhomia is assumed by Bhils in a spirit of boasting. Bhumijs that are among Kôls speak Koli. As to the supposed aborigines of Bengal, see *Bengal Asiatic Society's Journal*, Vol. IX, p. 606. Bhoomijas are the exorcists.—*Tickell*, p. 709.

PART II.—VOCABULARY.

Note by the Editor.

The following Vocabulary of the unwritten dialects of the aboriginal tribes is in all essential particulars the same as that left by Mr. Hislop, but has been re-arranged for this publication. In his manuscript, the alphabetical order of the words was not followed, though doubtless this would have been done had he lived to complete his work. He classified the English words according to subjects, beginning with nouns, which supplied the names of the primary objects of observation; such as the elements, the prominent features in the face of Nature, the minerals, and so on; then the relations in the human community, the members of the human body, the brute creation, the vegetable world. Next came numerals and adverbs. Then came a fairly large selection of adjectives, and, lastly, of verbs.

The English words having been thus classified, the design was to ascertain and record in the Roman character the equivalents in eleven unwritten dialects, namely Gondi, Gayeti, Rutluk, Naikude, Kolami Mádi or Mária, Mádia, Kuri or Muási, Keikádi, Bhatráin, and Párjá. Also in juxtaposition were to be entered the equivalents in the Teloogoo and Tamil languages. It will have been seen from the Essay that Mr. Hislop considered that some affinity was discernible between some of these aboriginal dialects and the Tamil.

But this classification by subjects, however convenient for the rough draft of a vocabulary, in which the words would be entered as they were ascertained from these wild people in the sequence of ideas, would not be suited for publication, when the object is to facilitate reference. It has, therefore, been necessary to re-arrange all the words strictly in alphabetical order.

In several parts of the manuscript Vocabulary, there are breaks and blanks where the work was left unfinished. And for the *verbs*, the equivalents are only given in the Kuri or Muási, and not at all in the Gondi and the other dialects. All the breaks and blanks in the Gondi have been filled up from information obtained at Nagpore, which can probably be relied on. But it has not been possible to supply satisfactorily the deficiencies in the other dialects. This much, therefore, is unavoidably left wanting.

The Vocabulary thus made up comprises some 362 words. Though perhaps tolerably full for an unwritten dialect, it probably does not contain *all* the words actually in use, or otherwise ascertainable. Indeed there are other and additional words used by, or known to, the Gonds of Nagpore. These have been recorded; but they have not been inserted in this Vocabulary, as it seemed better not to enlarge Mr. Hislop's plan, but to leave it in its originality as much as possible.

The Teloogoo and Tamil words have also been entered as given by Mr. Hislop. Several of the coincidences with the Tamil will be found to be interesting and important. In addition to what is said on this point in Mr. Hislop's Essay, I would adduce the following passage from the preface to H. H. Wilson's Sanskrit Grammar :—

"In the south of India cultivated languages of local origin are met with, largely supplied with words which are not of Sanskrit origin. There, however, as in the north, the introduction of Sanskrit was the precursor of civilization, and deeply impressed it with its own peculiarities. The spoken languages were cultivated in imitation and rivalry, and but partially aspired to an independent literature. The principal compositions in Teloogoo, Tamil, Canara, and Malayalam, are translations or paraphrases from Sanskrit works."

In this passage, Teloogoo and Tamil are clearly recognised as aboriginal languages.

In this Vocabulary, also, many words appeared to be borrowed from the Sanskrit, and where this is seemingly the case, I have noted it in the column of remarks.

Some words, also, now naturalized in the Gondi, such as the names of the superior sorts of weapons, are taken from the Hindoostanee, and were probably learnt by the Gonds from the Mahomedans.

Among Mr. Hislop's papers was found a printed copy of the narrative of a second visit to the Gonds of the Nerbudda territory by the Rev. J. G. Driberg and the Rev. H. J. Harrison in 1849, to which was appended a grammar vocabulary of their language. Doubtless Mr. Hislop intended to compare, or may have actually compared, that vocabulary with his manuscripts. But there is no record of such comparison to be found. The comparison has now been made, and may possess some interest, inasmuch as the Gonds whom Mr. Driberg met were those inhabiting the outskirts of the Nerbudda Valley to the north of, or on the northern face of the Sautpoora, or Puchmurree, or Mahadeva hills; whereas the Gonds whom Mr. Hislop met were those dwelling to the south of the range, and separated by mountain barriers from their northern brethren. Some words given in one vocabulary are not found in the other, and *vice versâ*; but, on the whole, that by Mr. Hislop is much the more complete and copious of the two. In many instances there is full atheement; in some, partial resemblance; and in some, difference. In every instance I have noted the result of the comparison in the column of remarks.

In reference to the short grammar given by Mr. Driberg, it may be added that Mr. Hislop does not appear to have commenced the preparation of any grammar, though doubtless he would have done so had he survived.

Also among Mr. Hislop's papers was found a printed copy of the transactions of the Bombay Geographical Society of the year 1846, which contained an account of the Gonds of the Gawil hills on the north of Berar, by Assistant Surgeon Bradley, then of the Nizam's Infantry. To this account was appended a vocabulary of the dialect of the tribes inhabiting those hills. This, no doubt, was intended by Mr. Hislop for purposes of comparison, though no record of such has been left. I find, however, on comparison that the words do not generally agree with the Gondi properly so called, nor with the Gondi words as given by Mr. Hislop and Mr. Driberg. But they do agree to a considerable extent with the Kuri or Muási words as given by Mr. Hislop, and with the words given by other authorities, as spoken by the Koorkus, and by the tribes inhabiting the hills to the south of Hoshungabad.

The result of this latter comparison has not been given in the column of remarks in the Hilsop Vocabulary now under consideration; but has been treated of in another part of this publication.

R. T.

VOCABULARY, AS LEFT BY MR. HISLOP.

English.	Gondi.	Gayeti.	Rutluk.	Ñaikude Gondi.	Kolami.	Mádi, or Mária.	Mádiá.	Kurí, or Muási.	Keikadi.	Bhatráin.	Parjá.	Teloogoo	Tamil.	Remarks by the Editor.
Above	Kis	..	..	..	..	..	..	..	Méle	..	..	Midá	Méle	Is given as Parro in Mr. Driberg's vocabulary.
After	Paja	..	..	..	..	..	..	..	..	..	..	Tarawata	Pirpadu	Gondi term not given by Mr. Hislop, but ascertained at Nagpore.
Air	Wadi	Wadi	Wadi Wadi	Gáli	Gáli	Wadi Wadigu	Wadi	Keyo	Gáli	Wále	..	Gáli	Wau, Káttu	In Sanskrit, Wayo.
All	Sabe	..	Save	Attana	Átte	Sab, Sabato	..	..	Aliveru	..	..	Antá	Yellám	Is given as Sabro in Mr. Driberg's vocabulary.
Alligator	Magod	Magod	Mogdal	Mosali	Mosali	Moyóri, Mosal, Yedumá	..	Mangar	Modalá	..	..	Mosali	Mudalai	In Sanskrit, Muggur.
Although	...	..	..	..	..	..	..	..	Eite	..	..	Ainappaty-Kinni	Agilum	There seems to be no term for this in Gondi.
And	Oondsy	..	..	..	..	..	..	..	..	..	..	Nunnú	Um	The Gondi word not given by Mr. Hislop, but ascertained at Nagpore.

English.	Gondi.	Gayeti.	Rutluk.	Naikude Gondi.	Kolami.	Mádi, or Mária.	Mádiá.	Kuri, or Muási.	Keikadi.	Bhatráin.	Parjá.	Teloogoo.	Tamil.	Remarks by the Editor.
Angry	Riswayál	..	..	..	..	..	..	..	Kowápadu	..	..	Kopaginchu	Kobapadu	The Gondi word not given by Mr. Hislop, but ascertained at Nagpore.
Animal	Janáwar	Janáwar	..	Janáwar	Janáwar	Bárangiwád	..	Jánwar	Janáwar	..	..	Murugamu	Murugum	There seems to be no original word for this in Gondi. The word given is borrowed from the Hindoostanee.
Answer (v.)	Pallosiana	..	..	..	..	..	..	..	Suninu	..	..	Jawabuiv-vu	Uttarvuko-du	The Gondi word not given by Mr. Hislop, but ascertained at Nagpore.
nt, black	Patte	Pate	..	Simál	Shimel	Pette, Pitti, Chutti	..	Cháti	..	..	..	Chimá	Yerumbú	The Gondi term corresponds with that given in Mr. Driberg's vocabulary.
Antelope	Koti	Koti	Harná	Sikárak	Kori	Koti, (m) Taluri, (f)	Yesarmow	Ghotári	Jinká	..	..	Jinká	Mán	
Ant, white	Udeli, Alu	Alu	Diwar	Sedal	Sedal	Yelam, Yelumi, Nusu	..	Ninder	..	..	..	Chedalu	Karayán	Is given as Dianri in Mr. Driberg's vocabulary.
Any	Bore, (m) Bati (f)	Bore, (m) Bati (f)	Bore	Yannakátir	Amdenen	Bortadi, Portáinda-ná Bánataki	..	..	Yedagao	..	..	Vedayná	Yedágilum	The Gondi term corresponds with that given in Mr. Driberg's vocabulary.
Arm	Kai	Kai	..	Ki	Kiyu	Kai-Dandá	..	Ti	Keiya	Kai	Pittá	Chei	Kai	Do. Do.

Arrive (v.)	Handana	..	..	..	..	..	..	..	Nilungo	..	..	Chéru	Séru	The Gondi word not given by Mr. Hislop, but ascertained at Nagpore. It is given as Aoville in Mr. Driberg's vocabulary.
Arrow	Tir	..	..	Tir	Murre	Kádi, Káni	Kádi	Tir	Tirkamtá	..	..	Ambu	Ambu	There seems to be no original Gondi word for this. The word given is borrowed from the Hindoostanee.
Aside	Oondikhak	..	..	...	..	..	..	..	Bagalno	..	..	Pakka	Pakkam	The Gondi word not given by Mr. Hislop, but ascertained at Nagpore.
Ask (v.)	Talkana	..	..	..	..	..	..	..	Kerungo	..	..	Adugu	Kél	Do. Do.
Back	Morchul, Parki	Pareká	Murchul, Pareke	Sarál	Ven	Murchuli, Molako, Piake	..	Bhawadi	Mudgu	..	..	Vipu, Yenná	Muduvú	....
Bad	Kharab	Ànemátal	Buro	Nasádin	Karáb	Lágor, Lágo	..	Karáb	Kettá	..	..	Cheddá	Kettá	Is given as Burtor in Mr. Driberg's vocabulary
Bag	Piwasi	Kothani	Jeke	Pisavi	Pisavi	Piwasi, Chanchi	..	Tēili	Pai	..	..	Chanchi	Pai	....
Bambu	Wadúr	Wadúl	Wandur	Yedul	Vetur	Yeduri, Veduri, Vedu	..	Máhat	Wadaru	..	..	Yedurú	Múngil	The Gondi term corresponds with that given in Mr. Driberg's vocabulary.
Bark	Tol	Tol	..	Chiltá	Chakkal	Tol, Tolá	..	Chali	Chaká	..	..	Chaká	Pattei	....

English.	Gondi.	Gayeti.	Rutluk.	Naikude Goudi.	Kolami.	Mádi, or Máría.	Mádiá.	Kuri, or Muási.	Keikadi.	Bhat-ráin.	Parjá.	Teloogoo.	Tamil.	Remarks by the Editor.
Basket	Wodi	Wodi	..	Burra	Topalá	Tukadi, Dutti	..	Dindna, Topla	Gula	..	..	Gampa Tatta	Kúdei	....
Be (v.)	Ám	Ingi	Inge	Attena	..	Dryaná	..	Danyá	Nilu	..	..	Awawalanu	Iru	The Gondi term correspond with that given in Mr. Driberg's vocabulary.
Beads	Poti	..	..	..	..	..	..	..	..	..	..	Pusi	Mani	....
Bear	Yedjál	Ádjál	Ádajal	Guddi	Kutti	Yedaju, Yaréd	..	Báná	Asolu	..	..	Gudelugu	Karadi	Is given as Wehtalle in Mr Driberg's vocabulary.
Beard	Dáditu	Dádi	Dádhing	Gaddam	Dilas	..	Gaddam	Dádi	..	..	..	Guddam	Dádi	....
Before	Munnai	..	..	..	..	..	..	..	Munnuki	..	..	Yedatta	Munne	The Gondi term not give by Mr. Hislop, but asce tained at Nagpore.
Behind	Paja	..	..	..	..	..	..	..	Pragu	..	..	Yenaka	Pinne	It corresponds with that give in Mr. Driberg's vocabu lary.
Belly	Pir	Pir	Pir	Pottá	Pottá	Pottá	..	Lai	Warg	Pottá	..	Pottá	Wairú	The Gondi term correspond with that given in M Driberg's vocabulary.

Below	Naili, Sir	..	..	..	..	..	..	..	Digu	..	..	Kinda	Kile	The Gondi term not given by Mr. Hislop, but ascertained at Nagpore. It is given as Tarri in Mr. Driberg's vocabulary.
Between	Nuddum	..	..	..	..	..	..	..	Naduwa	..	..	Naduma	Naduvu	The Gondi term not given by Mr. Hislop, but ascertained at Nagpore.
Bind	Dohtana	..	..	..	...	..	..	..	Kattapo-dungá	..	..	Kattu	Kattu	Do. Do.
Bird	Pitte	Pitte	Pithe	Pittá	Sidemugi	Pittá, Parittá	Pidho	Titit	Kunju, Piská	..	..	Pitta	Kuruvi	The Gondi term corresponds with that given in Mr. Driberg's vocabulary.
Bite	Kuskana	..	..	..	..	..	..	..	Kadi	..	..	Karuvu	Kadi	The Gondi term not given by Mr. Hislop, but ascertained at Nagpore. It corresponds with that given in Mr. Driberg's vocabulary.
Bitter	Kaitá	Keiemul	Keitá	Send	Chendu	Kahitá	Keile	Katik	Kachu	..	..	Chedu	Kasuppu	The Gondi term corresponds with that given in Mr. Driberg's vocabulary.
Black	Karyál	Kadiyal	Kariyal	Mulludi	Dowdan-karí	Káriyál, Jurtor, Karkál	Kariyál	Kende	Karupu	..	..	Nalupu	Karpána	Do. Do.
Blind	Andra	Andhamal	..	Guddi	Murtá	Kádál, Kondábeg	..	Andá	Guddukan-na	..	..	Guddi	Kuruttu	In Sanskrit, Andh.
Blood	Natúr	Natúr	Natúr	Netúr	Natúr	Netúr	Kanhántue	Pachna	Natho	..	..	Netrú	Rattam	The Gondi term corresponds with that given in Mr. Driberg's vocabulary.

English.	Gondi.	Gayeti.	Rutluk.	Naikude Gondi.	Kolami.	Mádi, or Mária.	Mádia.	Kuri, or Muási.	Keikadi.	Bhat-ráin.	Parjá.	Teloogoo.	Tamil.	Remarks by the Editor.
Blue	Nil	Kariyál	Nilo	Nil	Karinil	Nil, Togari	..	Nila	Nila	..	..	Nilamu	Nila	In Sanskrit, Nil.
Blunt	Bothad	..	Meidhákodi	Mondi	Meijá	Wumgutu, Horo	..	..	Mondi	..	..	Mondi	Mondiyana	....
Body	Mendol	Mendol	Madol	Men	Arkali	Mendul, Mendoli	..	Komor	Wodmu	..	..	Wollu	Wodambu	The Gondi term corresponds with that given in Mr. Driberg's vocabulary.
Bone	Padeká	Padeká	Hada, Padeka	Bokkál	Bokka	Pedeká, Bokairo	Atká	Hadi	Yamká	..	..	Bokka, Yemuka	Yelumbu	Is given as Harga in Mr. Driberg's vocabulary.
Bow	Kamta	..	..	Galal	Vil	Vilhu, Nungu	..	Kamta	Undelu	..	..	Undilu, Vilu	Vilu	The Gondi term not given by Mr. Hislop, but ascertained at Nagpore.
Box	..	..	..	Petari	Salad	Japi, Koska	..	Petali	Patti	..	..	Petti	Potti	....
Boy	Tuda, Pedgal	Pedgal	Pedaga	Dodhan	Podas	Pikor, Padalira	..	Ganda	Gundta	..	Toko	Pillawadu	Payan	The Gondi term corresponds with that given in Mr. Driberg's vocabulary.
Branch	Kándi	..	Jar, Khákaj	Pát	Komul	Kándáng, Kandairo, Kohuku	Dettee	Dangál,	Kala	..	...	Komma	Kelei	....

Brass	Pitur	Pitur	Pitur	Pital	Pital	Pitór, Molá	Pital	Pitar	Pitalá	..	..	Yittadi	Pitalei	The Gondí term is borrowed from the Hindí.
Bring	Táttana	..	..	..	..	..	..	..	Kunda	..	..	Tisukurá	Kondá	The Gondí term not given by Mr. Hislop, but ascertained at Nagpore. It corresponds with that given in Mr. Driberg's vocabulary.
Broad	Rund	Rudo	Chakro	..	Podam	Rund, Borilá, Godi	..	..	Sayal	..	..	Wedulpú	Agalamáná	....
Brother	Dádá (e) Tamúr (y)	Dádá	Dádá, Tamúr	Toren	Bhaw	Dada, Tomúr Tamwri	..	Dádá	Anná, Tambi	..	..	Anná (e) Tammudu (y)	Anná (e) Tambie (y)	The Gondí term corresponds with that given in Mr. Driberg's vocabulary.
Buffalo	Boda (m) Yedmi (f)	Boda (m) Yedmi (f)	Bodál (m) Ádami (f)	Helyá (m) Chir (f)	Sir (m) (f)	Yeliyál (m) Yermi (f)	Adami	Butkil	Hate (m) Baremádu (f)	Cher	Banktal	Barré, Géde	Yerumai	Do. Do.
Bullock	Kondá	Kondá	Kodám	Hed	Yed	Kondá, Gondá	Dhali Kondá	Dhobá	Potmád	Baddá	Bádi	Yeddu	Yerudú, Mádu	Do. Do.
Burn (v.)	Karustana	..	..	..	..	..	..	..	Chuttupodu	..	..	Veluginchu	Kolutu	The Gondí word not given by Mr. Hislop, but ascertained at Nagpore. It is given as Mastalle in Mr. Driberg's vocabulary.
Bury (v.)	Nissana	..	..	..	..	..	..	..	Mannukudu	..	..	Patthu	Pudal	Do. do. do. It is given as Mistalle in Mr. Driberg's vocabulary.
Butterfly	Pápe	Pápe	..	Pákoli	Urugumasal	Guge, Kuge	..	Kapuli	Kunju	..	..	Ákupitta	Pápátí	The Gondí term corresponds with that given in Mr. Driberg's vocabulary.

English.	Gondi.	Gayeti.	Rutluk.	Naikude Gondi.	Kolami.	Mádi, or Mária.	Mádia.	Kuri, or Muási.	Keikadi.	Bhatráin.	Parjá.	Teloogoo.	Tamil.	Remarks by the Editor.
Buy (v.)	Yáitana	..	..	..	..	..	..	..	Wángu	..	..	Konu	Vángu	Not given by Mr. Hislop, but ascertained at Nagpore.
By	Igat	..	..	..	..	..	..	..	..	..	..	Wullá	Nále	The Gondi term corresponds with that given in Mr. Driberg's vocabulary.
Calf	Kurá (m) Peiyá (f)	Kurá (m) Peiyá (f)	Kurrápadá, (m) Peiyá (f)	Lengá	Lenká	Peiyá	..	Gorá	Mátkuti	..	..	Peyá, Dooda	Kannukuti	Do. Do.
Call (v.)	Kaiyana	..	..	..	..	..	..	..	Kutápodu	..	..	Piluvu	Kupidu	The Gondi term not given by Mr. Hislop, but ascertained at Nagpore. It corresponds with that given in Mr. Driberg's vocabulary.
Cat	Bilál	Bilál	Bilál	Pilli	Pilli	Biláli Pusál	Bilái	Minnu	Puná	Bilar	Guku	Pilli	Púnai	....
Cheap	Sasto	..	Sasto	Chawaká	Soidadem	Sukhare, Kenawantu Kágántá	..	..	Agáwá	..	..	Sawaká	Maliváná	....
Cheek	Karvi	Korvi	Korvi	Pukhul	Dádá	Bhuká Phuká	..	Joka	Gandá	..	..	Buggalu	Kannangul	....
Chest	Cháti	Sáti	Máril	Arli	Arkil	Sáti, Arul	..	Cháti	Najgudu	..	..	Rommu	Márú	The Gondi term is borrowed from the Hindi.

Child	Chawá	Chawá	Chewá	Bala	Padas	Chawá	..	Tádei	Dadi	..	..	Bálá	Pullei	The Gondi term corresponds with that given in Mr. Driberg's vocabulary.
Chin	Hotáli	Thadawa	Tádawá	Gaddam	Gaddam	Thádawá Dadi	..	Dadi	Dadi	..	..	Geddamu	Dadi	....
Claws	Kojji	..	Kaye	Panja	Panja	..	..	Panj	Koikál	..	..	Gorlu	Negam	The Gondi term is given as Tirinj in Mr. Driberg's vocabulary.
Clean	Chokot	..	Sisa	..	Soita	Bidbid	..	Choka	Suddi	..	..	Subramu	Subramána	....
Cloth	Dhadotá	Dikadi	Dikadi, Chindrá	Kandwá	Sunge	Gende	..	Tutri	..	Gándá	Chindra	Batta	Tuni	The Gondi term is given as Dikri in Mr. Driberg's vocabulary.
Cloud	Bádal	Abhárwát	Bádar	..	Babiwátar	Abúl, Abarai	..	Bádal	Mod	..	..	Mogulu	Mugil, Pugar, Megam	The Gondi term corresponds with that given in Mr. Driberg's vocabulary.
Cock	Ghoghoti	Ghoghoti	..	Pot	..	Gogodi	..	..	Koi	Adad, Dada	Gopungdong, Hanpadar	Punju	Cháwal	Do. do.
Cold	Mudungtá	Mudnugtal	Marustá	Igam	Pani	Dalangtá, Kinda Keringtá	..	Chamrabáng Rarang	Idá	..	..	Challana	Sidalamana Kularu	Do. do.
Come	Wara	..	..	..	..	..	..	..	Wango	..	..	Ra	Va	The Gondi word not given by Mr. Hislop, but ascertained at Nagpore. It corresponds with that given in Mr. Driberg's vocabulary.

English.	Gondi.	Gayeti.	Rutluk.	Naikude Gondi.	Kolami.	Mádi, or Mária.	Mádia.	Kuri, or Muási.	Keikádi.	Bhatráin.	Parjá.	Teloogoo.	Tamil.	Remarks by the Editor.
Copper	Támbo	Támbo	Támo	Tambá	Támbá	Tamboi	Tam	Tamba	Rági	..	..	Rági	Tambrum Chembu	In Sanskrit, Tamra.
Cow	Tali, Muda	Mudá	Muda	Kutte	Kutte	Mure, Mura	..	Gai	Potamadu	Goe	Kitta	Au	Pasumadu	The Gondi term corresponds with that given in Mr. Driberg's vocabulary.
Crooked	Hekodal	Waritá	Wariál	Wánkade	Sarase	Waktá, Adám, Wadeg	Ádaphi	Kwocha	Wánká	..	..	Wankára	Kónalána	In Sanskrit, Wakra.
Crow	Kawal	Kawal	..	Kawala	Kaka	Kákadi Kakari	Kabal.	..	Koi	..	..	Kaki	Kaka	The Gondi term corresponds with that given in Mr. Driberg's vocabulary.
Cucumber	Wahaku	Wahaku	Wahakum	Parki	Kaikul	Kákadi Hiraka	..	Tákher	Káksdi	..	..	Dósakáya	Vélerekoi	....
Cut (v.)	Aska	..	..	..	..	..	..	..	Aru	..	..	Kói	Aru	The Gondi term not given by Mr. Hislop, but ascertained at Nagpore. It corresponds with that given in Mr. Driberg's vocabulary.
Dance (v.)	Yandana	..	..	..	..	..	..	..	Adu	..	..	Adu	Adu	Do. Do.
Darkness	Andhár	Narká	Sikáti	Chidedin	Ropálsát	Andhárá, Hikaráta	..	Indara	Irtu	..	..	Chíkati	Irutu	In Sanskrit, Undhkar. The Gondi term is given as Sikatti in Mr. Driberg's vocabulary.

Daughter	Miár,	Tudi	Mayá, Dali	Komal	Kumal	Miyar, Miyadi, Magei	Márdi	Konjái	Pomalpilla	Mal	..	Kútru	Magal	The Gondi term corresponds with that given in Mr. Driberg's vocabulary.
Day	Din	Din	Piyál	Pod	Páte	Peyál	Biyár	Din	Pugdu, Poddu	..	..	Dinamu Pugdu	Dinam Nal	In Sanskrit, Din. The Gondi term corresponds with that given in Mr. Driberg's vocabulary.
Deaf	Báhira	Báhira	Báhiral	..	Shewadá	Báhira, Boyál	..	Bahira	Chevda	..	..	Chovati	Chevudu	In Sanskrit, Buhir.
Dear	Kad	..	Mahanga	Piriyam	Kattamá	Padátán, Udu	..	..	Patu	..	..	Piriyamu,	Koraivu	....
Die (v.)	Sayana	..	..	..	..	..	..	..	Setupo	..	..	Chau	Savu	The Gondi term not given by Mr. Hislop, but ascertained at Nagpore. It corresponds with that given in Mr. Driberg's vocabulary.
Dirty	Gade, Surta	Surta	..	..	Mulepatti	Machata	..	Kumut	Kartu	..	..	Murko	Alukana	....
Do (v.)	Kim	Kim	Kim	..	..	Kimu, Kim	..	Deie	Sei	..	..	Cheyi	Sei	The Gondi term corresponds with that given in Mr. Driberg's vocabulary.
Dog	Nei	Nai	Nei	Átte	Átte	Neiyu Neio	Nei	Chita, Seta	Nai	Neta	Gusak	Kukka	Nai	Do. Do.
Door	Dwar	Dwar	Daridad	Dong	Satekotar	Dware Agei	..	Kora	Wasalu	..	..	Wakile	Wasal	Do. Do. In Sanskrit, Dwar.

English.	Gondi.	Gayeti.	Rutluk.	Naikude Gondi.	Kolami.	Mádi, or Mária.	Mádia.	Kuri, or Muási.	Keikádi.	Bhatráin.	Parjá.	Teloogoo.	Tamil.	Remarks by the Editor.
Driuk	Oondana	..	..	..	..	..	..	..	Kudi	..	..	Tagu	Kudi	Is given as Undalle in Mr. Driberg's vocabulary.
Dumb	Mukal	..	Bankor	..	Muti	Mukkál	..	Gungá	Kunda	..	..	Muga	Umayana	In Sanskrit, Mookal.
Early	Pihato	..	Tapane	Patadin	Itetullani	Sekári (morning, like quickly)	..	Sakal Parta	Jaldi	..	..	Tuwurga	Tuwaridama	Is given as Narkhey in Mr. Driberg's vocabulary.
Ears	Kavi	Kavi	Kavi	Kewul (pl.)	Kavvul (pl.)	Chouku Kewoku (pl.)	Kavi	Lutur	Suvi	..	..	Chevvalu	Kádugul	The Gondi term corresponds with that given in Mr. Driberg's vocabulary.
Earth	Dhartri	Dhartri	Dhartri	El	El	Dartri	Neli	Ote, Wote	Nard	Nindil	Tubo	Dharani Bhumi	Ulagum Buni	....
East	Khalwa	..	Dinukti	..	..	Porad pechina (Sun rises)	..	..	..	..	..	Túrpu	Kezsaku	The Gondi term not given by Mr. Hislop, but ascertained at Nagpore.
Eat (v.)	Tindana	..	..	..	..	..	..	..	Tin	..	..	Tinu	Tinu	The Gondi term corresponds with that given in Mr. Driberg's vocabulary.
Eight	Yermud	Yermud	Armur	..	At	Átte, Atu, Ermadi	At	Ilarku Ilariya	Yet	...	..	Yenimidi	Yettu	....

Eleven	Akra	..	..	..	Akra	Akra, Padanji	..	Geraku	Padronu	..	..	Padakóndu	Padinonru	The Gondi word not given by Mr. Hislop, but ascertained at Nagpore.
Eyes	Kan (s.) Kank (pl.)	Kark (pl.)	Kanak (pl.) Kadak (pl.)	Kandlu (pl.)	Kanul (pl.)	Kondá	Kodá	Met, Med	Kan	..	..	Kanlu (pl.)	Kangul	The Gondi term corresponds with that given in Mr. Driberg's vocabulary.
Face	Todi	Todi, Wan	..	Mokam	Mutti	Todi Moha	Dhodi	Chabu, Mou	Wai	..	..	Mokham	Mugum	....
Fall (v.)	Urrana	..	..	..	..	..	..	..	Bunduko	..	..	Padutum	Vizsa	The Gondi term not given by Mr. Hislop, but ascertained at Nagpore. It corresponds with that given in Mr. Driberg's vocabulary.
Far	Lak	Lak	Lab	Daw	Peredáw	Vilak, Jeku	Lap	Atár	Dúram	..	..	Dúramu	Dúram	....
Fat	Kodavinch, Tajo (adj)	Kodavij	Korbis, Karal (adj.)	Koru	Koraw, Kubamon (adj.)	Koduwasku, Koduanji, Kosela, Mendul, Berpor(adj.)	..	Charbi, Bedeka	Nono Todu (adj.)	..	..	Kovu Balupu	Koluppu Kozsuta	....
Father	Baba, Dada	Baba	Bawo, Dada	Tag	Bao	Baba	Bakdalta	Ba-Abba	Eiya Baba	Tata	Hap-pang	Abba	Appa	The Gondi term corresponds with that given in Mr. Driberg's vocabulary.
Fear (v.)	Varitana	..	..	..	..	..	..	..	Bitko	..	..	Jaduvu Biapadatam	Biapudu	The Gondi term not given by Mr. Hislop, but ascertained at Nagpore. It corresponds with that given in Mr. Driberg's vocabulary.
Feather	Marel	Mádar	Máder	Bul	Kadal	Burá, Pulá	..	Kata	..	..	..	Yerkalu	Iragu	Is given as Marchk in Mr. Driberg's vocabulary.

English.	Gondi.	Gayeti.	Rutluk.	Naikude Gondi.	Kolami.	Mádi, or Mária.	Mádia.	Kuri, or Muási.	Keikádi.	Bhatráin.	Parjá.	Teloogoo.	Tamil.	Remarks by the Editor.
Field	Neli	Nel	Ka	Khen	Senikikum	Gate, Seneiram	..	Kati	Kwala	..	..	Chenu, Polamu	Wail, Káshani	The Gondi term corresponds with that given in Mr. Driberg's vocabulary.
Fifty	..	..	..	..	..	Rand, visa, dahi (two, twenty, ten)	Adhei kodi (two and a half score)	..	..	..	..	Yabai	Ainbudu	There seem to be no Gondi word for this Known at Nagpore.
Finger	Wadanj	Wadinj	..	Vende	Vendal (pl.)	Wadas, Veras	..	Anduk	Warka	..	..	Véllu	Virul	The Gondi term corresponds with that given in Mr. Driberg's vocabulary.
Fire	Kis	Kis	Kis	Kich	Kis	Kis	Kis	Singal	Narpu	Kich	Sawal	Nippu	Nerupu	Do. Do.
Fish	Min	Min	..	Keiye	Kei	Min	Min	Kaku	Min	..	..	Chapa	Min	Is given as Mind or Mindk in Mr. Driberg's vocabulary
Five	Seiung	Seiyung	Seiyu	Panch	Aidu	Siyum, Siyu, Hium, Heingu, Aigu	Heigi	Maneiku	Anj	..	..	Aidu	Anjei	....
Flesh	Savi	Savi	Sachchi, Savi	Nanjud	Nanjudu	Ahi, Hawi Avi	..	Jilu	Kari	..	..	Nanjudu	Karí, Irachi	....
Flower	Pungár	Pungár	Pungár	Putá	Phuel	Pungár, Pungári, Puita	Pungár	Phul	Phuo	..	..	Phuo	Phuo	The Gondi term corresponds with that given in Mr. Driberg's vocabulary.

Fly	Visi	Visi	..	Ningál	Ningá	Visu, Visi, Nule	..	Ruku	Yi	..	..	Yige	Yi	The Gondi term corresponds with that given in Mr. Driberg's vocabulary.
Foolish	Gawar	..	..	..	Dadapan-hiren	Wosumbar-hal	..	Akalbang	Buddhiledu	..	..	Verry Debe Pichche	Mutál	Is given as Bhondu in Mr. Driberg's vocabulary.
Foot	Kal	Kal	Kal	Talgatta	Taral	Kal	Kal; foot only: Erp-wugi	Jang	Kal	..	..	Pádamu Kalu	Pádam	The Gondi term corresponds with that given in Mr. Driberg's vocabulary.
Forty	Rand, eisai (two, twenty)	..	..	..	..	Chalis, Rand visa	Rand kodi (two score)	..	..	..	..	Nalubai	Narpadu	Not given by Mr. Hislop, but ascertained at Nagpore.
Four	Nalung	Nalung	Nalu	Char	Naling	Nal	Nalgu	Upanku	Nal	..	..	Nalugu	Nangu	....
Fruit	Sudta, Pandu	Sadta	..	Pel	Panal	Pandi Kaja	..	Chali	Phalo	..	..	Pandú	Palam	In Sanskrit, Ful.
Get (v.)	Yaitana	..	..	..	..	..	..	..	Konda	..	..	Sampadin-chutum	Sambadi	The Gondi term not given by Mr. Hislop, but ascertained at Nagpore. It is given as Putile in Mr. Driberg's vocabulary.
Girl	Tudi, Pedgi	Pedgi Pekin	Pedagi	Pilla	Pilla	Pedi, Pekis	..	Erkon	Warponu	..	Toki	Pilla Pudehu Chinathe	Pen	The Gondi term is given as Ferdgi or Pekin in Mr. Driberg's vocabulary.
Give (v.)	Siana	..	..	..	..	..	..	..	Kudu	..	..	Ivu	Kudu	The Gondi term not given by Mr. Hislop, but ascertained at Nagpore. It is given as Siana in Mr. Driberg's vocabulary.

English.	Gondi.	Gayeti.	Rutluk.	Naikude Gondi.	Kolami.	Mádi, or Mária.	Mádia.	Kuri, or Muási.	Keikádi.	Bhatráin.	Parjá.	Teloogoo.	Tamil.	Remarks by the Editor.
Go (v.)	Handana	..	..	..	..	..	..	..	Ponga	..	..	Poutam, Vellutam	Po	The Gondi term not given by Mr. Hislop, but ascertained at Nagpore. It corresponds with that given in Mr. Driberg's vocabulary.
Goat	Bokadal (m) Yetti (f)	Bokadal (m) Yeti (f) Here (f)	Bukaral (m) Edi (f)	Meka	Meke	Bokada (m) Yatti (f) Here (f)	Edhi	Bongara, Siri	Ad	..	..	Meka	Adu	The Gondi term corresponds with that given in Mr. Driberg's vocabulary.
Gold	Sano	Sono	Sono, Sun	Sona	Sone	Chonos Sono	..	Sunna	Kali	..	..	Bangáramu	Pon	....
Good	Chokat	..	Tisa	Berindod	Dadam	Besh Nehana Neinatu	Nehana	Awal	Nalla	..	..	Chokamu Bága	Nalla	The Gondi term is given as Choko or Achcho in Mr. Driberg's vocabulary.
Grass	Jádi	Jádi	Jári	Gaddi	Gaddi	Jadi, Kar, Piri	..	Jará	Gadi	..	..	Gaddi	Pille	The Gondi term corresponds with that given in Mr. Driberg's vocabulary.
Grave	Gam	..	..	..	Mudusar	..	..	..	Gambher	..	..	Gambhiramu	Gambiramana	
Great	Fada, Paror	Sajor	Jetan	Dahud Dodo	Gubanda	Bedha, Beraha, Perama	..	Kat, Gad	Bardu	..	..	Pedda	Periya	Do. Do.
Green	Hirawa	Kache	Hariro	Pachaná	Pachchi	Arta, Artana	Hariyal	Hara	Pasuru	..	...	Pachoha	Patohai	....

Gum	Saver	Saver	Modegudi	Bikká	Banká	Hewar, Heveri, Kewakli	..	Tiki	Banki	..	..	Banká	Pisni	....
Hair	Chuti	Chuti	Robachuti	Til	Til	Kelku	Kalak	Katha, op, up	Meir	Choa	Higho	Ventrukalu	Meir	The Gondi term corresponds with that given in Mr. Driberg's vocabulary.
Half	Adho	..	..	..	..	Ardha	..	Adha	..	..	..	Ardha	Arai	In Sanskrit, Ardh.
Handsome	Sajari	..	Nehen Lachkut	Dadapata	Dadápan	Beshmukhami, Karkal	Nehana	Chajar	Nalla	..	..	Chakkadanamu	Sauindiyamaua, Alugu	Do. Soondur.
Hard	Sabado	Nimaro	Kurro	Gatt	Kupani	Gatti, Pugta	..	Kara	Gatti	..	..	Gatti	Gattiana	....
Hate	..	..	..	..	..	..	..	..	Dushmanisei	..	..	Punginchu	Pagai	....
Hatchet	Murs	..	..	..	..	..	..	..	..	..	..	Guddali	Kodali	....
Have	Mayana	..	..	..	..	..	..	..	Erku	..	..	Kalligiunduta	Vai Odatai	....
He	Hore	Wor	Ad	Ound, Ad	Ad	Woru, Oru	..	Hán	Ado	..	..	Wadu	Avan	The Gondi term is given as Wor or Wur in Mr. Driberg's vocabulary.

English.	Gondi.	Gayeti.	Rutluk.	Naikude Gondi.	Kolami.	Mádi, or Mária.	Mádia	Kuri, or Muási.	Keikádi.	Bhatráin.	Parjá.	Teloogoo.	Tamil.	Remarks by the Editor.
Head	Talá	Talá	Talá	Tal	Kupál	Tala, Talai	Tala	Dui	Talkai	Talu	Bo	Tala Talkai	Talai	The Gondi term corresponds with that given in Mr. Driberg's vocabulary.
Hear (v.)	Keinjana	..	..	..	..	..	..	..	Kar, Wei	..	..	Vinuta	Kell	The Gondi term not given by Mr. Hislop, but ascertained at Nagpore. It corresponds with that given in Mr. Driberg's vocabulary.
Heavy	Puhta	Pubata	Pukta	Vekam	Mop	Puhuta	..	Kamalba	Bhari	..	..	Bhaluvu	Báram	....
High	Phural	..	Uncho	Podam	Peratpodam	Berasta, Peragupa	..	Bharie	Yetu	..	..	Yettu	Wyaram	The Gondi term not given by Mr. Hislop, but ascertained at Nagpore.
His	Hona	Oná	Waná	Awanet Yenuet	Awanel	Woná Hatundu	Woná	..	Atuti	..	..	Vadiokka	Avanúdaya	....
Hog	Padi	..	Padi	Turre	Turre	Paddi, Patti	Pahi	Chukadi	Pani	Pendu	Jibi	Pandi	Panni	....
Hoof	Khuri	Khuri	Nejikhuri	Kur	Kur	Kuringe	..	Kudi	Kurrá	..	..	Gurisé Kurrumu	Negum Kulambu	In Sanskrit, Kshoor. It is given as Kurk in Mr. Driberg's vocabulary.
Horns	Kor, Kohak (pl.)	Kor Kohak (pl.)	Singikor	Komul	Pedata	Korru, Kor, Kohak (pl.) Baraya	..	Singi	..	..	..	Kommulu	Kodu Kombu	The Gondi term corresponds with that given in Mr. Driberg's vocabulary.

Horse	Kodá	Kodá	Kodá	Gurram	Gurram	Kodá, Gudá	Kodá	Ghodgi	Kudara	Guram	Kitá	Guram	Kudurai	The Gondi term corresponds with that given in Mr. Driberg's vocabulary.
Hot	Kástá	Kastal	Kasta	Ukhadá	Situr	Kasta, Kasinta	Kasta	Lolor	Udku	..	..	Uduku	Kaivulla, Veppum, Soodu	The Gondi term is given as Castal in Mr. Driberg's vocabulary.
House	Ron	Ron	Ron	Ella	Ella	Lon	Lon	Ura	Ud	..	..	Illu	Vidu	....
How	Bahoon	..	..	..	..	..	..	..	Yedanu	..	..	Yetla	Yeppady	The Gondi term not given by Mr. Hislop, but ascertained at Nagpore. It is given as Ba in Mr. Driberg's vocabulary.
How large	Bachor, Phura	..	..	..	..	..	..	..	Yentawasu	..	..	Yenta peddadi	Yevvalavu-periyadu	The Gondi term not given by Mr. Hislop, but ascertained at Nagpore.
How much	Bachola	..	..	..	..	..	..	..	Yentabaru	..	..	Yenta	Yevvulavu	The Gondi term not given by Mr. Hislop, but ascertained at Nagpore. It corresponds with that given in Mr. Driberg's vocabulary.
HumbleBee	Patte	Pate	..	Bangaro	..	Bungara	..	Bhawara	Yermu	..	..	Tumadalu	Bandu	....
Hundred	Nur	Nur	..	..	..	Nuru	Hein kodi (Five score)	Chovi	..	..	..	Náru	Náru	....
I	Anna	Nana	Nanna	An	An	Nanna, Nan	Ana	In	Nanu	..	..	Nenu	Nan	The Gondi term corresponds with that given in Mr. Driberg's vocabulary.

English.	Gondi.	Gayeti.	Rutluk.	Naikude Gondi.	Kolami.	Mádi, or Mária.	Mádia.	Kuri, or Muási.	Keikádi.	Bhatráin.	Parjá.	Teloogoo.	Tamil.	Remarks by the Editor.
Insect	Pudi	Pudi	Purush	Purre	Purel	Pudi Pette	..	Kide Takhur	Pulga, Busi	..	..	Purugu	Puchi	....
Iron	Kachchi	Kachchi	Kachi	Yinamu	Lokand	Kachi	Kachi	Loha	Ilmu	..	..	Inumu	Irumbu	The Gondi term corresponds with that given in Mr. Driberg's vocabulary.
It	Wur	Wur	..	..	..	..	..	..	..	..	..	Adi	Adu	The Gondi term is given as Ad in Mr. Driberg's vocabulary.
Ivory	Palk	Palech	Enibisa	Palko	Goral	Palku Palle	..	Kisá	Anakwora	..	..	Danthaomu	Tandam	....
Juice	Ras	Sawar	Rasad	Ir	..	Er	..	Da	Ras	..	..	Rasamu	Rasum	In Sanskrit, Ras.
Jumpabout	Dyana	..	..	..	..	..	..	..	Iteatidunku	..	..	Yeguruta, Dumkuta	Inga-anga-kudi	The Gondi term not given by Mr. Hislop, but ascertained at Nagpore. It is given as Daiktalle in Mr. Driberg's vocabulary.
Jump over	Dysibandana	..	..	..	..	..	..	..	Dunku	..	..	Dumkatam	Tándi kudi	The Gondi term not given by Mr. Hislop, but ascertained at Nagpore.
Jungle	Dongur	Dongur, Kheda	Jengur, Kheda	Adei	Adávi	Geda	..	Dongar	Kad, Phalar	...	..	Adavi	Kádu	....

Kill (v.)	Jukkana	..	..	..	..	..	..	..	Praname-du	..	..	Champuta	Kolhu	The Gondi term not given by Mr. Hislop, but ascertaiued at Nagpore. It corresponds with that given in Mr. Driberg's vocabulary.
Knee	Tonghade	Tonghade	Ghutawá	Tongal	Mudushul	Mindá	..	Tongará	Mokál	..	..	Mokallu	Mulangal	The Gondi term is given as Tongro in Mr. Drsberg's vocabulary.
Know (v.)	Mayana	..	..	..	..	..	..	..	Arjukango	..	..	Verugota	Ari	The Gondi term not given by Mr. Hislop, but ascertained at Nagpore. It is given as Pundalle in Mr. Driberg's vocabulary.
Lame	Langada	Langadal	Khāral	Langada	Janwatti	Kutta, Katal	..	Langa-dya	Kuntukála	..	..	Kunti	Nendi	The Gondi term appears to be borrowed from the Hindí.
Land crab	Kekada	Yete	Kekedá	Yendá	Yendá	Kekadei, Yatti	..	Kátkum, Kekade	Nand	..	..	Yendraka-ya	Nundu	....
Late	Usir	..	Ser, Serdu	Podkurtin	Gormatti	Mulpe, (evening)	..	Jerye	Mella	..	..	Mellaga, Alasiyam	Tamasam	....
Laugh (v.)	Kawana	..	..	..	..	..	..	..	Sri	..	..	Naúta	Sri	Gondi term not given by Mr. Hislop, but ascertained at Nagpore. It is viven as Kaoille in Mr. Driberg's vocabulary.
Leaf	Áki	..	Áki	..	Yegul	Áki	Áki, Maka	Chakam	Yela	..	..	Aku	Yelei	The Gondi term corresponds with that given in Mr. Driberg's vocabulary.
Lean	Sir	..	Bator	..	Teitan	Watitor, Vetita	..	Usuya	Nodundu	..	..	Chikina	Ileitta	The Gondi term is given as Sirtal in Mr. Driberg's vocabulary.

English.	Gondi.	Gayeti.	Rutluk.	Naikude Gondi.	Kolami.	Mádi, or Mária.	Mádia.	Kuri, or Muási.	Keikádi.	Bhat-ráin.	Parjá.	Teloogoo.	Tamil.	Remarks by the Editor.
Left	Dáwo	..	Dawo	Donki	Edamakei	Adanág, Dawar, Demar	..	Dawa	Pich	..	..	Yedama	Yeda, Pich	The Gondi term is given as Đero in Mr. Driberg's vocabulary.
Leg	Kal	Kal	..	Getal	Getal	Kalu	..	Jang	Mokal	Kalu	Susu	Kalu	Kal	....
Leopard	..	..	..	Chita	Chittar	Tumari, Niral, Nekali	..	Sonorá	Chite	..	..	Chirta	Chirtai	....
Light	Vedchi, Halko (adj)	Vedchi, Halko (adj)	Beijianjor	Vektín, Walang, Halká (adj)	Velang, Halke (adj)	Ves, Peinina-ta (adj) Peingina-ta (adj)	Hujaláhur	Ujawaro, Halka (adj)	Paymaro, Halka (adj)	..	..	Velugu, Suluvu(adj)	Velicham, Suchum	The Gondi term corresponds with that given in Mr. Driberg's vocabulary.
Lightning	Vij, Mirchatá	Vij	Bijuli	Merpate	Merpad	Mirchanta, Mirchanda	..	Charán-wo, Chiran	Minari	..	..	Merupu	Minnul	The Gondi term is given as Mitstata in Mr. Driberg's vocabulary.
Lips	Silvi	Sivli	Silvi	Peddel	Peddel	Hilivi, Pilivi, Gadam	..	Liur	Wordu	..	..	Pedivilu	Wodadu	....
Little	Thodko	..	Thoro	Torra	Turra	Ichun, Huduk	Hudu, Ugunam	Thani	Tode	..	..	Konchamu	Chinna	....
Live (v.)	Pissána	Pisina	Pistor, Biso	..	..	Pistor	..	Jiw	Pogasupon-ga	..	..	Jivinchata	Pizsei	The Gondi term corresponds with that given in Mr. Driberg's vocabulary.

Lizard	Kidúrdoke	Ijgur	Gharar khal	Pal	Sindrá	Doke	..	Chirmun-gi	Wona	..	..	Balli	Palli	....
Long	Leior	..	Leior	Podam	Pudam	Lakhu, Lati	..	Giling	Wasara	..	..	Podugu	Neglam	....
Loose	Dhilo-kia-na	..	..	..	..	..	..	..	Amtudun-ga	..	..	Wadulu	Vidu Thalathi	No Gondi word for this seems to be known at Nagpore.
Love (v.)	Jiwa lagana	..	..	..	..	..	..	..	Battisei	..	..	Mohinchuta	Unba	The Gondi term not given by Mr. Hislop, but ascertained at Nagpore. It is given as Ladkialle in Mr. Driberg's vocabulary.
Low	Neli	..	Nicho	Dubrak	Utten	Pedal	..	Ita	Gidda	..	..	Potti	Kizsa	....
Man	Mánwál	Mánwál	Manwol	Mas	Pedda	Manei, Koitar	Manei, Gaita	Koro	Managi	Manai	Angar	Manushi	Manidan	The Gondi term is given as Maurdsal in Mr. Driberg's vocabulary.
Mangoe	Marka	Marka	Wará	Mámadi	Mámdi	Marka, Makka	..	Amb	Mángái	..	..	Mamadikoi	Mangai	....
Mat	Kati	Kati	Kati	Sapa	Cháparas	Chapi, Dala, Sarpa	..	Boriya	Pai	..	..	Chapa	Pai	....
Merry	Khushyal	..	Sukhwar	..	Tudak	Manawal	..	Anandi	Kushi	..	..	Ulasámu	Kalipu, Ulasa	....

English.	Gondi.	Gayeti.	Rutluk.	Naikude Gondi.	Kolami.	Mádi, or Mária.	Mádia.	Kuri, or Muási.	Keikáḍi.	Bhat-ráin.	Parjá.	Teloogoo.	Tamil.	Remarks by the Editor.
Milk	Pal	Pal	Pal	Pal	Pal	Pal-u-e	..	Dudom	Pal	..	..	Palu	Pal	The Gondi term corresponds with that given in Mr. Driberg's vocabulary.
Mine	Nawa	Idana, Awá	Náwá	Anet	Aneten	Náwá	..	Ing	Namtu	..	..	Nayokka	Yennudaya	
Monkey	Kove	Mujal	Kevi, Puwal	Mui	Mui	Munj-u, or mus	Mujal	Sará	Kwoti	..	..	Koti	Kurangu	Do. Do.
Month	Maihana	Maihana	Mahina	Mahina	Mahina	Mahina, Hatu, Nalanjmen-di	..	Mahina	Mado	..	..	Nela	Madam	In Sanskrit Mas, in Hindi Mahina.
Moon	Nalej	Nalej	Nalej, Jagon	Nela	Nela	Nelanj-i-u	Chandanlej	Gumong, Chando	Nalou	Nalin	Atka	Yennala	Nela, Chandran	The Gondi term is given as Chandal in Mr. Driberg's vocabulary.
Mother	Ya, Ma, Bau	Dai	Dai, Ouwal	Amma	Amma	Yali, Awa	Maiyal	Aya, Ma	Amma	Yan	Yang	Amma, Tali	Tai	The Gondi term corresponds with that given in Mr. Driberg's vocabulary.
Mountain	Mattá	Matta	Mata	Seppa	Met	Metta	Madhá	Katadi	Gutta	..	..	Gutta	Malei	....
Moustache	Misháng	Michhe	Micehegam	Misal	Misal	Misa	Mishal	Mache, Musar	Misou	..	...	Misalu	Misle	....

Much	Wale	Wale	Walle	Dagár	Kub	Velle	Bel	Galetakig	Wanrási	..	..	Mikili	Michamana	The Gondi term is given as Pharol in Mr. Driberg's vocabulary.
Mud	Chikla	..	..	..	..	..	..	..	Burde	..	..	Burda	Cheru	The Gondi term corresponds with that given in Mr. Driberg's vocabulary.
Musket	..	..	..	Tupak	Tubak	Tupáki Topak	..	Bhanduk, Palita	Tubáki	..	..	Tupaki	Tubaki	....
Nail	Tidinj,	Tidinj	..	Gol	Goral (pl.)	Hidiaku (pl)	..	Nok, Nak	Goru	..	..	Goru	Negam	The Gondi term corresponds with that given in Mr. Driberg's vocabulary.
Narrow	Nirund	..	Sakro	..	Madikan	Uduku, Bonda	Hudul	..	Narká	..	..	Iruka	Nerukamana	....
Near	Karum	Karum	Karúm	Daia	Madawattan	Vere, Here	Hor	Merá	Kitte	..	..	Daggira	Kitta	The Gondi term is given as Karúmpt in Mr. Driberg's vocabulary.
Neck	Gudungá, Wadal	Wadel	Warer	Mak	Mak	Gúdangá, Vereri	..	Gungi	Partálá	..	..	Meda	Midam	....
New	Punál	Punál	Punál	Kottá	Kottá	Puná	..	..	Pudidu	..	..	Kotta	Pudisa	The Gondi term corresponds with that given in Mr. Driberg's vocabulary.
Night	Narka	Narka	Narka	Ale	Andhar	Narka	Narka	Rati	Namar	..	..	Ratri, Raju	Ratri, Irul	Do. Do.

English.	Gondi.	Gayeti.	Rutluk.	Naikude Gondi.	Kolami.	Mádi, or Mária.	Mádia.	Kuri, or Muási.	Keikádi.	Bhat-ráin.	Parjá.	Teloogoo.	Tamil.	Remarks by the Editor.
Nine	Naw	Naw	..	..	Naw	Nawe, Ermu, Tumadi	Naw	Areiku	Wamberu	..	..	Tommidi	Onbadu	In Sanskrit, Now.
Ninety	..	..	..	..	..	..	..	Nawad	..	..	..	Tombhai	Tunnúru	No Gondi term for this is known at Nagpore.
No	Halli	..	..	..	..	..	..	..	Illa	..	..	Ledu	Ille	The Gondi term not given by Mr. Hislop, but ascertained at Nagpore. It corresponds with that given in Mr. Driberg's vocabulary.
North	..	..	..	..	..	Adam	..	..	..	..	..	Utaram	Vadaku	The Gonds seem to have no term for this.
Nose	Masor	Masor	Masor	Mungol	Mungát	Mosor, Mosákei	..	Mu	Muku	..	..	Mukku	Múku	The Gondi term corresponds with that given in Mr. Driberg's vocabulary.
Now	Inga	..	..	..	..	..	..	..	Ipo	..	..	Ippudu	Ippo	
Oil	Ni	Ni	Ni	Nane	Nune	Ni, Nai, Niyu	Nei	Sunúm	Yana	..	..	Nune	Yennei, Nei, Ninam	Do. Do.
Old	Junalk, Sedal (age)	Junal, Sedal (age)	Sedhál, Seda (age)	Pátá, Pobalak (age)	Pát, Bubbak (age)	Padána, Purana, Muitor (age) Muido (age)	..	Dukra (age)	Pugadu, Kelava (age)	..	..	Pata, Musaliwadu (old man) Musalidi (old woman)	Pazsaya, Kizza (age)	Do. Do.

One	Undi	Undi	Wundi	Wákko	Okadu	Undi, Wunči, Wandi	Udi	Nekor	Wanu	..	..	Okati	Wondru	....
Onion	Oolli	..	..	Gaddá	Wuligadda	Wulli	Mati	Kandi	..	..	..	Uligadda	Vengayum	The Gondi term not given by Mr. Hislop, but ascertained at Nagpore. It is given as Gondri in Mr. Driberg's vocabulary.
Other	Doosro	..	Dusero	Inu	Vegare	Verre	..	..	Unonu	..	..	Vere	Vere, Inonu	The Gondi term not given by Mr. Hislop, but ascertained at Nagpore.
Ours	Mawa	Idana awa	Mawa	Amed	Anet	Mawa, Adunawand	..	Ńan	..	..	..	Manayokka	Yengaluda-ya	....
Palm (of the hand)	Hatteri	..	Latori	Talki	Árungkei	Nalla	..	..	Árakei	..	..	Arechei	Arunkei	The Gondi term corresponds with that given in Mr. Driberg's vocabulary.
Peacock	Mara, Mal	Mal	..	Lamani	Namali	Mal, Mallu	..	Mera	Namali	..	..	Namali	Mail	....
Plain	Ruphad	Pallá	Pallá	Talán	Meidan	Tallá	..	Raphad	Meidán	..	..	Beilu	Meidánam	....
Plantain	Ker, Kereng (pl.)	Ker	Kera	Kela	Kor	Kedi, Dugadi	..	Kete, Thora (wild)	Walasadi,	..	..	Artipandu	Wálapalam	....
Play (v.)	Gursana	..	..	..	..	..	..	..	Adu	..	..	Ádukóvata	Vileadu	The Gondi term not given by Mr. Hislop, but ascertained at Nagpore.

English.	Gondi.	Gayeti.	Rutluk.	Naikude Gondi.	Kolami.	Mádi, or Mária.	Mádia.	Kuri, or Muási.	Keikádi.	Bhat-ráin.	Parjá.	Teloogoo.	Tamil.	Remarks by the Editor.
Poison	Vik	Vik	Mahur	..	Singa	Yik-i	..	Bicho	Iko	..	..	Vishamu	Visham	....
Pull (v.)	Oommana	..	..	..	..	..	..	..	Gunju	..	..	Laguta, Gunju	Ila	The Gondi term not given by Mr. Hislop, but ascertained at Nagpore. It is given as Umille in Mr. Driberg's vocabulary.
Pumpkin	Paras	Kudeseni	Kubada	Rajkode	Topritik	Kumadi, Puka	..	Kural	..	..	..	Gummadi-kaya	Pusanikai	....
Push (v.)	Dhuklakhi-ana	..	..	..	..	..	..	..	Dubbuda	..	..	Toiata	Talla	The Gondi term not given by Mr. Hislop, but ascertained at Nagpore. Seems in part to be derived from the Hindi.
Put down (v.)	Watana	..	..	..	..	..	..	..	Tarliwei	..	..	Kindaun-chata	Kileveia	The Gondi term not given by Mr. Hislop, but ascertained at Nagpore. It is given as Dasialle in Mr. Driberg's vocabulary.
Quarrel	Kalagata	..	..	..	..	..	..	..	Chandapo-du	..	..	Keiyamu-cheiata	Sandaipoda	The Gondi term not given by Mr. Hislop, but ascertained at Nagpore.
Quarter	Pariá	..	..	..	..	Pau	..	Pasa	..	..	..	Paú Patika	Kal	....
Rain	Pirwáetá	Pirwata	..	Wana	..	Pirwanta	..	Dag	Mala, Maga	Wani	..	Wana	Mazshei	The Gondi term is given as Pirr in Mr. Driberg's vocabulary.

Rainbow	Gunel	Gunsl	Goragulel	Dhanu	Veldundá	Dumavilu	..	Damaku-to,	Arjunaba-nou	..	..	Dhánasu	Wanavil	....
Rat	Yelli, Mosal	Ali	Álimusal	Elká	..	Yelka, Umps	..	Puchi	Yeli	..	..	Elka, Mosali	Yeli	The Gondi term corresponds with that given in Mr. Driberg's vocabulary.
Raw (unripe)	Hivwo, Kai	Kái	Kacho	..	Keik	Kodukelá, Kaiar, Kai	Káyá	Kách	Kai	..	..	Kai	Kaí	....
Red	Lal	Bulal	Sundi	Yerodi	Yerrodi	Netral-i, Reugal, Pekieli	Lal	Ratta,	Yerpu	..	..	Yerupu	Sivapu	....
Remain (v.)	Man	Man	Man, Posa	Tak	..	Manu, Nilá	..	Dumáie	Nilu	..	..	Undu	Nila (stand) Irra (remain)	The Gondi term is given as Mandalle in Mr. Driberg's vocabulary.
Rice	Pariyak, Nuka	Pariyak, Nuka	Para, Nuka	Biam	Walkul	Nuka	Nuka, Wanji	Chawal	Nal, Arshi	Parkul (cleaned)	Káru-ng	Biyam, Nuka	Arsi	The Gondi term corresponds with that given in Mr. Driberg's vocabulary.
Right	Jewano	..	Jewono	Unaki	Unnakei	Tina-r-di	..	Jawane	Sot	..	..	Kudi	Valadu	Do. Do.
Ripe	Pandatál	Pandatá	Pandi	Panditin	Pannu	Muitá, Pandi	Padale	Biliye	Pala, Pagdu	..	..	Pandu	Pazsuta	....
Rise (v.)	Nittana	..	..	..	..	..	..	..	Ninduko	..	..	Legu	Yezsundra	The Gondi term not given by Mr. Hislop, but ascertained at Nagpore.

English.	Gondi.	Gayeti.	Rutluk.	Naikude Gondi.	Kolami.	Mádi, or Mária.	Mádia.	Kuri, or Muási.	Keikádi.	Bhat-ráin.	Parjá.	Teloogoo.	Tamil.	Remarks by the Editor.
River	Jhodi	Jhodi	Kurergangá	Peni	Peni	Berer-i-dota	..	Gada	Ár,	..	..	Yeru	Aru	The Gondi term is given as Dhoda in Mr. Driberg's vocabulary.
Root	Sir	Sid	Sid, Jari	Vel	Vendal	Yirku, Mada, Hisko, Veki	..	Jar	Budo	..	..	Véru	Véru	The Gondi term corresponds with that given in Mr. Driberg's vocabulary.
Rough	Kharbush-ál	Kor	..	..	Adenak	Merta	..	..	Kundukur-pa	..	..	Gurukyna	Karadana	....
Round	Gol	Wátarál	..	Watore	Gundu	Gommá	Gula	Gol	Gundra	..	..	Gundramu	Urandaya-na	In Sanskrit, Golakirt.
Run (v.)	Vittana	..	..	..	..	..	..	..	Wodu	..	..	Urkota	Woda	The Gondi term not given by Mr. Hislop, but ascertained at Nagpore. It corresponds with that given in Mr. Driberg's vocabulary.
Salt	Sawod	Sawod	Sawor	Sup	Sup	Áwori, Howar	Howar	Bulum	Upu	..	..	Uppu	Uppu	The Gondi term corresponds with that given in Mr. Driberg's vocabulary.
Sâmbar	Maw	Maw	..	Kadas	..	Máw	..	Roi	Manbot	..	..	Ambot	Kádimán	....
See (v.)	Hoorana	..	..	..	..	..	..	..	Parungo	..	..	Chudu, Chuchuta	Parka	Gondi term not given by Mr. Hislop, but ascertained at Nagpore. It is given as Hurille in Mr. Driberg's vocabulary.

Seek (v.)	Hoorana	..	..	..	..	..	..	..	Paru	..	..	Vedukuta	Tédu, Paru	The Gondi term not given by Mr. Hislop, but ascertained at Nagpore.
Sell (v.)	Mammana	..	..	..	..	..	..	..	Ichupodu	..	..	Ammuta	Vitka	The Gondi term not given by Mr. Hislop, but ascertained at Nagpore. It corresponds with that given in Mr. Driberg's vocabulary.
Seven	Yedung	Yeruug	Erug	..	Yed	Sátte, Satu, Yedu, Eirum	Sat	Yeiku	Yal	..	..	Yédu	Yézsu	....
Sharp	Sodta	Sorta	Tejdar	Dar	Sudi	Darwata, Horata	..	Borbor	Pudun	..	..	Churukyna	Kúrulla	The Gondi term corresponds with that given in Mr. Driberg's vocabulary.
She	War	War	Ad	Ad	Ad	Oru	..	Han	Ado	..	..	Ame	Aval	....
Shield	Dhar	..	..	Dhal	Dhal	Dhal, Dali Mogei	..	Dhal	Dhali	..	..	Dhalu, Kedemu	Kedayum	....
Short	Chodor	..	Chudur, Abado	Mota	Moda	Kande, Daktir	..	Kodar	Giddu	..	..	Kúrasa, Potti	Kuttamána Kullamana	The Gondi term not given by Mr. Hislop, but ascertained at Nagpore.
Shoulder	Sattá	Satta	Satti	..	Bujal	Hatta	..	Kánde	Bujo	..	..	Bhújamu	Buyam, Tól	The Gondi term corresponds with that given in Mr. Driberg's vocabulary.
Silver	Kuro	Kuro	Rup	Kure	Kurá	Kuro Rupo	..	Chándi	Wali	..	..	Vendi	Vellie	....

English.	Gondi.	Gayeti.	Rutluk.	Naikude Gondi.	Kolami.	Mádi, or Mária.	Mádia.	Kuri, or Muási.	Keikádi.	Bhatráin.	Parjá.	Teloogoo.	Tamil.	Remarks by the Editor.
Sing (v.)	Warana	..	..	..	..	..	..	..	Pada	..	..	Paduta	Páda	The Gondi term not given by Mr. Hislop, but ascertained at Nagpore. It corresponds with that given in Mr. Driberg's vocabulary.
Sister	Taka, Bai (e) Selod (y)	Bai, Selad	Bai, Selad	Bai	Torandál	Bai	Akka	Jiji	Akka, (e) Tangchi (y)	..	..	Ukka (e) Chella (y)	Ukka (e) Tangáchi (y)	The Gondi term corresponds with that given in Mr. Driberg's vocabulary.
Sit (v.)	Ooddana	..	..	..	..	..	..	..	Ukka	Und	Lesá	Kurchun-data	Ulkara	The Gondi term not given by Mr. Hislop, but ascertained at Nagpore. It corresponds with that given in Mr. Driberg's vocabulary.
Six	Sarug	Sarung	Sarug	Saha	Ar	Sarum, Saru, Harum, Aru	Harug	Tureiku	Ar	..	..	Áru	Áru	
Skin	Tol	Tol	..	Tolka	Tol	Tol	Tol	Katre	Tolu	..	..	Tólu	Tól	
Sky	Abhar	Abhar	Sargam	Ákásh	Abhár, Paiti	Ábá, Moyule	Desub	Agas, Badrájá	Máná	Bádar	Bileng	Akásamu, Minu	Wánam	
Sleep (v.)	Narmana	..	..	..	..	..	..	..	Tungu	..	..	Nidrapovuta	Túnga	Do. Do.
Small	Chudor, Loro	Chudor	Chudor	Chinná	Chinnam	Hudilá, Udlo	Hudili	Sang, Sani	Chinna	..	...	Chinna	Siria, Chinna	The Gondi term corresponds with that given in Mr. Driberg's vocabulary.

Smell	Mooskana	..	..	..	..	..	..	..	Musi	..	..	Vasana	Mara	The Gondi term not given by Mr. Hislop, but ascertained at Nagpore. It is given as Dengla in Mr. Driberg's vocabulary.
Smoke	Poyo	..	Kum	Duam	Pog	Dudom, Poyá	..	Dudur	Poga	..	..	Poga	Pugei	The Gondi term is given as Kumb in Mr. Driberg's vocabulary.
Smooth	Chopado	..	..	Sowan	Awdesak	..	..	Bulari	Samana	..	..	Nunupu	Semmamána	....
Snake	Tadas	Tadas	Taras	..	Pam	Taras, Tarasi	..	Bing	Pamu	..	..	Pamu	Pambu	The Gondi term correspond with that given in Mr. Driberg's vocabulary.
Soft	Naram	Naram	Kowaro	Mette	Mette	Gulgulâti, Pagwan	..	Lopot	Kulu	..	..	Mettana	Medwulla	
Son	Marri, Tudal	Marri	Marri	Kike	Kike	Marre, Magái	Mighi	Kon	Amilpilla (male child)	Chind	..	Koduku	Magan	Do. Do.
Sour	Savitá	Savitál	Nagul	..	Tiıre	Wovita, Weita, Pulla	Dhirdhira	Kataye	Pulpu	..	..	Pulchu	Pullippu	....
South	..	..	..	..	..	Adam	..	..	..	..	..	Dachanamu	Terku	There seem to be no word for this in Gondi.
Speak (v).	Wurkana	..	..	..	..	..	..	..	Pesu	..	..	Mattaladuta	Pesa	The Gondi term not given by Mr. Hislop, but ascertained at Nagpore. It is given as Wankille in Mr. Driberg's vocabulary.

English.	Gondi.	Gayeti.	Rutluk.	Naikude Gondi.	Kolami.	Mádi, or Mária.	Mádia.	Kuri, or Muási.	Keikádi.	Bhat-ráin.	Parjá.	Teloogoo.	Tamil.	Remarks by the Editor.
Spear	Bhala	Gorka	..	Barsi	Bhalas	Gorra, Gorka	..	Barchi	Barshi	..	..	Bhallamu	Wallayam	....
Square	Charkuntya	..	Khutul	..	Okesarase	..	..	Cherku-tya	Choukunta	..	..	Choukamy-na	Chakutkum	....
Stand (v).	Nittana	..	..	..	..	..	..	..	Ninduko	..	..	Niluvutá	Nila	The Gondi term not given by Mr. Hislop, bnt ascertained at Nagpore. It corresponds with that given in Mr. Driberg's vocabulary.
Star	Sukum	Sukum	Sukum	Sukha	Chukka	Uko, Huku	Hukam	Epal, Idiu	Chukka	..	..	Chukka	Tárakei	The Gondi term corresponds with that given in Mr. Driberg's vocabulary.
Steal (v).	Kallana	..	..	..	..	..	..	..	Tigudusei	..	..	Dongilin-chuta	Tiruda	The Gondi term not given by Mr. Hislop, but ascertained at Nagpore. It corresponds with that given in Mr. Driberg's vocabulary.
Stone	Kal	Kal	Kal, Pata	Gund	Dop	Kal	K al	Degá	Kal	..	..	Rai	Kal	....
Straight	Sarko	Kasnu	Kasum	Dadapad	Andidadam	Kasumi, Kasomue	Soj	Korá	Sukágá	..	..	Chakkaga	Nérana	....
Strike (v).	Jiana	..	..	..	..	..	..	..	Adi	..	..	Kottuta	Adia	The Gondi term not given by Mr. Hislop, but ascertained at Nagpore.

Strong	Jor	..	Garbhi	..	Dadapan, Soitan	Lawu	..	Kubaku	Joru	..	..	Balamyna	Balamulla	The Gondi word is perhaps borrowed from the Hindi.
Sun	Suryal, Din	Suryál Din	Surajá	Suryátali	Podh	Porde, Podudu, Yadde	Pod	Gomoi	Surya	Pokal	Si	Suryadu	Suryan	In Sanskrit, Surya. The Gondi term corresponds with that given in Mr. Driberg's vocabulary.
Sweet	Mingul	Mingul	Mithomi	Tirre	Send	Mingta, Mirangul	Milgale	Simel	Tipu	..	..	Tipu	Tittippu	The Gondi term is given as Minunktal in Mr. Driberg's vocabulary.
Sword	Talwar	..	Kiwotá	Tarwan	Talwar	Talwar	..	Talwar	Kati	..	..	Kati	Kati	The Gondi word is borrowed from the Hindi. There seems to be no original word in Gondi for this.
Tail	Tokár	Tokár	Tokár	Toká	Toká	Toká, Tokar	..	Chut	Toká	..	..	Tóka	Wal	The Gondi term corresponds with that given in Mr. Driberg's vocabulary.
Take (v).	Wontona	..	..	..	..	..	..	..	Yedutuko	..	..	Tisukòuta	Yeda	The Gondi term not given by Mr. Hislop, but ascertained at Nagpore. It is given as Yetalle in Mr. Driberg's vocabulary.
Take away	Wontona	..	..	..	..	..	..	..	Yedu	..	..	Tisukupo	Yedtapo	Do. as Woyalle, Do.
Tear	Sarotana	..	..	..	..	..	..	..	Pichpodh	..	..	Chimputa	Kizsi, Picha	Do. as Sarretalle, Do.
Teeth	Palapal-k (pl.)	Pal-k (pl.)	Palak (pl).	Palku (pl.)	Palkul (pl.)	Pal, Palku (pl.)	Palaku (pl.)	Tiding	Pal	..	..	Panlu	Palgal	....

English.	Gondi.	Gayeti.	Rutluk.	Naikude Gondi.	Kolami.	Mádi, or Mária.	Mádia.	Kuri, or Muási.	Keikádi.	Bhat-ráin.	Parjá.	Teloogoo.	Tamil.	Remarks by the Editor.
Ten	Daha	Daha	Pad	..	Daha	Daha, Dase, Pade	Das	Gelku	Patu	..	..	Padi	Pattu	....
That	Hud, War, Wor	Wor	Wor	Ad	Atol	Woru, Oru, Attu	..	Hardi	Ture	..	..	Adi	Adu	....
Theirs	Hon, Wora, Wura	Adawonan	Hadenal	Awaned	Awareten	Wona Adunmon-andana	..	..	..	..	..	Wariyokka	Avargalu-daya	....
Then	Anni	..	..	..	..	..	..	..	Apo	..	..	Appudu	Appo	....
There	Hukkai	..	..	..	..	..	..	..	Akada	..	..	Akkada	Ange	The Gondi term not given by Mr. Hislop, but ascertained at Nagpore. It is given as Hoga in Mr. Driberg's vocabulary.
They	Hurk, Wurk	Wor	..	..	Awar	Woru	..	Arko	..	..	..	Wáru	Ávargal	....
Thigh	Kudki	Kudki	..	Ranku	Kudukul	Kudki	..	Bulu	Toda	..	..	Toda	Todai	The Gondi term corresponds with that given in Mr. Driberg's vocabulary.
Thine	Niwá	Niwá	Niwá	Inet	Ineten	Niwá	..	Ama	Nimtu	..	..	Niyokka	Unnudaya	....

Thirty	Tisa	Tisa	..	..	..	Tis, Dedhvisa	Didhakodi	Tis	(Cant count above vis)	..	..	Muppai	Muppadu	....
This	Yer (m) Id (f)	..	..	Id	Idda	Veru, Viru, Attu	..	..	Kite	..	..	Idi	Idu	....
This also	Adundai	..	..	..	..	..	..	..	Idikuda	..	..	Iduini	Idu-um	....
Thou	Imme	Ime	Imá	Niwa	Niwa	Nima	..	Am	Ninu	..	..	Nivou	Ní	....
Thousand	Huzar	Hazar	..	..	..	Achari	..	..	..	..	..	Vei	Aezam	....
Three	Muud	Mund	Mund	Mundi	Munding	Mundu	Mund	Akor, Apkor	Munu	..	..	Mudu	Múndru	....
Three quarters	..	..	..	..	..	..	..	Afapasa	..	..	..	Muppátika	Múkkal	....
Thunder	Garjaná	Garjaná	Garjaná	Garja	..	Garjit, Uram	..	Sadiwo	Garchiri	..	..	Urumu	Muzsakam	....
Tiger	Puli	Burkál	Pulial (m) Bagheli (f)	Pul	Pul	Burkal, Dual	Burkal	Kula	Puli	Du	Gikkal	Puli	Puli	The Gondi term corresponds with that given in Mr. Driberg's vocabulary.

English.	Gondi.	Gayeti.	Rutluk.	Naikude Gondi.	Kolami.	Mádi, or Mária.	Mádia.	Kuri, or Muási.	Keikádi.	Bhatráiu.	Parjá.	Teloogoo.	Tamil.	Remarks by the Editor.
To	..	..	..	..	..	..	..	..	Ku	..	..	Ku	Ku	....
Tobacco	Bhangi	..	Tamak	Tambáku	Pok	Dningá, Poga, Pokka	Poga	Tamaku	..	..	..	Pogáku	Pugellei	In Sanskrit, Tumal.
Today	Naind	..	..	..	..	..	..	..	Iuanu	..	..	Nedu	Innaki	The Gondi term not given by Mr. Hislop, but ascertained at Nagpore.
Toe	Wadanj	Wadanj	Wadanj	Vende	Getal, Vendal	Kaliwadasku	..	Jangan-duk	Warka	..	..	Kaluvelu	Kalvirul	
Tomorrow	Nadi	..	..	..	..	..	..	..	Nalaka	..	..	Répu	Nalaki	Do. Do.
Tongue	Wanja,	..	..	..	..	..	Wanja	..	..	..	..	Nálika	Nak	The Gondi term is given as Wanjar in Mr. Driberg's vocabulary.
Tree	Mará	Mada	Mará	Chet	Mot	Mara	Bhanda	Sing	Maro	Mareng	Lánta	Chettu	Maram	The Gondi term corresponds with that given in Mr. Driberg's vocabulary.
Turmeric	Kamká	Kamká	Kamka	Pasáp	Pasapul	Kanka, Kamka, Gamka	..	Kesang	Majal	..	..	Paspu	Manjal	....

Twelve	..	..	..	..	Bara	Bara, Padaran-du	..	Baraku	Panind	..	..	Panindu	Pannirendu	....
Twenty	Visa	Visa	..	..	Vis	Bis, Visa, Irwa	Bis	Bis	Vis	..	..	Iruwei	Irupadu	The Gondi term is borrowed from the Hindi
Two	Rand	Rand	Rand	Indi	Inding	Randu	Rand	Barkoo	Rand	..	..	Randu	Irendu	....
Ugly	Chokat hilli	..	Buro	..	Wadinasat-ti	Lagor, Katta	Banomyo	..	Gidadu	..	..	Vikáramy-na	Andakeda-na	....
Village	Nar, Nak (pl).	Nar	..	Ur	Ur	Nar-u, Nagu	Nar	Gawa	Uru	..	..	Úru	Úr	The Gondi term corresponds with that given in Mr. Driberg's vocabulary.
Waist	Nadi, Nani	Nadi	Nadinnani	Mulke	Mulke	Nadi, Nanni Mokchul	..	Mejang	Nadu	..	..	Nadumu	Nadu	....
Wake (v).	Chaitoana	..	..	..	..	..	..	..	Yedi	..	..	Melkóuta	Yelundru	The Gondi term not given by Mr. Hislop, but ascertained at Nagpore.
Walk (v).	Takana	..	..	..	..	..	..	..	Nadu	..	..	Naduvuta	Nadā	Gondi term not given by Mr. Hislop, but ascertained at Nagpore. It is given as Takille in Mr. Driberg's vocabulary.
Want	..	..	..	..	..	..	..	..	Paje	..	..	Káwalenu	Vendia	....

English.	Gondi.	Gayeti.	Rutluk.	Naikude Gondi.	Kolami.	Mádi, or Mária.	Mádia.	Kuri, or Muási.	Keikádi.	Bhat-ráin.	Parjá.	Teloogoo.	Tamil.	Remarks by the Editor.
Water	Yer	Yer	Er	Ir	Ir	Er, Yegu	Per	Da	Tanni	Nir	Dong	Nilu	Tunnir	....
Wax	Men	Men	Mewana ..	Menam	Menam	Watte	..	Meina	Meinou	..	..	Meinamu	Mozsugu	....
We	Amot	Mamad	..	..	Anandun	Mam	..	Ále	Nang	..	..	Manamu	Nangul	....
Weak	Dhilo	..	Itore	..	Sadamtari-kam	..	..	Bangbal	Dila	..	..	Balahinamu	Balainama-na	....
Weep (v).	Adana, Arana	..	..	..	..	..	..	..	Agu	..	..	Yeduta	Azsu	The Gondi term not given by Mr. Hislop, but ascertained at Nagpore.
West	Paroy	..	Dinbudti	..	..	Porad, Eriana	..	..	..	..	..	Paschamu	Merku	Do. Do.
What	Bang	Badanga	Badáng	Táne	Táneten	Bara	Bara	Tune, Yo	Yendu	..	..	Yimi	Yenna	
When	Baska	..	..	..	..	..	..	..	Yepo	..	...	Yeppudu	Yeppo	Do. Do.

Where	Bugga	..	..	..	..	..	..	..	Yekada	..	..	Yekkada	Yenge	The Gondi term not given by Mr. Hislop, but ascertained at Nagpore.
Which	Bad	Bad	Bako	Yand	Yetten	Bona, Patenind	..	..	..	..	..	Yedi	Yedu	….
White	Pándari	Pandari	Pandaro	Touda	Telodi	Pándari, Viditor	Padaral	Pulung	Vella	..	..	Tellupu	Velley	….
Who	Mare	Bor, Boni	Bor	Yenendiw	Niveniv	Boru, Poniuda	Bor	Tuni, Eiye	Yedu	..	..	Yevaru	Ar	The Gondi term corresponds with that given in Mr. Driberg's vocabulary.
Why	Bassáti	..	..	..	..	..	..	..	Yenátuku	..	..	Yenduku	Yen	The Gondi term not given by Mr. Hislop, but ascertained at Nagpore. It is given as Barri in Mr. Driberg's vocabulary.
Window	..	..	..	Bagga	Kidakis	Arri, Hari, Magei	..	..	Kidaki	..	..	Didi, Kidiki	Palagani	….
Wings	Mare	..	..	..	Redapal	Mare, Maráki	..	Panko	..	..	..	Rekka	Rekkai	….
Wise	Shahanál	..	Akaldar	..	Soitabudhi	Seleseinal, Putako	..	Churta, Diand	Buddhi-mandu	..	..	Buddhi-mantudu	Budhi	….
Within	Rappu	..	..	..	..	..	..	..	Wulle	..	..	Loga	Wulle	The Gondi term not given by Mr. Hislop, but ascertained at Nagpore.

English.	Gondi.	Gayeti.	Rutluk.	Naikude Gondi.	Kolami.	Mádi, or Mária.	Mádia.	Kuri, or Muási.	Keikádi.	Bhat-ráin.	Parjá.	Teloogoo.	Tamil.	Remarks by the Editor.
Without	Bahro	..	..	..	..	..	..	..	Beilu	..	..	Beita, Vina	Veliye, Tavira	The Gondi word not given by Mr. Hislop, but ascertained at Nagpore. Seems to be borrowed from the Hindi.
Women	Ad	Ad	Or	Áima	Pilákun	Adu, Ar, Enchaira	..	Japai	Pondu, Badi	Haial	Anvon	Ádadi	Pendu	The Gondi term corresponds with that given in Mr. Driberg's vocabulary.
Wood	Katiya, Geda	Katiya	Katiya	..	Sivvá	Katiyá	..	Subá	Muddu	..	..	Kutte	Viragu, Marram	In Sanskrit, Kasht. The Gondi term corresponds with that given in Mr. Driberg's vocabulary.
Work	..	..	..	..	..	..	..	..	Pani	..	..	Pani	Velei	No Gondi term for this is ascertainable at Nagpore.
Wrist	Mungut	..	Guti	Mangat	..	Gutkeiyu	..	Malgati	..	..	..	Manykattu	Manikai	The Gondi term not given by Mr. Hislop, but ascertained at Nagpore.
Ye	Immet	Im	..	..	Niwa	Mirad	..	Ape	Ne	..	..	Miru	Ningul	....
Year	Sal	Sal	Barsa	Yadel	Salber	Salmeda	..	Sal	Wotkál	..	..	Yadádi	Warushum	Is borrowed from the Hindi.
Yellow	Kamkal	..	Pilo	Piwala	Biwaras	Kankal, Puwarali	..	Sarsang	Manja	..	..	Pasupu	Manja	....

Yes	Hingi	..	..	..	..	..	...	..	Ámbo	..	..	Avunu	Am	The Gondi term not given by Mr. Hislop, but ascertained at Nagpore.
Yesterday	Nadi	..	..	..	..	..	..	..	Ninná	..	..	Ninna	Nétu	Do. Do.
Young	Riyor	Rayo	Reior	Mindegi	Mindegi	Leior, Neio	..	Jawán	Gowadá	..	..	Pasi	Yilia	....
Yours	Niwa, Miwa	Idawonan	Miwa	Imed	Yeinnaton	Miwa, Aduniwand	..	...	..	..	..	Niyokka	Ungaludaya	....

NOTE.—In this Vocabulary the Gondi verbs are all given in the infinitive mood, which may be known by the termination "ana"

Note by Editor on the following Supplement to the Hislop Vocabulary, as respects the Gondi dialect only.

Mr. Hislop's Vocabulary is so far comprehensive, that perhaps it may be well to make it as complete as possible, according to the means available at Nagpore. The following list of English words is given, which appear to be useful, although they did not enter into Mr. Hislop's scheme. And the synonyms are given in Gondi as ascertained from Gonds at Nagpore. Though the population of Nagpore is not, of course, Gond, still the Deogurh Gond Rajah and his dependants live there; and there are Gond Ozhas (or minstrels) there also, on whom Mr. Hislop used to rely as being of some authority on these points. But in offering this brief Supplement, I by no means intend it to be supposed that this list includes all the remaining Gondi words, or that there are no other words. Indeed there may be many others, and doubtless there must be such.

R. T.

SUPPLEMENT TO THE HISLOP VOCABULARY, AS RESPECTS THE GONDI DIALECT ONLY.

English.	Gondi.	English.	Gondi.
A.		Autumn ..	Kahlai
Able (v) ..	Parintona	Awake ..	Chaitoayana
Abuse ..	Rángana	Axe ..	Mars
Ache ..	Karawullana	**B.**	
Acid ..	Suwitál	Bald ..	Tal
Active ..	Tapur	Bake ..	Atana
Add ..	Jumma	Bard ..	Pataree
Adopted son ..	Koratai aitoor chhava	Bare ..	Koottaka
Adore ..	Poonjakiana	Barley ..	Jou
Afternoon ..	Piyal	Barren ..	Wanjooli
Age ..	Woi	Base ..	Hulko
Aged ..	Seira	Bathe ..	Yarekiana
Agree (v) ..	Sarko ayana	Battle ..	Tarotantor
Aim (v) ..	Hindanlawai kim	Battleaxe ..	Pharchia
Alight ..	Ruggana	Bawl ..	Killitana
Angry ..	Rees	Beads ..	Poting
Annual ..	San	Beak ..	Chachu
Another ..	Dusro	Bear ..	Yedjal
Appear ..	Disana	Beat ..	Jiana
Arise ..	Taidana	Beauty ..	Sajro
Armpit ..	Kootling	Bed ..	Bichona
Arms ..	Partal	Bee ..	Phukee wissing
Ascend ..	Tárgana	Beginning ..	Mohtur
Ass ..	Gadhal		

English.	Gondi.	English.	Gondi.
B—continued.		Cattle	.. Dobalk
Believe (v)	.. Man tatana	Cease	.. Kamma kakisana
Bell	.. Tápper	Change	.. More kiana
Belt	.. Naree dohta	Chaste	.. Sutro
Bend	.. Bagaikiana	Chastise (v)	.. Soeto kiana
Best	.. Bako	Chew	.. Kachkana
Betroth	.. Kulloo dohtana, Paring	Chirp (v)	.. Chir chir kiana
Big	.. Paror	Clear (v)	.. Oota kiana
Bloom	.. Poongaroayana	Climb	.. Targana
Bosom	.. Chhati	Club	.. Kutka
Brackish	.. Kharo	Cocoanut	.. Naral
Brave	.. Hatal	Colour	.. Rango
Bread	.. Sarei	Conquer	.. Myana
Breast	.. Chati	Cook	.. Attana
Breath	.. Waree, Naiskana	Country	.. Dess, Dehar
Bright	.. Jhalka manta	Cousin	.. { Yaina (Mothana ther's son) Tummo Cook }
Brother-in-law	.. Sairndo Koko (wife's brother)	Creep	.. Ghursay mayana
Brown	.. Bhurka	Cripple	.. Langra
Bud	.. Jewai	Cry	.. Arana
Bull	.. Kurra	Cub	.. Piela
Bush	.. Jhoorpuree	Cultivate	.. Julekiana
C.		Cup	.. Wate
Carry	.. Tahtana	Custardapple	.. Cheeta-far
Cart	.. Gadda	**D.**	
Castle	.. Killa	Dagger	.. Soorie

English.	Gondi.	English.	Gondi.
D.—*continued.*		Enter	.. Wasi handana
Dash	.. Aptikiyana	Err (v)	.. Bhulai matana
Daughter-in-law	.. Korial	Escape	.. Soddaisihundana
Dawn	.. Pahto	Evening	.. Nulpay
Dearth	.. Ankro	Evil	.. Burte
Deep	.. Khole	**F.**	
Deer	.. Kurs	Fair	.. Goro
Destroy	.. Burtai kiana	Faithful	.. Sooda
Dig	.. Katana	False	.. Khotal
Dirt	.. Gaday	Family	.. Kutum
Distant	.. Luk	Famine	.. Mahang
Drag	.. Umana	Father-in-law	.. Murial
Dread	.. Varitana	Feed	.. Teehtana
Dream	.. Kanchkana	Feel	.. Pundana
Dress (v)	.. Pondana	Fever	.. Yerki
Drive	.. Hakle kiana	Fight	.. Tarotana
Drop	.. Arootana	Fill	.. Neihetana
Drown	.. Murutana	Find	.. Puttana
Dry	.. Wattal	First	.. Pehlo
Dwell	.. Mandana	Flint	.. Garee
E.		Float	.. Pohay mayana
Egg	.. Mes	Flow (v)	.. Pong-in-tana
Elephant	.. Yani	Fly	.. Paritana
End	.. At	Food	.. Nehna
Enemy	.. Dandi	Fool	.. Khotal

English.	Gondi.	English.	Gondi.
F.—*continued*		Hasten	Lahki kiyana
Forenoon	Piyal	Hatchet	Murs
Forest	Kaira, Dongur	Hate	Burte kiana
Forget	Bhule mayana	Have	Erana
Forgive	Dam tindana	Heal	Nehen ayana
Fort	Killa	Heap	Rási
Foul	Brote	Hear	Kenjana
Fowl	Pitte	Heart	Boka
Fox	Khekreo	Heat	Kahlaimat
Fragrant	Makmak	Heel	Moorwing
Friend	Sungo	Help	Asrokiana
Fruit	Kaya	Hide	Tole
Full	Nintal	Hill	Matta
G.		Hip	Kula
Girdle	Nuri dohta	Hit	Jeana
Give	Siyana	Hold	Biana
Glad	Nehna	Honey	Phukey
Grain	Danáng	Hunger	Karu
Grandfather	Tado	Hunt	Shikar
Graze	Mehtana	Hurt	Khosre
Grove	Gurba	Husband	Muido
H.		J.	
Hand	Kyk	Jackal	Kolial
Hang (v)	Tang kiana	Join	Misre mayana
Hare	Malol	Jump	Dyana, Dehkana
Harvest	Sugge		

English.	Gondi.	English.	Gondi.
K.		**M.**	
Keep	.. Irrana	Mad	.. Pisal
Kindle	.. Massiana	Madness	.. Pise
King	.. Kural	Maize	.. Makaik, Making
Kiss	.. Burrana	Make	.. Kiana
Kneel	.. Tongurotek kiana	Marry	.. Marmingkiana
Knife	.. Surie	Meat	.. Khandk
Knot	.. Gattee	Midday	.. Dopuhri
L.		Mill	.. Jatta
Lamb	.. Patru	Mix	.. Milaykiana
Lamp	.. Diwa	Moist	.. Pahoa
Last	.. Pujjat	More	.. Unde
Lay	.. Irsiyana	Morning	.. Sukkare
Lead	.. Sieo	Mother	.. Awal Ya
Leech	.. Juroo	Mother-in-law	.. Porar
Lick	.. Nakana	Mount (v)	.. Turgana
Lie	.. Lutkowarukana	Mouse	.. Yelle Mssal
Life	.. Jiwa	Muscle	.. Sirang
Lift	.. Tahtana	Music	.. Bujanaikana
Like (v)	.. Dilte wayana	**N.**	
Lip	.. Silvi	Naked	.. Kuttake
Live	.. Pissana	Name	.. Pallo, Parol
Load	.. Wajje	**O.**	
Look	.. Hurana	Oath	.. Aura
Lose	.. Khowakiana	Once	.. Oondi pullo
Lost	.. Khoe mat	Ox	.. Kunda

English.	Gondi.	English.	Gondi.
P.		Restore	.. Malochiana
Pair	.. Jora	Right	.. Chokote, Oojo
Panther	.. Cheetál	Roast	.. Bersana
Parrot	.. Raglio	Rob	.. Kullaua
Pass	.. Haudana	Rock	.. Tonging
Pasture	.. Akur, Gohtan	Roll	.. Gurbare mayana
People	.. Lokoork	Rot	.. Karitana
Perspire	.. Aipurepasitana	Rotten	.. Karita
Pursue	.. Wittana	Rub	.. Malaikiana
Pig	.. Puddy	Rush	.. Seritana
Pigeon	.. Parua	**S.**	
Plough	.. Nagur	Sacrifice	.. Taruhsiana
Poet	.. Patari	Sand	.. Waroo
Powder	.. Burko	Sandy	.. Warwat
Prick	.. Gadustana	Savage (adj.)	.. Kore matal
Purchase	.. Sambakeyana	Save	.. Pisutana
Q.		Say	.. Indana
Quail	.. Batte	Scream	.. Kilitana
Quarrel	.. Tarotana	Season	.. Ghalumb
Quick	.. Jhupna	Seed	.. Vijja
Quiver	.. Peti	Seldom	.. Bapore
R.		Send	.. Rohtana
Real	.. Khurro	Separate	.. Agrokiana
Reap	.. Kocle	Serve	.. Chakrikana
Reside	.. Mandana	Sew	.. Wulchana

English.	Gondi.	English.	Gondi.
S.—*continued.*			
Shake	.. Hala kiana	Squirrel	.. Varche
Shameful	.. Basro mal	Starve	.. Karu mayana
Sharpen	.. Sorstana	Stay	.. Posana
Shave	.. Koritana	Stink	.. Dyngana
Sheep { (he) (she)	.. Maindal .. Maindral	Stomach	.. Paddo
Shine	.. Jhalkai mayana	Stray	.. Doundai mayana
Shoe	.. Sarpok	Stretch	.. Sahtana
Shoot	.. Sistjiana	Suffer	.. Ganja mayana
Shout	.. Killitana	Sugar	.. Sakur
Shut	.. Mochchisiana	Summer	.. Dokalumb
Sickle	.. Sattár	Sunrise	.. Dinpasit
Sickness	.. Yerki	Sunset	.. Noolpay
Silent	.. Kamme kiana	Swear	.. Arutana
Silly	.. Bhoral	Swim	.. Pohe mayana
Silver	.. Khuro		
Sink	.. Morohtana	**T.**	
Sister-in-law	.. Sairndar	Talk	.. Warkana
Slip (v	.. Ghasraina	Taste	.. Naka
Slow	.. Hallo	Tell	.. Wurkana
Smallpox	.. Wunk	Thief	.. Kullay, Luarial
Solid	.. Ninthal	Think	.. Mao kiana
Son-in-law	.. Sare	Thirst	.. Wutkee, Wusta
Soon	.. Jhapna	Thumb	.. Unktia
Sow	.. Yeddana	Top	.. Parro
Spit	.. Uskana	Torch	.. Duty
Spring	.. Dekana (v)	Touch	.. Ittana

English.	Gondi.	English.	Gondi.
T.—*continued.*			
Town ..	Dugro Nar (large village)	Wedded ..	Marmina
Turban ..	Phag	Wet ..	Pahna
U.		Wheat ..	Gohk
Uncle ..	Kakal	Wicked ..	Burtore
V.		Wife ..	Maiju
Victory ..	Mytur	Wind ..	Dhundar
Voice ..	Lange	Wine ..	Kall
W.		Winter ..	Pieni Ghalumb
Wait ..	Possna	Wither ..	Akiaral
Wake ..	Chaitomandana	Wolf ..	Landgal
Wander ..	Bhullay mayana	Wonder ..	Achrit kiana
War ..	Taro tanto	Work ..	Wanari kiana
Warm ..	Kastal	World ..	Manial, Doonya
Waste (v) ..	Boortai kiana	Worm ..	Kitkur, Purk
Watch ..	Kaipana	Worship ..	Punja kiana
Wed ..	Marming kiana	Wrestle ..	Dhawari kiana

NOTE.—In this Supplement the Gondi verbs are all given in the infinitive mood, which may be known by the termination "ana"

Note by the Editor regarding the Muási, or Kuri, dialect.

It will have been seen that Mr. Hislop in the Essay points out that the Kûrs, or Muásis, are distinct from the Gonds, at least in language; and that Kuri, or Muási, is not, as may have been supposed by some, a dialect of Gondi. Mr. Hislop indicates that the error may have arisen from expressions used by Dr. Voysey when, many years ago, he supplied a brief vocabulary of the language spoken by the tribes of the hills lying between Hoshungabad and Berar. This region is believed to be the real home of the Kûrs, or Muásis.

The vocabulary which Dr. Voysey gave in 1821 is to be found in Vol. XIII, Part I, of the Journal of the Asiatic Society. Several of the words agree with the Kuri, or Muási, as given by Mr. Hislop.

Dr. Bradley's list has been adverted to in this publication in a previous Note (see Preface to the Hislop Vocabulary). Many of those words also agree with the Muási in Mr. Hislop's Vocabulary.

In 1863, Major Pearson (the Conservator of Forests in the Central Provinces) furnished to Mr. Hislop a few words spoken by the Koorkus, whom he considers to be the same as the Muásis; and that memorandum is found among Mr. Hislop's papers. A few of the Koorku words agree with those in Dr. Bradley's list.

In 1865 Mr. C. A. Elliott, Settlement Officer of Hoshungabad, transmitted a Memo. on the Koorkus of Kalibheet (in the hills south-west of Hoshungabad), to which a short vocabulary is attached. Of these words, many agree with those given by Mr. Hislop and the other officers above mentioned.

For many of the Kuri words then, there are data obtained by various persons at various times and places, and I have caused a comparison to be entered of the points of agreement.

R. T.

COMPARATIVE VOCABULARY OF THE MUASI, OR KURI, DIALECT.

English.	Mr. Hislop. Muasi.	Mr. Elliott.	Dr. Voysey.	Dr. Bradley.	Major Pearson.
Air	Koyo	Koyo	..	Koeyo	..
Bambu	Mahat	Mad	Mat	Mat	..
Bedstead	..	Parkhum	Parkoum	..	..
Blood	Pachna	Puchna	..	Puchna	..
Body	Komor	Komur	..	..	..
Buffalo	Butkil	Bitkil	Butkil	..	..
Cat	Minnco	Meenoo	..	Munoo	..
Cowdung	..	Sena	Shena	..	..
Fire	Singal	Seengul	Singhel	Singhul	..
Fish	Kaku	Kakoo	..	Kakoo	..
Flesh	Jilu	Jeeloo	Jeloo	Zulo	..
Lightning	Chiran	Cheerun	..	Cheerun	..
Plantain	Kete	Kere	..	..	..
Star	Epal	Eefeel	Ipeel	Ephill	..
Stone	Dega	Gota	..	Yotha	Deegah
Sun	Gomci	Gomuj	..	Gomoi	..
Tiger	Kula	Koolla	Koda	..	Kootar
Tooth	Tiding	Tirinj	..	Terring	..
Tree	Sing	Seeng	Seeng	Sing	Seeng
Water	Da	Da	Da	Dhee	..

PART III. SONGS.

Note by the Editor on the Gond Songs.

THESE Songs were reduced to writing in the Gondi language by Mr. Hislop in his own handwriting. He obtained them from a Pardhán priest of the Gonds at Nagpore. Having made a very complete and accurate copy in Gondi, in the Roman character of course, he began to translate by entering over each Gondi word the counterpart in English. But at his death he had proceeded only a short way with the last named part of the task. His translation did not comprise a fourth of the whole—and even then it was only in detached fragments; and in no place was it consecutive. But, inasmuch as he had reduced to writing these lengthy Songs with so much care, it seemed very desirable to bring into an available and intelligible shape an unfinished work, which he regarded as of much importance, as evidenced by the admirable industry which he must have devoted to it. Moreover it was found quite possible to do this, inasmuch as the very Pardhán who recited the Songs to Mr. Hislop was still at Nagpore; and being versed both in Hindi and Mahrattee, was able to interpret the Gondi, word for word, into those languages from which the rendering into English was easy. Moreover, assistance was obtainable from the Rev. Baba Pandurang (of the Free Church of Scotland Mission), who was Mr. Hislop's native assistant, and his companion in several tours, and who frequently was employed by Mr. Hislop in obtaining information. I, therefore, entrusted to Mr. Pandurang, as being specially qualified, the task of comparing Mr. Hislop's manuscript with the recitations of the Pardhán, and of ascertaining the English equivalent for every word.

Thus is reproduced Mr. Hislop's manuscript of the Gondi, with Mr. Pandurang's equivalent in English entered over each word.

From this detached verbal translation I have myself prepared the following consecutive English version, adhering as nearly to the original as may consist with the easy understanding of the sense, and preserving the precise order of the lines. And I have supplied notes explaining the passages which seemed to need explanation.

The Songs form a sort of rude epic, full of episodes and

digressions, but preserving a thread of narrative connection from beginning to end. I have divided them into five parts, according as the sense of the piece indicated the propriety of such division. They are indeed recited or sung in parts, or in whole; but such parts would not necessarily correspond with the parts into which I have ventured to subdivide the pieces.

But, as already mentioned, these Songs were very lengthy in the original. While, on the one hand, many passages are curious, others vividly illustrative of Gond life and reality, and others remarkable in their way; yet, as might be expected, many passages were redundant, others frivolous, others improper or objectionable. All passages clearly belonging to any of the latter categories have been cut out. And the original whole has been thus pared down to about one half. And it has been found practicable to do this, without at all impairing the sense or breaking the sequence of the story. Even in this abridged shape the Songs are long, being some 997 lines in the Gondi.

The Songs and the Notes will speak for themselves. It will be seen therefrom, that they are to some extent worthy of being selected for the laborious treatment which Mr. Hislop bestowed upon them. For they are the best Gond pieces extant; and they comprise a sort of compendium of Gond thoughts and notions. Though abounding in things borrowed from the Hindus, they are yet possessed of much originality, and in many passages they are, so to speak, redolent of Gondism.

They have never before been reduced to writing, but have been for many generations sung or said by the Pardhân priests, to circles of listening Gonds, at marriages, and on other festive occasions. They are for the most part old, perhaps even ancient, though much obscured by modern interpolations and additions. And though the first original must be older than the Hindus, yet the framework of the Story, as it now exists, must have been composed subsequently to the arrival of the Aryan Hindus among the aborigines of Central India. Beyond this most vague estimate, it is impossible to say how old or how new these pieces may be. For the Gondi being unwritten, and the Pardhâns being unlettered, none of these men can explain the history of the Songs. A Gond will refer the enquirer to the Pardhân. Then one Pardhân will say that he learnt the piece by heart from the mouth of another, perhaps aged, Pardhân, who will say that he learnt it from another Pardhân before him, and so on. This is all that can be ascertained at Nagpore at all events.

R. T.

ABSTRACT ENGLISH VERSION, BY THE EDITOR.

PART I.

The Creation of the World and of the Gond people, and the bondage of the Gonds.

1. In the midst of twelve hills, in the glens of seven hills, is Lingawângad, or mount Lingawan.

2. In that mount is a flower tree named Dati; thence for twelve koss there is no dwelling—

3. Caw saying there is no crow, chirp saying there is no bird, roar saying there is no tiger.

4. Then, what happened? God spread betelnut, and called Nalli yado rishi [saint].

5. When an order to the vakeel (servant) Narayan was made, he heard it, and went running

6. To Kurtao Subal to ask him. He said there are sixteen threshingfloors of Teloogoo gods,

7. Eighteen threshingfloors of Brahmin gods, twelve threshing-floors of Gond gods. Thus he was asking for gods.

8. So many gods! where are they? their tidings I seek.

9 What did he begin to say? He said thus:

---

1. The twelve hills and the seven valleys are the same as those hereafter to be mentioned (see Part IV., line 85), as the place chosen by the Gond gods for their local habitation. Lingawângad—this name has nothing particular about it, but seems intended merely to introduce the story of Lingo.

2. The flower tree is the same as that mentioned in Part II., line 2, as that from which Lingo was born.

3. This is a forcible Gond idiom for expressing utter silence, and aptly describes the solitudes which are frequent among the homes of the Gond people. The phrase is also known to the Hindus of these parts.

4. Betel-leaf and nut are frequently mentioned in all the Parts. The idea is Hindu.

5. This Narayan must be the same as the Narayan of the Hindus. Or perhaps, in reference to the belief of the common Hindus, the Sun is meant.

6. Kurtao Subal—this name appears to be of Gond origin, and not a Hindu name, which is worthy of remark, inasmuch as the other names in this part of the story are Hindu.

7. The term threshingfloor is supposed to be here intended to express some indefinite number. Mahadewa is said to have had a threshingfloor in a field, whereon he created the Gonds. Thus the pure Gonds are called threshingfloor Gonds. The idea has been extended as a metaphor to other races. And each race is represented by its special divinities.

10. There (the god) Mahadewa was ruling from the upper sea to the lower sea.

11. What was that Mahadewa doing? He was swimming like a roller stone: he had no hands no feet:

12. He remained like the trunk (of a tree).

13 Gowara Parwatee (his wife) having stood, began to ask Narayan—

14. Who art thou? He said, I am Bhagawán's (god's) Subadar (deputy).

15. She said, Why hast thou come so far? I came to see Mahadewa.

16 Gowara Parwatee came. Narayan having gone to the banks of the Narbadda, stood there.

17. The Raja Mahadewa was swimming and came up.

18. Then Parwatee, with joined hands, stood, and so did Narayan.

19. Then said Mahadewa, For what has thou come? where are the gods of the twelve threshingfloors of the Gonds?

20. What did he say, Kurtao Subal? what did he say to Mahadewa?

21. Perform devotion (tap) for twelve months, and then you will come to know the names of them.

22. Five and six months passed; at the end of it, the devotion was finished.

23. Then came Bhagawán and stood close to Mahadewa, and called to him—

24. Thy devotion is finished, emerge out of the water. He said, how shall I

25. Emerge? I have no hands, no feet, no eyes.

---

10. And the subsequent lines comprise distorted versions in Gondi phrase of portions of the Hindu mythology.

14. The Mahomedan word Subadar is known to the Mahrattas as well as to the Gonds. The Gonds may have borrowed it straight from the Mahomedans.

19. Twelve is probably a number of mystic significance, though sixteen is the number used in the subsequent passages. Perhaps here allusion is made to the twelve tribes of the Gonds.

21. The "tap," or devotion, is a regular Hindu ceremony.

26. Then Mahadewa received man's form.

27. Thus man's form complete was made in the luminous world.

28. He raised his eyes and saw Bhagawán (god); but he (Bhagawán), immediately disappeared.

29. Mahadewa said, It is not well that God should not be seen (actually visible). Hear, O God, my story.

30. My devotion is fruitless; I received a man's form, which is not well.

31. Then he began to establish a (tap) devotion.

32. At the end of nine months and nine days his boil moved and burst—

33. Kalia Adao was born. Then Mahadewa what did he say?

34. Said Mahadewa to him, Establish a tap (devotion).

35. He (the Kalia Adao) began a devotion; one month, two months passed, when a boil arose in his hand.

36. The boil burst and sixteen daughters were born out of it. Then said he,

37. What! why are these daughters born?

38. I shall have cause to cast my head down. Whence shall I bring husbands for them?

39. He took hold of them and threw them in the water. After the throwing

40. The water was dried up, and sixteen sorts of earth were produced.

41. (He said) I shall perform devotion, and then I shall be at peace.

42. He then established a devotion, and a boil arose in his hand:

43. Twelve threshingfloors of Gondi gods were born.

44. Hither and thither all the Gónds were scattered in the jungle;

---

33. Kalia Adao is believed to be the same personage as Kurtao Subal.

37. These sixteen daughters may perhaps be in allusion to the sixteen Gond goddesses mentioned in Part II., line 253; and this view is borne out by the Pardhán who recites the Song.

41. Whether the sixteen kinds of earth have any special purport, is doubtful. The Pardhán who recites the song, says that the phrase merely refers to the several sorts of soil known to the people; such as black loam, reddish earth, sandy ground, gravel, and the like.

45. Places, hills, and valleys were filled with these Gonds.

46. Even trees had their Gonds. How did the Gonds conduct themselves?

47. Whatever came across them they must needs kill and eat it;

48. They made no distinction. If they saw a jackal they killed

49. And eat it; no distinction was observed: they respected not antelope, sambur, and the like.

50. They made no distinction in eating a sow, a quail, a pigeon,

51. A crow, a kite, an adjutant, a vulture,

52. A lizard, a frog, a beetle, a cow, a calf, a he and she-baffalo,

53. Rats, bandicoots, squirrels—all these they killed and ate.

54. So began the Gonds to do. They devoured raw and ripe things;

55. They did not bathe for six months together;

56. They did not wash their faces properly, even on dung hills they would fall down and remain.

57. Such were the Gonds born in the beginning. A smell was spread over the jungle

58. When the Gonds were thus disorderly behaved; they became disagreeable to Mahadewa,

59. Who said, The caste of the Gonds is very bad;

60. I will not preserve them; they will ruin my hill Dhawalagiri;

61. I perceive here and there smells. So said Mahadewa. Call the Gonds

62. Said he to Narayan: He went, and called them,

63. And brought them into the presence of Mahadewa.

64. When they were standing, Mahadewa arose and looked, and saw all the Gonds come.

65. He spoke within himself, and took them away into his valley.

66. He made them to sit in a line, and he sat at the head of them.

---

47. This somewhat sarcastic description, which follows, of the habits of the Gonds is probably of Hindu suggestion.

67. He took substance from his own body, and made it into a squirrel.

68. Thus he made a squirrel while bathing, and gave it life.

69. When he made it alive, he caused it to run away.

70. With its upright tail the squirrel ran from the midst of them.

71. The Gonds saw it running, and they pursued it.

72. As the Gonds were pursuing it, some said, kill it, kill it!

73. Another said, catch it; it will serve as a nice roast.

74. So saying, some seized a stick, some a stone;

75. Some seized a clod: their waist cloths were shaking: their hair began to fly about.

76. The squirrel entered a hole (which) was god's prison on earth.

77. The Gonds also followed it up to the hole.

78. All the threshingfloor Gonds ran into the cave.

79. Thus all the Gonds ran; the rest, four in number, remained behind.

80. They came to Parwatee: she was sleeping. In the meantime

81. She awoke. She cared for the Gonds. She said, For many

82. Days I have not seen my Gonds;

83. There used to be noise in mount Dhawalagiri,

84. But to-day there is silence. For many days there has been a smell (of Gonds),

85. But to-day I perceive no smell;

86. They must have gone somewhere.

87. Mahadewa is not to be seen, where did he lead them? Thus said Parwatee.

88. She ascended Dhawalagiri, and saw no Gonds. Then she said

89. To Mahadewa, My Gonds do not appear, where have they gone?

---

79. See Note on line 7. The term threshingfloor Gonds means the regular Gonds created by Mahadewa.

80. The number of four persons, which appears, too, in subsequent parts of the Story might be thought to have some significance; but none is ascertainable.

90. Mahadewa arose and placed a stone sixteen cubits long at the entrance of the cave, and thus shut in the Gonds.

91. He stationed Bhrasmasûr (a giant) to guard it. Still Parwatee remained asking (after them).

92. Then said Mahadewa, Dhawalagiri began to be odorous, and I fell into a rage thereat;

93. But four Gonds have survived, and they are fled. So said he.

94. Then Parwatee thought in her mind, My Gonds are lost.

95. The four Gonds who fled travelled onward over hills.

96. Thence they went and saw a tree rising upright, as a Date tree, which they climbed, and looked (about them).

97. They said there is no hiding place visible for us.

98. But one of them looked and saw a place named Kachikopa Lahugad.

99. They went by the jungly road and reached that place.

100. There the four brothers remained.

101. When the Gonds were not to be found, Parwatee began to feel regret for them.

102. She then commenced a devotion (tap):

103. Six months passed

104. Parwatee ended her tap. Bhagawán (god) meanwhile was swinging (in a swing).

105. He said, What devotee at my resting time has begun a devotion; Narayan, go and see to it.

106. Narayan went to see; ascending a hill, he came to Parwatee,

107. And stood while Parwatee was performing her tap, and saying, My threshingfloor Gonds do not appear;

---

91. This Bhasmasûr seems to be one of the giants of Hindu mythology.

99. The name Kachikopa Lahugad appears frequently in the Story, but there is no known place particularly of that name. The meaning in Gondi is the "Iron Valley—the Red Hills;" a nomenclature very applicable to the mineral products and external aspect of many hills in the Gond country.

104. The name God Bhagawán occurs frequently in all the Parts. It is borrowed, of course, from Hinduism. It is remarkable, however, that this name should be used especially, as the Gonds have an idea of their own for the one great God, Supreme over all the gods, who is named Bara Dèo. But the name Bara Dèo is not used any where in these Songs.

108. Therefore I commenced my devotion. When Narayan heard this, he ran; resting and running, he came to Bhagawán and said—

109. Parwatee is performing a devotion, and says my threshing-floor Gonds do not appear; where have they gone?

110. Bhagawán said, Go and tell her I will make her Gonds visible.

PART II.

The Birth, Life, and Death of Lingo.

1. Then care fell to Bhagawán (god). There was a tree :
2. It was blossoming. Then, said he, One of its flowers shall conceive.
3. By God's doing, clouds and winds were loosed. A cloud like
4. A fan arose : thunder roared, and lightning flashed;
5. The flower burst, clouds opened, and darkness fell; the day was hid.
6. A heap of turmeric fell at the fourth watch of the night.
7. In the morning, when clouds resounded with thunder, the flower opened
8. And burst, and Lingo was born, and he sprang and fell into the heap of turmeric.
9. Then the clouds cleared, and at the dawn Lingo began to cry.
10. Thereat, care fell upon God: the (face of Lingo) began to dry amidst the powder.
11. But by God's doing, there was a Ficus tree, on which was honey—
12. The honey burst, and a small drop fell into his mouth.
13. Thus the juice continued to fall, and his mouth began to suck.
14. It was noon, and wind blew, when Lingo began to grow.
15. He leapt into a swing, and began to swing, when day was set
16. Lingo arose with haste, and sat in a cradle swinging.
17. Lingo was a perfect man: water may be stained, but he had no stain whatever.

---

8. Lingo, or Lingal, is a sort of prophet among the Gonds. Though he appears throughout this Story in the character of a devout Hindu, yet the name is of Gond origin. Sometimes Bhân (Gondi for devotee) is affixed to his name, and sometimes Pariûr (Gondi for Saint.)

18. There was a diamond on his navel and sandle wood mark on his forehead. He was a divine Saint. He became two years old.

19. He played in turmeric, and slept in a swing. Thus days rolled away,

20. He became nine years old; he was ordered not to eat anything from off the jungle trees or thickets.

21. Lingo, in his mind, said, Here is no person to be seen; man does not appear, neither are there any animals;

22. There appears none like me; I will go where I can see someone like myself.

23. Having said so, one day he arose and went on straight.

24. He ascended a needle-like hill; there he saw a Mundita tree;

25. Below was a tree named Kidsadita: it blossomed.

26. He went thither, and having seen flowers he smelled them.

27. He went a little beyond, upon a precipitous hill, and climbed a tree.

28. Then he looked around and saw smoke arising from Kachikopa Lahugad.

29. What is this? said he; I must go and see it.

30. He ascended, and saw the smoke. The four brothers quickly brought their game, and began to roast it; they began to eat it raw or cooked.

31. In the meantime Lingo went there. They saw him and stood up; he stood also;

32. Neither spoke to the other. The four then began to say within themselves,

33. We are four brothers, and he will be the fifth brother. Let us call him.

34. We will go and bring him Then they went.

35. They came to (the place) where he was. Who art thou? asked they of Lingo.

---

18. These are Hindu distinctions.

36. Lingo said, I am Saint Lingo; I have a knot of hair on my head.

37. The four brothers said, Come to our house.

38. They took him home. While some game was lying there,

39. Lingo said, What is this? (They said) it is game that we have brought.

40. What kind of game is this? Lingo asked. They said, It is a pig.

41. He said, Give me its liver. There was no liver there. Then they said,

42. Hear, O brother, we have killed an animal without liver!

43. Then Lingo said, Let me see an animal without liver.

44. Then care fell upon them. Where shall we show him an animal without a liver? said they.

45. One said, Hear my word! He is a little (fellow), we are big men; we will take him to the jungle among large stones.

46. Among thorns in thickets and caves we will roam; he will get tired, and will sit down;

47. He will be thirsty and hungry, then he will propose to return.

48. With Lingo, they, with bow and arrow in their hands, went by the jungle road.

49. Onward they went, and saw an antelope. Lingo said, Kill it!

50. It had a liver. Then came a sambur, kill ye it!

51. It had a liver. A hare came, and he said, kill ye it!

52. It had a liver.

53. Thus the devout Lingo did not tire. These four brothers were tired.

54. For water they thirsted. On a steep they ascended to look for water;

---

36. Again a Hindu mark in contradistinction to Gonds.

39. This and many subsequent passages contain life-like descriptions of the hunting pastimes of the Gonds.

55. But no water appeared, so they descended from the hill.

56. Thus they came to a thick jungle of Anjun trees, where thorny plants blockaded the road.

57. They came and stood. A little water appeared. They plucked Palas (Butia) leaves, and made them into a trough;

58. They drank water with it, and were much refreshed.

59. Lingo said, What are you doing sitting there? (They said) we cannot find an animal without a liver.

60. If we don't find it we will leave off mentioning the name (of such a creature). This is a good place;

61. After scraping the ground, and cutting down trees, we will sow rice.

62. (Lingo said) I will sleep a little; you make a field ready.

63. The four brothers brought hatchets, and they all four began to cut the Anjun trees.

64. (Lingo) fell asleep, and he dreamed a dream. In his dream

65. He saw the twelve threshingfloors of Gonds, and he was afraid.

66. He awoke, and returned while the four brothers

67. Cut down the tree: their hands were blistered, and each blister was as large as an Awala fruit.

68. They threw down their hatchets and came to Lingo,

69. (And said) our hands are blistered, therefore we threw down our hatchets.

70. They went aside, and sat down. Then arose Lingo and held a hatchet in his hand,

71. And went on cutting trees; the trees fell, their roots were dug up.

72. Thus he began to cut down jungle. In an hour he made a good field.

---

56. The Anjun tree *(Hardwickia binata)* was probably more abundant at former periods. It still is found, but it is no longer plentiful in the Gond country.

65. See the previous note explaining the term threshingfloor. Allusion seems here to be made to the twelve tribes.

70 to 76. Comprises regular description of the cultivation so well known in recent times as *Dhya*.

73. (They said) our hands are blistered and not one tree have we cut down,

74. But Lingo in one hour has cut down several trees;

75. He has made the black soil (appear), and has sown rice and hedged it round;

76. He has made a door to it, and has made a shutter (for the door).

77. Then they arose and took their homeward road, and came to their own houses.

78. On the first day of the rainy season a little black cloud appeared:

79. Wind blew violently; it was cloudy all day; rain began to fall;

80. Rills in the open places were filled knee deep; all the holes were filled (with water).

81. When the rain had poured for three days, the weather became fair: rice began to spring;

82. All the fields appeared green. In one day the rice grew a finger's breadth high;

83. In a month it rose up to a man's knee.

84. There were sixteen scores of Nilgais (deer), among whom two bucks (uncle and nephew) were chiefs.

85. When the scent of rice spread around, they came to know it; thither they went to graze.

86. At the head of the herd was the uncle, and the nephew was at the rear.

87. With cracking joints the nephew arose; he leaped upwards.

88. With two ears upright, and with cheerful heart, he bounded towards his uncle,

89. (And said) some one has a beautiful field of rice: it must be green tender fodder.

90. To us little ones give that field, the sixteen scores of deer will go there;

---

84. The term "sixteen scores" is frequently used; for instance, sixteen scores of Gonds are spoken of. No particular significance is ascertainable; perhaps the term may only be an idiom for a large number.

91. After eating rice we will come back. (The uncle said) O nephew, hear my words! Take

92. The name of other fields, but not that of Lingo's field, (otherwise) he will not preserve even one of the sixteen scores of deer for seed to carry on the species.

93. The nephew said, You are old, but we are young; we will go.

94. Arriving there we will eat. If any one sees us we will bound away;

95. We will make a jump of five cubits, and thus escape; but you, being an old one, will be caught.

96. Therefore you are afraid to go, I will not hear your word; don't come with us.

97. So said the nephew. With straight tails and erect ears they turned back.

98. The uncle was grieved. Then he arose and went after them;

99. They left him far behind. The herd came near the fields;

100. But the nephew and the deer began to look for a way to enter it, but could not find one.

101. The deer said, Your uncle was the wise one amongst us, of whom shall we now ask advice?

102. We have left him behind (instead of him), you are our chief.

103. The nephew said, Do as you see me doing before you.

104. He put himself in front, when one of the deer said:

105. At first, your uncle told you that this is Lingo's field, but you did not hear;

106. Look behind and before you (be prudent). So said the deer.

107. But the nephew said, We will not keep an old one's company.

108. So he, being in front, gave a bound, and was in the midst of the rice,

109. And stood; then all the deer came after him leaping.

110. After him came the uncle to the hedge and stood.

111. All the deer were eating rice. But the uncle could not find his way.

112. Being old, he was unable to leap the door of the field of rice.

113. They went from thence and leaped back over the hedge, when the uncle said to them:—

114. Hear, O sixteen scores of deer, you have eaten this field! Father Lingo when he comes to it

115. What measures will he adopt? Then the nephew, who was behind, came in front,

116. And said, Hear, O friends and brethren! flee from this place, but hear my word.

117. As you flee keep your feet on leaves, and stones, and boughs, and grass, but don't put your feet on the soil. So said the nephew.

118. As he told them, so they did—all the sixteen scores of deer began to run,

119. And left no marks nor traces.

120. Then they stopped: some remained standing, some slept.

121. In the midst of the flower fragrance was Lingo sleeping, while half of the night was passed.

122. In his dream he saw a field eaten by deer, and all the rice becoming spoilt.

123. Then Lingo departed, and took his road to Kachikopa Lahugad.

124. Hence he departed, and went to the brothers and said, O brothers! out of your house come ye;

125. Hear one word: the deer have eaten our field of rice.

126. The four brothers said we need rice to offer our firstfruits (to the gods).

127. Then Lingo said, Hear, O brethren! our rice has been eaten up;

128. It has been spoilt; we have no firstfruits. Lingo said, We will offer the liver of these deer as firstfruits;

129. Then I will remain as a devotee, otherwise my power will vanish.

130. I fill my stomach by the smelling of flowers;

131. But how will the Gonds fill their bellies, there is nothing for their eating—

132. The rice has been spoilt by the deer. So said Lingo.

133. The four brothers said we will take in our arms, bow and arrow.

134. With anger against the deer they came to the field, and entered in the midst of it.

135. When they came in the centre they saw only black soil.

136. Only rice stubble appeared, and Lingo saw nothing.

137. Then his anger arose from the heel to the head, and he bit his finger on the spot;

138. His eyes became red. Where are the deer? said he, look for them?

139. They looked, but did not see anywhere the footprints of deer.

140. Near a tree they beheld some foot-marks; they looked at it.

141. As they went they beheld a jungle trodden down; then some traces appeared.

142. Onward they went, but did not see the deer, they beheld a peepul tree.

143. Lingo said, I will climb the tree, you stand below.

144. From the top he looked, and the deer were visible. He said,

145. The deer are in sight, some are seated, some are sleeping, some are leaping about.

146. You four brothers separate yourselves on four sides with your arrows,

147. And allow not one of the deer to escape.

148. I will shoot them from the tree and you shoot from below.

149. Having heard this, the four brothers went and ambuscaded on four sides.

150. They shot their arrows from four corners, while Lingo shot from the tree.

151. The uncle (the buck) and one deer alone survived; they had aimed at them also, but the arrow fell from Lingo's hand.

152. He said to himself, when the arrow fell out of my hand, That must have been a good omen.

153. That uncle is a devout follower of the servant of god, and has not eaten anything.

154. But the two survivors began to run; then these four brothers went after them in pursuit, saying, We will catch them here or there.

155. But the two could not be found; then the brothers turned and looked around.

156. The eldest brother said, Hear, O brethren! These two have escaped, and Lingo

157. Has remained behind at a distance from us. Let us return, said the eldest brother.

158. When they returned, Lingo asked them, Where have you been?

159. They said, The two survivors have fled and cannot be found, so we have returned to you.

160. He said, I will show you something; see if anywhere in your

161. Waistbands there is a flint; if so, take it out and make fire.

162. Then they took out pieces of flint and began to make fire,

163 But the matches did not ignite. As they were doing this, a watch of the night passed.

164. They threw down the matches, and said to Lingo, Thou art a Saint;

165. Show us where our fire is, and why it does not come out.

166. Lingo said, Three koss (six miles) hence is Rikad. Gawadi the giant.

167. There is fire in his field; where smoke shall appear, go there.

168. Come not back without bringing fire. Thus said Lingo.

169. They said, We have never seen the place, where shall we go?

170. Ye have never seen where this fire is? Lingo said;

171. I will discharge an arrow thither.

172. Go in the direction of the arrow; there you will get fire.

173. He applied the arrow, and having pulled the bow, he discharged one:

174. It crashed on breaking twigs and making its passage clear.

175. Having cut through the high-grass, it made its way and reached the old man's place (above mentioned).

176. The arrow dropped close to the fire of the old man, who had daughters.

177. The arrow was near the door. As soon as they saw it, the daughters came and took it up,

178. And kept it. They asked their father, When will you give us in marriage?

179. Thus said the seven sisters, the daughters of the old man.

180. I will marry you as I think best for you;

181. Remain as you are So said the old man, the Rikad Gawadi.

182. Lingo said, Hear, O brethren! I shot an arrow; it made its way.

183. Go there, and you will see fire; bring thence the fire.

184. Each said to the other, I will not go: but (at last) the youngest went.

---

180. This Rikad Gawadi, a sort of giant, is a name of doubtful origin. The Gawadi may be a corruption of Gawali, or Gaoli,—a cowherd. The Gaolis were powerful in the early days of the Gond people, and established a dynasty of their own in the Gond country.

184. The picture of the old man sleeping in the midst of his field, so well fenced round, (to keep off wild beasts) and by the fireside (to preserve him from the night damps of the forest), is a true representation of the habits of the Gonds.

185. He descried the fire, and went to it; then beheld he an old man looking like the trunk of a tree.

186. He saw from afar the old man's field, around which a hedge was made.

187. The old man kept only one way to it, and fastened a screen to the entrance, and had a fire in the centre of the field.

188. He placed logs of the Mohwa and Anjun and Saj trees on the fire.

189. Teak faggots he gathered, and enkindled flame.

190. The fire blazed up, and, warmed by the heat of it, in deep sleep lay the Rikad Gawadi.

191. Thus the old man like a giant did appear. When the young Gond beheld him, he shivered;

192. His heart leaped; and he was much afraid in his mind, and said:

193. If the old man were to rise he will see me, and I shall be eaten up;

194. I will steal away the fire and carry it off, then my life will be safe.

195. He went near the fire secretly, and took a brand of Tembhur wood tree.

196. When he was lifting it up a spark flew and fell on the hip of the old man.

197. That spark was as large as a pot: the giant was blistered: he awoke alarmed,

198. And said, I am hungry, and I cannot get food to eat any where; I feel a desire for flesh;

199. Like a tender cucumber hast thou come to me. So said the old man to the Gond,

---

187. The Mohwa is the tree from the flower of which the Gonds obtain their favourite liquor.

188. The Teak tree is still found, though somewhat dwarfed, in most parts of the Gond country.

200. Who come within. The old man followed him. The Gond then threw away the brand which he had stolen.

201. He will come again, was not caught. Then the old man, being tired, turned back.

202. 'Then what happened? the old, and came near the fire and sat, will come What nonsense is this

203. A tender prey had come within my reach;

204. I said I will cut it up as soon as I can, but it escaped from my hand!

205. Let it go: it will come again, then I will catch it. It is gone now.

206. Then what happened? the Gond returned and came to his brethren,

207. And said to them, Hear, O brethren! I went for fire, as you sent me, to that field; I beheld an old man like a giant.

208. With hands stretched out and feet lifted up, I ran. I thus survived with difficulty.

209. The brethren said to Lingo, We will not go. Lingo said, Sit ye here.

210. O brethren, what sort of a person is this giant. I will go and see him.

211. So saying, Lingo went away and reached a river.

212. He thence arose and went onward. As he looked, he saw in front three gourds.

213. Then he saw a bamboo stick, which he took up.

214. When the river was flooded

215. It washed away a gourd tree, and its seed fell, and each stem produced bottle gourds.

216. He inserted a bamboo stick in the hollow of the gourd and made a guitar.

217. He plucked two hairs from his head and strung it.

218. He held a bow and fixed eleven keys to that one stick, and played on it.

219. Lingo was much pleased in his mind.

220. Holding it in his hand, he walked in the direction of the old man's field.

221. He approached the fire where Rikad Gawadi was sleeping.

222. The giant seemed like a log lying close to the fire: his teeth were hideously visible;

223. His mouth was gaping. Lingo looked at the old man while sleeping.

224. His eyes were shut. Lingo said This is not good time to carry the old man off while he is asleep.

225. In front he looked, and turned round and saw a tree

226. Of the peepul sort standing erect; he beheld its branches with wonder, and looked for a fit place to mount upon.

227. It appeared a very good tree; so he climbed it, and ascended to the top of it to sit.

228. As he sat, the cock crew. Lingo said, It is daybreak;

229. Meanwhile the old man must be rising. Therefore Lingo took the guitar in his hand,

230. And held it; he gave a stroke, and it sounded well: from it he drew one hundred tunes.

231. It sounded well, as if he was singing with his voice. Thus (as it were) a song was heard.

232. Trees and hills were silent at its sound. The music loudly entered into

233. The old man ears; he rose in haste, and sat up quickly; lifted up his eyes,

---

217. This two stringed guitar (jantar) is a favourite instrument with the Gonds.

234. And desired to hear (more). He looked hither and thither, but could not make out whence the sound came.

235. The old man said, Whence has a creature come here to-day to sing like the maina bird?

236. He saw a tree, but nothing appeared to him as he looked underneath it.

237. He did not look up; he looked at the thickets and ravines, but

238. Saw nothing. He came to the road, and near to the fire in the midst of his field and stood.

239. Sometimes sitting, and sometimes standing, jumping, and rolling, he began to dance.

240. The music sounded as the day dawned. His old woman came out in the morning and began to look out.

241. She heard, in the direction of the field, a melodious music playing.

242. When she arrived near the hedge of her field, she heard music in her ears.

243. That old woman called her husband to her.

244. With stretched hands and lifted feet, and with his neck bent down, he danced.

245. Thus he danced. The old woman looked towards her husband, and said, My old man, my husband,

246. Surely that music is very melodious. I will dance said the old woman.

247. Having made the fold of her dress loose, she quickly began to dance near the hedge.

248. Lingo said in his mind, I am a devout Lingo; God's servant am I.

---

238. The Gonds are very fond of boisterous dancing.

249. I (wear) my dhotee (cloth round the loins) down to my heels, and (keep) a knot (of hair) on my head, and on the navel a diamond, and on my forehead a sacred mark.

250. Water may possess a stain, but I have none. I am Lingo. I will make the old man and old woman

251. To dance the Gond dance. I will sing a song, and cause them to dance, if I be Lingo.

252. Lingo worshipped his god, and invoked Budhal Penta, Adul Penta,

253. The sixteen satiks (goddesses) and eighteen flags, Manko Raytal, Jango Raytal, and Pharsa Penda,

254. And said, Salutation (to you Gods)! He, holding his guitar in his hands, sung various tunes.

255. Is my guitar an allurement to them? So said Lingo. He stopped the guitar.

256. From on high he saluted the uncle, Rikad Gawadi, the old man;

257. Who looked towards the top of the tree, and said, Salutation to you, O nephew!

258. Well hast thou deceived me and caused us to dance Whither hast thou come, nephew?

259. (Let) us embrace each other. Lingo descended from the tree,

260. And going to the old man, held his hand, and said, Uncle, salutation to you!

261. They met together: nephew became known to the uncle, and the uncle to the nephew.

262. After the meeting was over, the nephew held the uncle's hand.

263. They both came near the fire, and sat. O nephew, whence hast thou come? asked the uncle.

---

249. These are Hindu marks in contradistinction to Gonds.
253. These names belong to Gond gods and goddesses.

264. I have killed sixteen scores of deer; we want to roast their liver to eat.

235. We were trying to make fire fall from the flint, but fire fell not.

266. You possess fire in your field, therefore I discharged an arrow.

267. It came near your fire. It arose and fell at the door of your daughters.

268. The daughters have lifted it up and carried it away. Have you no sense, uncle?

269. I sent my brother to fetch fire, and you ran to eat him.

270. If you had caught him, you would have eaten him up; and where should I have seen him again?

271. The uncle said, I made a mistake; O nephew, the thing that I did is past.

272. He replied, O uncle, I have killed sixteen scores of deer! Go and eat their flesh as much as you like.

273. Thus said Lingo. Then the old man said, Hear, O nephew, my word. There are seven sisters, my daughters;

274. I have them here. Take them away. Having first bound their eyes,

275. Lingo thence arose, and stood before the uncle and said, I am going uncle,

276. Receive my salutation. Lingo thence went by the way to the house where the old man's daughters were.

277. Having arrived, he stood at the door. Lingo appeared a youth of twelve years

278. Or as sixteen years old; in front he looked foppish, like a young man;

279. From behind he looked like a devout Brahmin. He appeared as a good man.

280. The seven sisters from within the house came to Lingo, and regarded him

281. As a young man. They came out and stood before Lingo.

282. Tell us, said the seven sisters, who art thou? tell us.

283. He said, Thy father is my uncle, and thy mother is my aunt.

284. I am devout Lingo, the servant of God. I am Lingo.

285. Hear, O sisters! my arrow came to your house and fell; I have been in search of it for a long time.

286. My four brothers are sitting in the jungle; and I have killed sixteen scores of deer;

287. They are also in the jungle, and my brothers are sitting near them.

288. I have come here for fire: it is very late.

289. My brothers must be expecting fire; they must have felt hunger,

290. And thirsty they must have become; where will they get bread?

291. Thus said Lingo. Then the seven sisters, what did they begin to say.

292. Hear, O brother, our word. Thou art a son to uncle, and we are daughters to aunt.

293. There is a good relationship between you and us; how can you leave us?

294. We will come along with you; therefore, don't say No.

295. If you like to come, be ready soon, and take the onward road, said Lingo.

296. They took the bedding for their beds, and their clothes, and gave the arrow to Lingo.

297. Lingo in the front, and they in the rear, began to tread the way.

298. The brothers were sitting and looking, and saying when will he come?

299. They beheld him from a far; and said, Hear, O brothers, our Lingo appears!

300. They arose and looked, and saw Lingo, and behind him the seven sisters.

301. They said, With whose daughters, or whose daughters-in-law,

302. Is he coming? Look, O brethren! they are of good appearance.

303. If Lingo give them to us, we would make them our wives. So said the brethren.

304. Lingo came near and stood, and said, Hear, O brethren, my word!

305. These seven sisters are the daughters of our uncle: they have come;

306. Take out your knives, and give to them the livers of the deer.

307. They took out the livers: some brought faggots and enkindled fire;

308. On its blaze they roasted flesh, and set it on the ground.

309. Offer this liver in the name of God.

310. So said the four brothers. Lingo arose.

311. They began to eat, while Lingo did not eat. then he said,

312. Let the seven sisters quickly go back, their father will abuse them.

313. Hear, O sisters! Go quickly, or else your mother will abuse you.

---

309. This offering of the liver to God seems to have been borrowed from the Hindus.

314. They replied, and said, Hear, O Lingo! Thou who art called good, may we call you bad ?

315. We will not go, we will stay. Whither thou shalt go, thither we will follow thee.

316. The brethren said, Hear, O Lingo, these seven sisters say well !

317. Say thou yes to them, O brother, we will marry them.

318. We will make them our wives. Hear, O Lingo, such is our word.

319. He said, Take these as wives in marriage, and I shall be greatly pleased.

320. Take them here in marriage, I will give you leave to make them your wives.

321. They said, If you see any one of them to be good-looking, you take her.

322. If any be inferior, we will take her.

323. He said, Hear my word, O brothers ! I do not need this.

324. I promised to give them to you; they are of no use to me.

325. So, said Lingo, if you marry them they will serve me.

326. They will be my sisters-in-law. You are older, and I am younger.

327. They can give me water and bread, and spread a bed for me:

328. I will sleep on it. They can give me a bath; my clothes they will wash.

329. They will be my sisters-in-law, and like my mothers they shall be.

330. So said Lingo. When Lingo said they will be my mothers, the suspicion of the four vanished.

331. They went to Lingo, and asked him: O Lingo, marry us quickly !

332. Lingal intor Padan kinja nawa palo ima handaki
Lingo says O Pardhan hear my words you go

333. Kachikopa Lahugad
Kachikopa Lahugad

334. Aga koitork mantork horkunige handaki
There Gonds are to them go

335. Hanjikun ima nitki sewa dharnirknit
After going you stand salam (make) to the head man

336. Nawa jahar mikun yavvi ihun indaki iun vehtur
My salutation to you may reach this tell thus say

337. Hona palo kinjtur bor Padal agatal pasitur Kachikopa
His word heard that Pardhan thence departed Kachikopa

338. Lahugadta sariya handa latur
Lahugad way to go began

339. Bor Padal horkna hatur rachadi niltur bor Padal
That Pardhan their went in compound stood that Pardhan

340. sewa dhanirknit
salam (made) to the landlord

341. Ana miwar Padana andan dada nakun Padal kitur
I your Pardhan am brother I Pardhan was made

mawor Lingal mikun nhanirk kitur
our Lingo you lord made

342. Lingal mihigi rohtor miwang tudik bade mantang
Lingo me sent you daughters possess therefore

343. mawor Lingan rohtor miwang tudikun talkana
our Lingo sent your daughters to ask

344. madming
in marriage

345. War hudsikun amot kikom
Bride having seen we will join them

Nalurkte tamurk inda laturk Lingan mawa sewajahar
The four brothers to tell began (to) Lingo our salutation

346. vehakun sikom
tell we will give

347. Padal sewa kitur tanara natenda sari bitur Linganiga
Pardhan salutation made to (his) town way took to Lingo

348. hatur
went

349. Ibun itur bor Padal Linganige mawor Lingal kintorte
Thus said that Pardhan to Lingo our Lingo (what) does

350. Lingal mihigi rohtor miwang tudik bade mantang
Lingo me sent you daughters possess therefore

351. Thus ended the marriage. When some days passed, the eldest brother said, Hear my word, O brethren.

352. Lingo has done good to us, and brought wives to our houses.

353. But Lingo is without a wife: he thought of our good, but not of his own,

354. So we will reckon him as our father.

355. We will kill game, and bring flowers for Lingo. Let him sit in a swing.

356. So said the four brothers.

357. Lingo sat in a swing, and the seven sisters swung the swing.

358. The four brothers took their bows and arrows, and repaired to the jungle.

359. After that, what happened? The seven sisters said within themselves, Hear, O sisters. This Lingo

360. Is our husbands' younger brother, and we are his sisters-in-law; we are at liberty to laugh with him;

361. We can pull him by the hand, and we can make him to speak with us.

362. Lingo does not laugh with us; he neither speaks nor looks towards us; he has closed his eyes:

363. But he shall laugh, and we will play with him. So saying,

364. Some held his hand, and some his feet, and pulled him, but Lingo moved not his eyes;

365. He did not speak or laugh with them.

366. Then Lingo said to them, Hear, O sisters. You have held my hands

---

354. This marriage bower is characteristic of the Gonds: but is not unknown to the Hindus.

367. And feet, and pulled them; but remember you are my sisters.

368. You are my mothers; why do you deal so with me? I am God's servant.

369. I don't care though my life be sacrificed, but I will not speak with you, nor look at you, nor laugh with you. So said Lingo. Having heard this, .

370. The eldest sister said, Hear, O sisters. Lingo speaks not to us, looks not towards us.

371. They began to embrace him. Then Lingo became angry: the anger ascended from the heel to his head;

372. Thence descended into his eyes and down to his feet. Lingo looked before him

373. But saw nothing, save a pestle for cleaning rice.

374. He descended from off his swing and took the pestle in his hand,

375. And soundly flogged his sisters-in-law. As he was beating them,

376. The seven sisters began to flee before him like bellowing cows.

377. Thence he returned, and having come to his swing,

378. In a swing he slept. Thus these seven sisters had received a sound beating.

379. They returned to their house, and having each one gone to her room,

380. The seven sisters slept in seven places; and Lingo slept in a swing.

381. Thus noontide came, and the time for the returning of the four brothers arrived.

382. Some of them had killed an antelope, some a hare, some a peafowl,

383. Some a quail; some brought flowers.

384. They came into their house and set their burdens down, and said, Let us go to our Lingo;

385. We will give him flowers; he may be expecting us. They entered the house.

386. They came near Lingo and stood, and saw him sleeping.

387. They said, There is no one here. Lingo is sleeping; our wives do not appear.

388. Then we will come and awake Lingo. Thence they returned

389. To their houses, and going to their rooms, they began to look.

390. They (the women) were feigning sleep, and panting, as if fear had come upon them. Then the husbands asked them,

391. Why are you sleeping? and why don't you swing Lingo? They replied, Hear our words

392. How Lingo, your brother, dealt with us. How long shall we hide this disgrace?

393. He allows you to go to the jungle, and behind your back he shamefully maltreats us.

394. Such is the conduct of this Lingo. We have kept quiet till to-day;

395. Now we will not stop quiet We will go back to our father's place.

396. We will not stay here. Can one woman have two husbands?

397. The brethren said, We told Lingo at the first

398. That there were seven sisters, and that he might choose one from amongst them,

399. And that we would marry the rest. But he said,

400. They are my sisters, they are my mothers.

401. Thus said that sinner, wicked and ill-conducted, that Lingo.

402. While we were out hunting, he deceived us. We will take

403. Him to the jungle, and, having killed him, we will pull out his eyes.

404. Up to this day we have killed antelope and hares;

405. But to-day we go to hunt Lingo, and after killing him we will take out his eyes,

406. And we will play with them as with marbles; and then we will eat food and drink water.

407. Then they came to Lingo. and stood before him and said, Rise, O Lingo, our youngest brother!

408. Lingo said, Why, brethren,—why have you not brought the game and the flowers to me? and why have you come so soon?

409. They said, There is a large animal; we hunted it hard, but it did not fall:

410. It does not flee, it stands still only; we are tired of discharging our arrows at it.

411. Lingo arose from the swing and sat, and looked towards his brothers.

412. I will kill that animal. So said Lingo.

413. Lingo thence arose and came out of the house, and said, Come, O brothers. Where is the animal?

414. In front Lingo, and in rear the four brothers walked towards the jungle.

415. It is a very large animal, said they; and saying thus, they searched for it among trees and grass.

416. Lingo said, If it has gone, let it go.

417. Lingo went under a Char tree and sat. Then they said, O brother!

418. Sit here, and we will bring water. So saying, yonder they went.

419. Being amongst the trees, they said among themselves, Good Lingo is seated in the shade,

420. This is the right time to effect our desire. The four took four arrows and shot :

421. One arrow hit the head, and the head split open ;

422. One hit the neck, and it bowed down ; one hit the liver, and it was cleft.

423. Thus Lingo breathed his last !

424. The four brothers came up to Lingo and stood,

425. And said, Draw a knife, and we will take out his eyes. They drew out a knife and

426. Took out his two eyes, and said, Cover him.

427. So they took some twigs and covered Lingo.

428. Then they said, We have killed Lingo, who was wicked.

429. They plucked some green leaves of the trees and made a cup of them,

430. And placed in it the two eyes of Lingo, and one tied it to his waistband.

431. They walked towards their house, and at evening time they arrived home.

432. One said, Hear, O wives ! Kindle fire quickly,

433. And light a lamp. They drew the stalks of flax from the eaves of the house roof and enkindled fire.

434. One said, It is a fine light, let us play at marbles.

435. They took out both the eyes, and said, O seven sisters ! you also join in play.

436. They brought the eyes, and placed one on the east side, and the other on the west ;

437. And the brethren, sitting close, held the marbles between the joints of their fingers.

438. Then began to play at marbles with the two eyes ; and their game lasted an hour.

PART III.

The revival of Lingo, and his delivery of the Gonds from bondage.

1. What did god (Bhagawán) do now?
2. Rayetal, Pharsi Pen, what did they in the upper world?
3. In the courts of god all the minor divinities sat.
4. God spake to them—Hear, O friends, Can you tell in what world the body (of Lingo) is fallen?
5. Will any of you trace it and go on this errand?
6. They made the preparation of betelnut, and threw it before the saints.
7. God said, Take this up, and come and tell me.
8. But none of the saints took it up.
9. Then God became angry, and began to reproach them.
10. God arose, and with a potful of water washed his hands and feet.
11. After washing, he, from the substance of his body created a crow, and sprinkled water of ambrosia on it,
12. And thus made it alive, and named it Kagesur; and held it in his hand,
13. And said, Go to the jungle, and make a search between hills, glens, lanes; amongst trees, in rivers, and water.
14. Thence the crow departed, and roamed over the upper world.
15. But did not find the body of Lingo anywhere; thence he came to the lower world and began his search.

---

1. This scene in the courts of god above, must probably be of Hindu imagining, as the word used is Bhagawán. But the great god of the Gonds *may* be meant; only if that supposition be entertained, it is observable that the Gond term Bura Deo is term seldom used.
2. These are Gond gods.
12. The crow's name—Kagesur—is apparently of Gond origin.

16. When it came to the jungle of Kachikopa Lahugad, it searched in the valleys there.

17. Its sight fell on the twigs, it came to them and sat, and searched the twigs.

18. It saw Lingo lying there looking as if smashed, and without eyes.

19. This the crow observed, and flew away and came to the upper world.

20. Perching on god's hand, it sat. God asked it, Where have you seen him?

21. It said I came to the jungle of Kachikopa Lahugad, I saw a man there in a cave.

22. When god heard this he became silent, and understood the truth of it;

23. And then said, It was in that very jungle that Lingo was born from a flower of the tree.

24. And has never been there since. He took nectar

25. From out of his fingers and called Kurtao Subal, and said to him:

26. Take this and sprinkle on the liver, belly, and head of the body.

27. Thus, the crow in front, and Kurtao Subal behind, went to Kachikopa Lahugad.

28. Kurtao Subal said, Hear, O crow. Here is my Lingal.

29. Ambrosia was brought, and dropped into his mouth, and sprinkled over his head and body: then Lingal's head began to unite,

30. And his flesh became warm.

31. Lingo rose

32. And sat up. Looking towards the crow, he said, I was fast asleep;

33. Where are my brothers?

34. I see only a man and a crow, and I don't see my brothers. After this

35. Kurtao Subal replied, Where are your brothers?

36. You were dead, your body was lying here; we came and restored you to life;

37. The brothers you enquire about have killed you, and gone away.

38. Then said Kurtao Subal, what do you say to going? Lingal, addressing the crow, said—

39. I will go to my sixteen scores of Gonds.

40. I will go and see them, and speak to them.

41. The crow and Kurtao Subal started in one direction,

42. And Lingo took another road.

43. Lingo, while crossing the mountains and jungle, was benighted.

44. Then Lingo said, I will stay here alone;

45. Tigers and bears may devour me.

46. He went to a large Niroor tree.

47. When he climbed to the top, the night came on :

48. Wild cocks crowed, peacocks cried, antelopes were afraid,

49. And bears wagged their heads, jackals yelled, and the jungle resounded.

50. At midnight Lingo saw the moon, and said to himself:

51. The day is approaching, and while the stars are still visible, I will ask them about my Gonds.

52. At the third watch of the night, the cock crowed:

53. The morning star appeared, the sky became red.

54. Lingo, descending from the tree, ran towards the sun and saluted him;

55. And said, I want to know where my sixteen scores of Gonds are?

56. The sun said, I am engaged in the service of God during the four watches of the day,

---

39. The number of sixteen scores of Gonds, which frequently recurs, is doubtless intended for some original tribal sub-division of the people, although the number may not be reconcilable with the tribes as now declared to exist.— See for further specification, Parts IV. and V.

57. And have not seen your Gonds.

58. Lingo went to the moon,

59. Saluted and asked her if she knew anything

60. About his sixteen scores of Gonds. The moon replied:

61. I travel all night, and during the day am engaged in the service of God;

62. Therefore I know not.

63. Lingo then went to black Kumayat,

64. Saluted him, and asked him, where are my sixteen scores of Gonds.

65. He replied: Hear, Lingo: Mention about anyone but Gonds.

66. The Gonds are foolish like the ass.

67. They eat cats, mice, and bandicoots;

68. They also eat pigs and buffaloes; they are of such a bad caste.

69. Why do you ask me about them?

70. At the source of the Jumna river, on the Dhawalagiri mountain,

71. Mahadewa has caught the Gonds,

72. And has confined them in a cave, and shut its mouth with a stone of sixteen cubits long.

73. Basmasûr the giant has been appionted to guard it and watch the place.

74. After hearing this, Lingo set out, and walked night and day,

75, Making devotion. After twelve months had expired, the term of his devotion was complete,

76. When the golden seat of Mahadewa began to shake (from the effects of Lingo's devotion).

---

63. This name—black Kumayat—is obscure. It is believed to refer to some Hindu saint, especially if taken in connexion with the remark that follows.

67. This severe remark upon the Gond people is doubtless of Hindu derivation.

77. Then Mahadewa said, What devotee has come to Dhawalagiri and has performed devotions to me,

78. Rendering me under obligation to him?

79. As he was wondering and searching,

80. He went towards Lingo, stood at a distance, and recognized him.

81. Lingo did not shake his head, or lift his foot, or open his eyes.

82. His flesh was consumed; his bones only remained. Thus Lingo was found on the thorns.

83. Whereupon Mahadewa said,

84. What do you ask for?—ask what you wish, and it will be granted.

85. Lingo replied:

86. I want nothing but my sixteen scores of Gonds.

87. Mahadewa replied:

88. Make no mention of Gonds; ask for any kingdom, or for any amount of money which you can enjoy,

89. And remember me. Thus said Mahadewa: To which Lingo did not agree.

90. On his again asking for the Gonds, Mahadewa disappeared and consented to give them to him,

91. Saying: Hear, Lingo. Your Gonds are below the earth, take them away.

92. Lingo rose, saluted him, and went on. After this,

93. Narayan said: Hear, Mahadewa: All these Gonds

94. Were well concealed and were forgotten; if they were dead, it would be a pleasure to me.

95. If they come out alive from below the earth, they will act as usual:

96. They will eat buffaloes, birds, such as pigeons, crows and eagles, and vultures.

---

82. The phrase, on the thorns, alludes to a heap of thorns which the devotee prepared in order that he might lie on them by way of penance.

96. This and the following lines contain reflections on the Gonds from a Hindu point of view.

97. They will alight here and there; smells will arise, bones will be scattered, and make the earth look very bad.

98. The respect for mount Dhawalagiri will be lost.

99. Mahadewa, hearing this, replied: Hear, Narayan, I have passed my word.

100. I have erred, but will not change my word.

101. Narayan then addressed Lingo:

102. Hear, Lingo. Bring me the young ones of the black bird Bindo for an offering;

103. After that you may take the Gonds away.

104. Lingo went and reached the sea, where there was nothing but water visible;

105. And on the shore he saw the young ones of the black bird. The parent bird

106. Had gone to the jungle. This bird was such, that

107. For food it killed the elephant, and ate its eyes; and breaking its head, brought the brains for the young ones to eat.

108. There had been seven broods, at seven different times;

109. But they had been devoured by a sea-serpent, called the Bhowrnag. Lingo went near.

110. After seeing the young ones, he said to himself: If I take them in the

111. Absence of their parents, I shall be called a thief; I will therefore

112. Take them in the presence of the parents, and will be true to my name.

113. He slept near the young ones with comfort.

114. A large snake, as thick as the trunk of the Itumna tree, appeared

---

105. The episode about the bird Bindo, and the sea-serpent, and the shore of the ocean, cannot be of Gond origination. The ideas and the imagery are quite beyond the Gonds. The fable must be derived from the Hindus, though I am not sure that the name Bindo occurs in their books. However, there is a great bird in Hindu mythology, described as "the king of the feathered tribe and the remorseless enemy of the serpent race." But his name is Garúda.—See H. H. Wilson's Vishnu Purâna, page 149.

115. With a hood as large as a basket for winnowing corn. This serpent, called the Bhowrnag, came out of the water to eat the young ones.

116. The young ones were terrified on seeing the serpent, and began to cry.

117. Lingo, taking an arrow, and fixing it in his bow,

118. Shot the serpent, and then cut it into seven pieces, which he immediately

119. Brought and laid at the head of his bed, and covered them up.

120. Then the male and female of the black bird returned from the jungle.

121. They brought the carcase of some camels and some elephants, together with some eyes and lips of elephants,

122. As food for their young ones.

123. But the young ones refused to eat;

124. When the female said to the male;

125. Notwithstanding my having had young seven times,

126. I am like a barren she-buffalo; if these young ones are spared

127. I shall be like a mother of children. What evil eye has been cast on

128. My young ones, that they do not eat!

129. The male bird, alighting from the tree, saw a white object lying below, where was Lingo.

130. He then exclaimed: Here is a man, and that is why our young ones do not eat.

131. Let us kill him and extract his brains;

132. Our young ones will then take their food.

133. Hearing this, the young ones said:

134. You have brought food for us, but how shall we eat it? You are our parents,

135. You leave us alone, and go away to the jungle;

136. Who is there to protect us?

137. The serpent came to eat us.

138. This man whom you see, has saved our lives.

139. Give him first to eat, we will then take our food; unless he eats, we will not eat.

140 After hearing what the young ones said,

141. The mother flew down from the tree, and coming near Lingo,

142. And lifting up the cloth with which he had covered himself, saw the seven pieces of the Bhowrnag serpent.

143. Seeing this she began to exclaim:

144. This is the serpent that has always eaten my young ones, and rendered me childless!

145. Had this man not been here it would have devoured these also.

146. Addressing Lingo, she said: Rise father,—rise brother; who are you, and

147. Where have you come from? You have saved the lives of our young ones, and you have become our grandfather.

148. Whatever you say, we will listen to it.

149. He said:

150. O bird, I am a devotee, a worshipper of the Deity.

151. Tell us, the bird said, what has brought you here.

152. Lingo replied, I want your young ones.

153. On hearing this the bird began to cry bitterly,

154. And, opening her eyes, she said:

155. I would give you anything

156. Except my young ones.

157, Lingo said:

158. I will take your young ones merely to show them to Mahadewa.

159. In reply to this, the black Bindo said:

160. If Mahadewa wants us, I am ready to go.

161. Saying this, the female bird carried the young ones on one wing,

162. And Lingo on the other. The male Bindo then said, Hear me, Lingo;

163. You will feel the effects of the sun, why then should I remain here?

164. The female Bindo then flew towards the sea.—

165. The male Bindo flying over her, and using his wings as a shelter for Lingo.

166. It was six months' journey to the residence of Mahadewa; but starting in the morning

167. They alighted at mid-day in the court-yard of Mahadewa.

168. Narayan seeing them from the door, went to Mahadewa and said:

169. Here is Lingo and the black Bindo birds which he has brought.

170. Mahadewa exclaimed: O Narayan!

171. I foresaw this, and you would not believe me when I told you

172. That Lingo would bring the birds.

173. Mahadewa then said: Hear, Lingo: I give you back your sixteen scores of Gonds;

174. Take them, and go away.

175. Lingo then saluted Mahadewa and went to the cave, and taking the name of the Great god,

176. And that of the god Rayetal, he made Basmasûr, the giant, to walk in front of him.

177. Reaching the cave, he lifted up the stone, sixteen cubits long, and laid it aside.

178. The Gonds coming out of the cave and seeing Lingo, cried,

179. We have no one but you.

---

175. This is the Bura Deo, or Great god of the Gonds.
176. Reyetal is a Gond god.

180. Mahadewa gave flour of wheat to some, flour of millet to others,

181. And rice to others.

182. The Gonds went to the river and began preparing their food.

183. Some of the Gonds said that they had been confined and punished severely.

184. On hearing this, Lingo said:

185. You are now at the river, cook and eat, and then complain.

PART IV.

The subdivision by Lingo of the Gonds into tribes, and the institution of the worship of the Gond gods.

1. Lingo kneaded the flour and made it into a thick cake, and cooked pulse, and satisfied all the Gonds.
2. Then clouds arose, and it began to rain.
3. When the rivers flooded and the flood began to roll, all the Gonds spoke:
4. O Lingo, much rain has come up and is falling.
5. Then all these Gonds began to walk in the middle of the river.
6. From among all these Gonds, four persons with Lingo remained.
7. Lingo, having seen this, began to say: Hear, O brethren;
8. This river is flooded, how shall we cross it?
9. More clouds came up, and darkness fell,
10. When those four persons and Lingo began to speak—
11. Hear, O brethren, what shall we do, and how shall we go on? the day is departing.
12. Now Dame the tortoise, and Pusi the alligator, were playing in the water.
13. They came to them out of the water, and began to speak:
14. Hear, O brethren, why do you silently stand and cry?
15. They said: Our sixteen scores of Gonds have all gone, and we only have remained;
16. O brethren, how shall we go? They said: Sit on us, and we will take you across.

---

6. The four persons who remained with Lingo when the rest crossed the river seem to be the same as the four who remained behind when all the rest entered the cave.—See Part I., line 79.

12. The episode of the tortoise and the alligator is of Gond origin. The Gonds are said to hold the tortoise sacred even now, and never to catch it themselves, and even to procure its release if caught by others.

17. If you keep your oath we will take you across the river.

18. They replied: Hear, O sisters. You are Pusi the alligator, and you are Dame the tortoise.

19. These four persons who are before you will keep their oath first of all.

20. If any beat you we will not allow it, or if any (try to) catch you we will prevent it.

21. You shall be the eldest sister of us four persons, said they.

22. Dame the tortoise, and Pusi the alligator, came before the face (of the Gonds), and those persons sat on the alligator's back, leaving Lingo alone to sit on the back of the tortoise.

23. The alligator went first, and then followed the tortoise in the flood.

24. The wicked alligator, having taken them into the midst of the water, began to drown them.

25. They began to cry. Then the tortoise spoke: Hear, O Lingo.

26. Stretch thy hand and drag them off, and make them sit on my back.

27. Lingo, having stretched his hand, caught them and dragged them away, and made them sit on the tortoise's back.

28. Then the tortoise took the four men on his back and went across the river;

29. And they fell at its feet, and said: Hear, O tortoise, we will not become faithless to you.

30. Then those four went by a jungly path, and ascended one hill,

31. And descended another. Thus they went forward.

32. They began to cut trees and build houses, and they remained (not together), but here and there.

33. Fields and houses were formed by the Gonds, and that town became large.

---

33. From this line to line 37 is a description of the scattered settlements made by the Gonds in the forests. The name Nar Bhumi is the Gondi term for a city; it has no further significance.

34. A bazaar (periodical market) was held in Nar Bhumi (the name of the town).

35. Then Lingo began to say: Hear, O brethren. If you will sow millet, it will spring up.

36. Thus twelve months passed, and Nar Bhumi began to appear excellent.

37. Those who had no bullocks received them.

38. Those who had no carts received carts: thus all the houses of the city became prosperous.

39. All the Gonds came to Lingo, and sat close to each other in rows,

40. While Lingo stood in the midst of them, and began to speak:

41. Hear, O brethren. All you Gonds understand nothing.

42. You do not know whom to call brother, and whom father,

43. Or other relative; from whom to ask a daughter, and to whom to give your daughter;

44. With whom to laugh. Then those Gonds began to say:

45. O Lingo, you possess great and good understanding; do as you

46. Have said with all your might, and make tribes of us.

47. Then Lingo, out of the sixteen scores of the Gonds, separated four scores, and told them to rise.

48. He caught one of them by the hand, and said: O friend, become Manawaja.

---

34. This bazaar is an exact allusion to the periodical markets (on some fixed day of the week), which are to this day held by the hill people, even amongst the wilds of the mountains.

35. The command of Lingo to the Gonds to sow millet (jowaree) is in advertence to their progress in agriculture. Their practice is first to sow rice, which is easily produced. As their resources increase, they begin to raise a little millet, which requires more care and resource.

37 and 38. Though the words are simple,—merely that the Gonds received bullocks, and then carts,—yet they are pregnant with actual meaning, which is this. In the earliest stages the Gonds lived first on fruit and game, as described in Part I. Then, as specified in Part II, line 63, *et passim*, they cut down trees, and burn them for ashes, which fertilizes the ground, and makes it yield, from seed sown without ploughing or other agricultural operation. As they advance they begin to cultivate with bullocks and ploughs; and then, lastly, as their villages improve, they use carts to carry grain to market, and especially to convey the wild fruits and other produce of the jungles. These several stages of progress are visible to this day among the the Gonds.

47. Though this and the subsequent lines refer to some tribal distribution, yet the division must not be regarded as at all complete; and it only partially corresponds with the best received specification of the twelve Gond tribes.

49. Then (that man) became Manawája. Then he caught another by the hand, and said: Become, O friend, Dahukwaja;

50. And he became Dahukwája. He then caught

51. Another by the hand, and said: O friend, Be Koilabutal; and he became Koilabutal.

52. Then he caught another by the hand, and said: You become a wild Koikopal;

53. And he became Koikopal. Thus the four scores were divided.

54. Out of the remaining twelve bands, four more were separated:

55. The first band he made to be Koorkus, and the others he made to be Bhils.

56. The third he made to be Kolâmi, and the fourth he made to be Kotolyâl. Thus eight bands

57. Were divided. There (still) remained eight bands. Then what followed? After the third of the month Weishák

58. Arrived, then Lingo said: Come, O brethren, we cannot see God

59. Anywhere; let us make a god, and we will worship him.

60. Then all the Gonds with one voice

61. Said—Yes, O brethren; bring a goat

62. Five years old, a crowing cock one year old, a three year old calf, a cow

---

48. Manawaja means one who casts and fashions the images of the gods. The exact derivation of the term is not ascertainable. It is the name of a class, or perhaps even of a tribe among the Gonds.

49. Dáhukwája,--the term means drum-sounding, and is applied to a particular tribe among the Gonds.

51. Koilabutal is the actual name of one of the tribes of the Gonds.

53. Koikopal is also the name of a tribe.

55. Koorku is the name of a tribe inhabiting the same hills as the Gonds, but supposed to be distinct from them in race, and certainly distinct from them in language. The name Bhil refers to the well-known tribe of that name, who are, however, considered to be distinct from the Gonds, and inhabit the hills to the westward of the Gond country.

56. The name Kolami belongs to one of the regular Gond tribes. Kotolyâl is the name of a tribe also: the word is derived from the Gondi word for a log of wood.

57 The month Weishák (May) is borrowed from the Hindus. The Gonds have no names of their own for the months.

63. Two years old; and call two of the

64. Manozas (bards). Then they named one god Ghagara Pen (the Bell god).

65. Lingo said: Bring a chouri (fan) made from the tail of the wild cow.

66. Then, said Lingo, open the shop (of the ironsmith), and make the god Parsapôt of steel.

67. Go to the jungle and cut a bamboo stick, and bring it.

68. Keep their god in Dhanegāon, and the seven sisters, goddesses (satiks), in Anegāon.

69. In the morning, Lingo arose and went to a river and bathed, and wore a dhote (cloth round the loins),

70. And applied the tika (sacred mark) to his forehead. What! says he. Hear, O brethren, to the Ozas (bards).

71. Call two Dahaking drummers; and they called them, and brought the Stick god. Then

72. Lingo bound the Chain god to the stick, and placed another stick in the god Pharsapôt; and the Gungâwan Chawor (the cow-tailed fan) was waved over it; and with joined hands then said: Hail! Pharsa (Pen).

73. He lifted the stick, and the gods Manko Rayetal, Jango Rayetal,

74. And Pharsa Pen came and stood (there); and Lingo was possessed of them.

75. Then Lingo became a man devoted to god, and moved and jumped much:

76. Lingo (was) in front, and behind were goats, cocks, a calf. And all the Gonds

---

64. Manoza, or Oza, are regular names for the bards or minstrels, so common amongst the Gonds. The Ghagara Pen, or Bell god, is one of the Gond gods, formed by stringing together a set of small tinkling bells.

65. This sacred fan (Gungâwan Chour, or Chowri) is well known among the Gonds; but the idea is believed to be borrowed from the Hindus.

66. The god Pharsapôt, or Pharsa Pen, is represented by a spear, and is one of the regular Gond gods. Pharsa also means a trident in Gondi. Iron-ore is obtained in most parts of the Gond country.

67. This is the Stick god, well known among the Gonds, and represented by a bamboo. The bamboo is plentiful generally in the Gond country.

68. Dhanegāon and Anegāon are names of villages without any particular meaning. The seven sisters are goddesses, well known to the common Hindus as well as to the Gonds.

72. The Chain god is represented simply by an iron chain, and is worshipped by the Gonds under the name of Sâkla Pen.

73. Manko Rayetal and Jango Rayetal are known to be members of the Gond pantheon. The Pardhân who recites this Song declares them to be the wives of the god Pharsa Pen.

77. Assembled in one place. Having left the village Dhanegaon,

78. They came, and began to say this is a thick jungle.

79. Then the Gonds (called on the gods) to stand still.

80. They fell at the feet of the gods, and asked where they should make seats for the gods of each band.

81. Then all the Gonds came in front and, with joined hands, stood,

82. And began to ask Pharsa Pen; who replied: Hear, O brethren.

83. Between twelve glens and seven dales go, and make place for (us gods).

84. Then in front went the Stick god, and behind followed all the Gonds.

85. They arrived, and after alighting they began to pick up grass and lift stones.

86. Then said Lingo,

87. Hear, O brethren. Do you see yonder a

88. Bijesal tree? Go and cut it, and make a kettle-drum from its wood. They, taking an axe, went and cut it.

89. Some held a pitcher, and brought a pitcherful of water; some digged earth, and

90. Made a platform, and placed on it the Stick god. Some said: Our drum is not ready,

91. Burn this fire in front and light the lamp.

---

79. The Gonds calling on the gods to stand still has a particular meaning, which is this. The people are marching in a sort of rude procession into the heart of the forest; and their gods, consisting of a sacred string of bells, a sacred spear, a sacred chain, a sacred bamboo stick, and a sacred fan, being waved about, *are being carried by priests and bearers along with the multitude.* Then the bearers of these consecrated emblems are ordered to stop; and thus it is phrased that the gods are made to stand still.

81. This standing on one leg and with joined hands is a Gond practice, probably learnt by them from Hindu devotees.

83. The twelve hills and the seven dales are the same as those mentioned in the opening line of Part I. It is an established phrase among the Gonds.

84. The Stick god leading the way, means that the sacred bamboo was carried in front.

88. The Bijesal (*Pterocarpus Marsupium*) tree is still common among the Gond forests.

92. They wetted five tolas' weight of vermilion in ghee, and threw five tolas of ral (resin) on the fire.

93. Then sat Lingo with joined hands before the god Ghangara (the bell god).

94. Ghangarang began to jump about, and possessed the body of Lingo. Pharsa Pen began to play also.

95. Then they took a pitcherful of daru (liquor),

96. And sprinkled it on the stick, and said: Hail to you Pharsa Pen!

97. And, with joined hands, they fell at his feet. While they were falling at his feet,

98. The god Rayetal possessed the body of Lingo, who moved and danced much.

99. Then he began to speak thus: Bring to me victims,—

100. Goats of five years old. After bringing the goat they fell at its feet

101. And washed its head, and applied vermilion, and poured daru (liquor) into its ears.

102. Then after catching the goat by the feet, they threw it before the god:

103. And the god Rayetal possessed the body of the goat, which began to shake its head, ears, and whole frame very much.

104. Then two or four persons ran and caught it, and threw it down

105. Before the god, and killed it. Then blood was sprinkled around.

106. And they placed the head before the god, and took the body.

107. Then a white cock, a year old, was brought, and they killed it.

---

98. Rayetal is the Sun god among the Gonds.

100. The lines which follow give an account of the sacrificial ceremonies still used by the Gonds.

108. And began to play a good tune on the Kingree (one-stringed guitar) and the drum.

109. The god derived pleasure therefrom. Then two feet of

110. A calf were washed, and (so) was its mouth; vermilion was applied to its forehead.

111. (Then) they threw them (the other animals) down, and killed them too.

112. The head of the calf was placed before the god. Then said Lingo: Hear, O brethren;

113. Remove quickly the skin of the calf and roast its liver.

114. They brought stones and made an oven, and placed a pitcher on it.

115. The pitcher was filled with water, and flesh was put in it.

116. The leaf of the Eyn tree (was) cut and brought, and made into plates.

117. And in a brass plate they placed cooked rice, liver, flesh, and they lighted four lamps, and took and placed them before the gods.

118. Some made an offering of silver pieces as a present to the god.

119. Thus a heap of silver up to the knee (of a man) was gathered before the god.

120. Then (Lingo) spoke: Hear, O brethren: The offerings are good in the courts of the god.

121. (There is) no one to receive these offerings.

122. Hear, O brethren: From the midst of all (these Gonds) some one should become a Pardhán,

123. And we will give (this offering) to him.

124. Then Lingo looked well among the company and (saw) an old, hoary haired man first of all;

---

122. The introduction of the Pardhán, a sort of priest among the Gonds, is here made by the Pardhán who recites this very Song, for the glorification of himself and his class. The Pardháns are well known in this capacity.

125. And having looked on him, held his hand and said:

126. Become a Pardhán, and we will give you much wealth and clothes;

127. We will give you a horse, and whatever you ask us we will not refuse.

128. Well, brother, (said the) old man, I am (fit for nothing but) to sit and eat.

129. All saluted him; and some gave clothes, some gave silver pieces,

130. Some gave him a pipe.

131. As they were rising, Lingo said: Hear, O brethren and friends.

132. Then (said they) what shall we do, O brethren? He rose, and made

133. Seven persons out of them to stand aside, and said to them, You become a family of seven.

134. He then made six persons to stand aside,

135. (And said) You become a family of six. He took five more aside,

136. And made them to stand, and breaking surface of the earth, a family of five were formed.

137. To the remaining four he said: Be divided into families of four and five.

138. After saying this, he reminded them to keep their promise with the tortoise.

---

127. The present of a horse is a mark of high honour. The god Koda Pen, or horse-god, is sometimes worshipped by the Gonds, and sometimes there are sacred images of this animal.

128. The man here gives a true description of the character of the Pardháns, who are averse to any sort of industry.

133 to 137. This arrangement of some of the people into families of seven, of six, of five, and of four, might at first appear obscure, but it refers to the division of the people into sects, who worship—some, seven gods; some, six; some, five; some, four. It is well known that some Gonds are seven-god-worshippers, others six-god worshippers, and so on.

138. The covenant with the tortoise refers to the episode mentioned in the preceding line 12 of this Part.

139. Then they all made salutation. Lingo said: O brethren, look yonder towards the gods.

140. All persons looked behind, but Lingo vanished and went to the gods.

141. While they were looking behind, they said: Where is our Lingo gone?

PART V.

The institution by Lingo of the rites of Marriage among the Gonds.

1. After the Pardhán had been made, he said: I will go to look for a partner (wife) for you Gonds.

2. Lingo (told) the four Gonds, and all the Gonds, small and great, to gather in one place and hold a council;

3. And said: Hear, O brethren; I will send the Pardhán—commune with him.

4. Then they sent for water, and put rice in it.

5. If the rice sticks or adheres, then we will send him; if not, we will not send him.

6. Then came all the Gonds, and stood before and behind Lingo.

7. (He said) cast two whole grains of rice in water. Then they threw rice in water.

8. The two grains of rice joined one to the other.

9. Then Lingo looked with his eyes, and said within himself: Just as I said, so it has happened; our marriage omen is good. Hear, O brethren.

10. (Let us) send our Pardhán to look for a wife.

11. The Pardhán became ready.

12. Lingo said: Hear, O Pardhán, to my word. Go to Kachikopa Lahugad,

13. There are (many) Gonds; go to them only.

14. When you reach their house, salute the head man;

15. And say Lingo has sent salutation, may it reach you.

---

1. It is still the recognized duty of a Pardhán to negotiate marriages among the Gonds.

2. The four Gonds are doubtless the same as those who figured in Part I. at the cave, and in Part IV. in the river. They are chiefs. Beyond this there is no special meaning ascertainable.

4. This description of the omen is the same as that still used by the Gonds.

16. Hearing Lingo's words, the Pardhán departed, and began to go on the way towards Kachikopa Lahugad.

17. Having reached it, he stood before the house and saluted the head man,

18. And said : I am your Pardhán, I was made Pardhán by Lingo your lord.

19. Lingo has sent me to you, because he knows that you possess daughters; to ask them in marriage he has sent me to you.

20. If I see a fit person I will join her in marriage.

21. Then the four brothers said: Give our salutation to Lingo, and tell him that we will not reject his proposals.

22. Then went the Pardhán (back) to his town, and came to Lingo

23. And said to Lingo: They told me to tell you that whatever Lingo does, to that we will consent.

24. Let him give our daughters to any one (he likes), said the four brothers.

25. So the Pardhán went to ask them for their daughters.

26. When he reached the place, he saluted the landlord, and called for a pitcherful of water, and performed the omen.

27. Then the four brothers saluted the (new) son-in-law.

28. After washing the feet of the Pardhán, they made him to sit in their house.

29. The Pardhán said: To make sure of this, (let us) go to the liquor shop.

30. Whatever Lingo told the Pardhán about marriage ceremonies, so the Pardháns now tell the Gonds to do.

31. Assemble five daughters and grind turmeric.

32. Make an offering to the domestic gods first;

33. Then (offer) saffron to all other gods by their names.

---

29. This refers to the fatal habit among the Gonds of ratifying everything with a drinking bout. The liquor is made from the flower of the Moha tree, so abundant in the Gond forests.

30. The description of the marriage ceremonies, which follows, is said to be correct and authentic.

31. Turmeric is grown in the Gond country.

34. Drink, wash the feet, (present) salutations, join your hands—

35. Spread the blanket, and make all the Gonds sit on it. Bring a pitcherful of liquor to the side of the bridegroom, and half a pitcher to that of the bride.

36. Then make all the women, both small and great, sit down.

37. Keep the full pitcher of liquor on the right side, and the half-full pitcher on the left.

38. Call (for) two more pitchersful of liquor, and drink according to custom.

39. Keep in a brass plate a lamp, some grains of rice, two pice, some betelnut, and a box of kuku (red powder), with gulal powder (red ochre). Apply a tika (sacred mark) to the front of the pitcher,

40. Then apply the mark to the pitcher-man, then to all the rest.

41. Break the pitcher, and let the women on the bride's side sing—

42. "A pair of blankets having been spread: O father, you have lost your dearest daughter.

43. O father, for the love of liquor you have lost your dear daughter."

44. Then distribute liquor cups, first to the pitcher-man,

45. And after he has drunk, then to all the rest of the company.

46. Salute (one another) and thus observe the custom.

47. (Then should) follow eating and drinking.

48. Next, at the time of departure, only those on the bridegroom's side must follow with the departing, and salute them.

49. Embrace, and then return to your house; and when the bridegroom reaches his house,

---

35. The spreading of these rough woollen blankets (sheep abound in the Gond country) is an integral part of the ceremonies.

38. The frequent mention in this and in following lines of liquor and drinking, are indicative of the customs of the Gonds; and on these occasions the women drink as much as the men.

50. Then his feet should be washed, and let all the guests on the bridegroom's side drink.

51. What happens next? Women should grind turmeric. Then what song is to be sung?

52. The Bhawajai (brother's wife) should say, Sing the bridegroom's song; and the bridegroom may say, Sing the Bhawajai's song.

53. After this, let all (the women) sing—let them grind saffron, and after making powder of it,

54. Let the Bhawajai sing, and say, Brother, sing a song.

55. After grinding saffron, wave a lamp; and in a brass plate keep saffron, and the preparation of betel-leaf with a whole nut.

56. Let there be a box of kuku (red powder), some grains of rice, and a waving lamp.

57. Bring in a pot of water, and hold liquor in a bottle named Lauguyal.

58. Then depart from the house. Let musicians be in front, and let the bridegroom follow them

59. With singing of songs. The saffron should be carried to the god Bhimsen;

60. Then to Mata, the goddess of the town; then to Matamai; fourthly, to the boundary gods.

61. Fifthly, to the god Hanuman; sixthly to the Pandhari god; seventhly, to the manes of the dead; then sing a song to Bhimsen.

---

52. Bhawajai, the elder brother's wife, is always an important personage on these occasions. If there be no such person actually, then some female relative is chosen to take the part.

57. Lauguyal is the common Gondi name for an earthen wine bottle.

59. Bhimsen is, of course, a Hindu mythological personage; but he is venerated as a god by the Gonds.

60. Mata and Matamai represent the small-pox: the names are doubtless borrowed from the Hindus. Mata is also one of the seven sisters alluded to in the preceding line 273, Part II. The fact of Mata being also the goddess of the town, indicates that the disease is frequently present and permanently dreaded, partly owing to the dirty and unwashed condition of the Gonds. The boundary gods merely allude to an imaginary demarcation among the hills; the Gonds do not put up land-marks.

61. Hanuman, the monkey god, is of course adopted from the Hindus. The Pandhari, the god of the land, is a Mahratta name. The shades of the dead (Sanyal Pen) are much venerated by the Gonds.

62. Then the song of oil offering should follow.

63. Then visit the domestic god. Let the bridegroom put a ring and chain on his neck,

64. And present grains of rice in his hand.

65. Let one woman stand in front, and the rest behind him.

66. Give a blanket to the bridegroom; apply the tika (mark) of rice.

67. Then, what song will they sing?. That song will be thus:

68. O brother, apply rice to the father with laughing countenance.

69. Apply with a smile a tika to your mother, O brother.

70. Apply with a smile a tika to your sister, O brother.

71. Apply with a smile a tika to your grandfather, O brother.

72. Apply with a smile a tika to your grandmother, O brother.

73. Apply with a smile a tika to your brother's wife, O brother.

74. Then bring the bridegroom home and wash his feet, and make him sit down.

75. Then sprinkle saffron (water) and apply saffron to the bridegroom.

76. What song shall we now sing? O Pardhán, our household priest, sing thus:

77. Tell, O father, tell us some story about our ancestors.

78. At bathing what song will they sing? They will sing thus: "Your body

79. Is like the plantain pith, and elegant is the nose of our brother."

80. Let the (bridegroom) bathe, and let all the (women) sing.

---

66. The tika mentioned in this song is the sacred mark borrowed from the Hindus.

76. This calling on the Pardhán to sing a song of the Gond traditions is exactly what occurs on these occasions.

79. The plantain tree is grown in the Gond country, and is found wild in some parts. The Gond race have small noses; and they would esteem a marked prominent nose as beautiful.

81. Let four women cause the bridegroom to be sent for. After this

82. Take the bridegroom into the house, and make him sit there.

83. Place around him four pots fastened together with thread, and

84. Surround the whole by one thread connecting all.

85. On the bridegroom's head hold cakes placed on an iron spoon,

86. And let five women hold their hands suspended over his head.

87. Then pour oil on the cakes, and then on his head

88. Pour water; then bathe him with water.

89. Then what custom follows? When the brother's wife covers a vessel on her lap, then the bridegroom should put a copper pice in it.

90. Then let him throw water till her body is wetted.

91. Bhawajai (brother's wife) will throw water also, and then let him bathe.

92. After bathing, what is to be done? Apply kuku (red powder). What song should be sung?

93. Women, holding betelnut to his mouth, and holding kuku (red powder) to his forehead, shall sing: "What Raja's son is this?"

94. Then what follows? Apply rice, then sing as follows:

95. "The Bhawajai (brother's wife) has not put oil in the lamp." She will say, in front is the bridegroom, and behind is the bride.

96. Then at the same time the drum should be sounded;

97. And with pipes; then should follow all the musicians with cheerful hearts.

98. Let (both) young and old men be merry, and raise up the bridegroom with force.

99. And make him sit on a heap of cowdung, and dance gladly around him.

100. One woman, having lifted up the seat on which the bridegroom bathed, should dance also.

101. One having taken a waving lamp, let her dance also.

102. Then let all dance and sing; first one may (lead), then let all follow him.

103. Thus ends the bathing—the bathing ceremony of the bridegroom.

104. What then follows? Make the bridegroom to be seated, and let four women lift him.

105. After raising him, let him be taken home, and having seated him bring the wedding cakes.

106. The cakes having been eaten, all begin singing.

107. As they move round (turn in the dance), let him wipe his hand on the garment of Bhawajai (brother's wife).

108. What then happens? What is the eating and drinking to be?

109. Bring a pitcher full of liquor to the house, and keep it there; and call the guests into the house, and make them sit down. Call women, both young and old, and likewise make them sit down.

110. Apply first a tika, sacred mark, to the pitcher(of liquor), and then to the pitcher-man,

111. Then to all (the company).

112. After applying the tika (mark) to the lid of the pitcher, open it and distribute the liquor.

113. Serve on the plates millet, and peas, and chillies,

114. A little salt, and serve as god (blessed you).

---

99. This sitting on a heap of cowdung is a Gond custom. But the idea of cowdung being particularly desirable, must have been learnt from the Hindus.

115. After eating is ended, then cause the hands to be washed in a brass plate. This is the eating custom—so do.

116. After rising, what follows next? Let the preparation be made for going to the bridegroom's house.

117. Call one woman, and place on her head a pitcher, and on it a burning lamp, and around it let a betel-leaf be fastened.

118. Then let all the women in procession pass.

119. When all is ready, let the bridegroom with all the company depart from the house.

120. First, take the names of the gods, and so let them depart.

121. After their departure, let them offer preparation of betel to the god Maroti, and let the bridegroom fall at its feet.

122. With the musicians beating their drums, let all take their homeward way.

---

121. The god Maroti is the same as Hanumán, or the monkey-god of the Hindus.

FINIS.

PART I.

Gond Songs as reduced to writing in the Roman character by Mr. Hislop, with the English equivalents as rendered by him also; the whole having been now examined and corrected by Mr. Pandurang.

The Creation of the World and of the Gond people, and the bondage of the Gonds.

1. Parin matan gondite yedung matan sandite
Of twelve hills in the ravines of seven hills in the glens
Lingawangad rehemand
Lingawangad (mount Lingawan) is remaining

2. Hadu gadterapo pahindi pungar mada agatal bara
Of it (in the) midst datti flower tree (was) thence twelve
kosk wasti halle
(for) coss (is) dwelling no

3. Kaw itke kawal halle chi itke pite halle raghum
Caw saying crow (there is) no chirp saying bird there is no roar
itke pulli halle
saying tiger (there is) no

4. Aske bang ata Bagawantal vida mandekitur Nalli Yadow
Then what happened god betel-nut spread Nalli Yadow
kiesia
called

5. Aske hukum kar Narayantun hukum kenstur vichike
When an order to this vakeel Narayan was made he heard it came
torat
running

6. Kartaw Subainge hon pusi kiya latur sola kadang
Kurtao Subal near him to ask he began sixteen threshingfloors
Telanganang
Teloogoo (where are)

7. Atara kadang Bamanang parin kadang Koya penk
Eighteen threshingfloors of Brahmin twelve threshingfloors of Gondi gods
ihun pusi kindor penk
thus he was asking gods

8. Ichong penk baga manda ihun idena batani talash
So many gods where are they thus of them tidings seek

9. Veru bango wadki lator
He what to say began

10. Hagada Raje madu Raji Mahadewan parrainta dariawa khalwa
There (ruler) Raja was King Mahadewa up to sea downward

11. Veru Mahadewan bahun mandur warula kaltleka
That Mahadewa how was he roller-stone (for pounding curry) like
yet para poheman-dur
water on he was swimming

12. Venu keik halle kalk halle dhundmundleka rehe mandur
To him hands were not feet not trunk like he was remaining

13. Gowra Parbatal wasi niltu Narayantun pusi kiya latu
Gowra Parbati having come stood to Narayan to ask begun

14. Ime boni andi ana Bhagawantana Subadar andan
Thou who art I of Bhagawan Subadar I am

15. Aske ime bartun wati Mahadewa baga mantor honu
And thou why hast come Mahadewa where is he

16. Idu munne ata pajaye Narayan Narbaddat Gunga adina thadit paro hanji nila latork
She first came after Narayan Narbadda Gunga of bank on having gone to stand began

17. Pope masike Raja Mahadewa waya latur Parbatal keik jodi kiai nila lata
Swimming Raja Mahadewa to come he began Parbati hands joined having to stand began

18. Pajadal Narayan horunde keik jodi keya laturk
Behind her Narayan he also hands to join began

19. Aske Mahadewa bang inta ime bartun watal parin kadang Koia penk awu baga manda
Then Mahadewa what says thou (for) what hast come twelve threshingfloors of Gond gods they where are

20. Usade bang indur bor Kartao Subal veru banga indur ime Mahadewa
Then what he says who Kartao Subal he what says to Mahadewa

21. Bara mahinana tapu kim munne mikun idena malum aial
For twelve months devotion do hereafter to you their news known (will be)

22. Seiyung mahinang atung sarung mahinang atung parotapsha atu
Five months passed six months became devotion finished

23. Aske Bhagawantal wasi niltur Mahadewa itke haka situr horu
Then Bhagawan having come stood close to Mahadewa so a calling gave him

24. Niwa tapu atu inga ime yeta bahero pasiya ana bahun pasika
Thy devotion is finished now thou water out of emerge I how shall emerge

25. Nakun hallekeiku nakun halle kalku nakun halle kanku
To me no hands to me no feet to me no eyes

26. Aske veru Mahadewaun tala atu talatun chutingatung kanku randute pasitung
Then to him (that is) to Mahadewa head became to head hair became eyes two became

27. Sabe mányana murat bane matur jagne vedachi atu
All man's form was made (in) world (of) light become

28. Ahune kanku tahachi hudtur veru Bhagawantal matkasi
Thus eyes having raise he saw him Bhagawán having seen
hatur
went away

29. Bhalo ata halle nakun pen dista halle ichor batu
Well has not become to us god appeared not so much story
kenja penti
hear O God

30. Nawa tapu waya hatu nakun manyana murat siti idu bhalo
My devotion in vain has gone to me of man's form gave this well
halle ata
has not happened

31. Unde veru tapu mandi kitur
And he devotion established

32. Nawa masu nowodinku atung poda wortu
Nine months nine days became boil burst

33. Kali Adaw peida atur horu Kali Adaw peida atur aske
Kalia Adao born was that Kalia Adao born was then
Mahadewa bang itu
Mahadewa what said

34. Aske honu Mahadewa bang itur ime tapu kime
Then to him Mahadewa what said thou devotion do

35. Boru Kali Adaw tapu kitur undi mahina atu randu mahinang
Who Kalia Adao devotion did one month become two months
atung hana kalkeidun poda watur
became to his hand boil came

36. Hadu podha wortu sola tudik jalme matung aske veru itur
That boil burst sixteen daughters born were then he said

37. Iwu tudik bartun peida atung
These daughters wherefore were born

38. Nawa sir tala aial iveruku ana bagador mangal talka
My head below will be to these I of what place husbands should bring
ihun itur
so said

39. Aske tudikun bisi yettapo wadsi situr aske watneke
Then daughters having caught in water he threw after throwing them in
yer
water

40. Soke matu sola bhar dhartari peida atu
Dry it become sixteen kinds of earth produced were

41. Nana unde tapu kika aske nawa jiwate shanti wayar
I more devotion will do then my mind (at) peace will be

42. Aske veru Kartaw Subal tapu mandi kitur vena keide podha watu
Then he devotion established in his hand boil came

43. Parin kadang kora penk jalme matung
Twelve threshingfloors of Gond gods were born

44. Koitork pagare maturk beke hake
Gonds spread over hither thither

45. Koitork aturk jagang jagang matang matang gonding ghoding
Gonds became from place to place on hill to hill in valley to valley

46. Madak madak Koiturk aturk horkna karar batal mandana
Tree to tree Gonds became their honor how must be

47. Bati distu adan jiana tan tindana
If any thing appeared to must kill it and eat

48. Halle samje maiwa kolyal bhalyal adan jiana tan tindana
No distinction must know jackal those killed to it they must eat

49. Halle samje maiwa kurshu mawku
No distinction must be antelope (deer) sambur

50. Halle samje maiwa tan tindana halle samje maiwa uti pural
Not knew distinction sow must eat not knew distinction quail pigeon

51. Halle samje maiwa kawal gidal tan tindana dokum baj
Not knew distinction crow kite must eat adjutant vulture

52. Dokke paune kida kituk muda piya yermi halyal
Lizard frog beetle cow calf she and he-buffalo

53. Yalk ghusing warcheng ihun tinda latur
Rats bandicoots squirrels so to eat began

54. Itork horku Koiturk peida aturk bange kocho bange pakko tindana
Such these Gonds born were some raw some ripe must eat

55. Sark mahinang yer kiwa halle dhad gatna todi norwa
Six months bathing must not be done nicely face must not be washed

56. Gagara gutate kudsi mandana itur
In dunghill having fallen must remain

57. Itork Koitork pahile mas peida aturk sabdan gude deing latu
Such Gonds first time were born in all the jungle a smell began

58. Ihun Koiturk bedangal iturk aske Mahadewatun nadan lagtu
Such Gonds without order became then to Mahadewa disagreeable they became

59. Ide Koirtona jatu bhurtai mantor
(Thus) Gonds caste bad was

60. Irwa halle ihun itur boru Mahadewa nawa Dhawalagiri nas kiturk
(I will) keep not so said who Mahadewa my Dhawalagiri they have spoiled

61. Beke hake deingta ihun itur verkun kesitarat
Hither thither smell comes so said to them call

62. Ihun itur Narayan handa latur horkun kesi latur torat
So said Narayan to go began to them to call began he brought

63. Munne Mahadewa
In presence of Mahadewa

64. Nilutur Mahadewa techi hud tur sabe Koitork waturk
Made them stand Mahadewa having risen he saw all Gonds come

65. Ihun tanwa dilte itur horkun tanwa bowante kesitarát
So in his mind said to them into his own cave called

66. Horkun wori wori upustur poraing kak lana utur
To them in lines he caused to sit to one end himself sat

67. Tanwa menduda neiyul tantur adena warehe bane kitur
Of his own body the dirt he took off of it a squirrel he made

68. Ital kitur yer kinake warche kitur tanu sajjio kitur
Thus did (while) bathing squirrel made to it living made

69. Tanrapo jiva wadtur tana igetal sute kiyald
Into it life threw from near himself he let it go

70. Usade sarko tokar kiyal horkunrapodal sudital latu
Then straight its tail it made through midst of them to escape it began

71. Ade hudturk Koitork tan paja vita laturk
Then saw Gonds it behind to run (they) began

72. Paja viti laturk bore indur jimtro jimtu
Behind they (to) run began some one said kill O kill

73. Bore indur bimtro bimt bako aplotun chakana aial
Another one said catch O catch good to us a kabab will be

74. Ihun indurk borku Koitork bore him katka bore him tongi
So said they who Gonds some seized a stick some seized a stone

75. Bore him dhakala pendati langoti burbur nair tudi latang
Some seized a clod of lips cloth was shaking sending to fly began

76. Beke mandot rapo penyade bhuyartrapo ade rapo soditur
It into a hole (god's prison) on the earth into it did enter

77. Warchi tanpaja Koitork sodita laturk
The squirrel after Gonds to run began

78. Parin kadang Koiturk soditar laturk bado bhuy artrapo
Twelve threshingfloors (of) Gonds to run began where in the cave

79. Aske sab Koiturk soditurk towha nalurk pistur
Thus all Gonds ran when four remained

80. Parbatin nind lagsi achalate
They came to Parwati she sleeping was in the meantime

81. Nind ugade towha Parbatin chiuta lagtu
Sleep opened when to Parwati care fell

82. Ichong diyáng mawá Koitork matork disork
Many days my Gonds were not seen

83. Dhowlagiaite kalla andu
On my Dhawalagiri noise was going on

84. Nend kameke átá ichong diyang deing gund
To-day silence has become so many days smell was

85. Nend deingo ihun itu
To-day smell is not so said

86. Bangena bange atu
Some where must be

87. Mawor Mahadewa disor Koitorkun beke atur itke ahun
My Mahadewa not to be seen Gonds whether has he led so
itu Parbatal
said Parwati

88. Towha Doulagiriparo tarksi hudtur bagane Koiturk
When Dhawalagiri having ascended saw where (no) Gonds
disork ihun itu
appear so said she

89. Mahadewtun puse kitu mawark Koiturk disork ihun
Mahadewa asked my Gonds appear not so
Koitork sodinake hudtur
Gonds entering I saw not

90. Mahadewa tetur sola kutang tingi darwajate kechi
Mahadewa arose sixteen cubits long a stone on the door he laid
situradtongi jake kitu Koiturk
(with) that stone he shut in Gonde

91. Basmásur deituna pahara nilochi situr Parbatal puse kitu
Basmásur, the demon to guard he stationed Parwati to ask began
báde ihun kiti nawa
why so is done

92. Dhawalagiri karab kiturk nakun songu watur anahun kitan
Dhawalagiri bad made to me anger came I thus did
ihun itur
so said

93. Tanrapo nalurk pisturk hork soditurk ihun itur boru
From them four have survived they fled so said who
Mahadewa
Mahadewa

94. Parbatal tanwa mante itur Koiturk mure maturk
Parwati in her mind said Gonds lost are

95. Nalurk Koiturk agatal soditurk undi mata tarksi
Four Gonds thence fled one hill ascending

96. Munne mada látu sanaghanjisendá tánparo laturk
A little forward a tree was straight gone like (a date tree) on it they climbed
agatal hadturk
thence they looked

97. Makun maknal jaga diso
To us a hiding place is not visible

98. Warur hudtur undi jaga dista inda latur bagate
One looked a place appears to say began on one side
dista Kachikopa Lahugad
appeared

99. Ad donguda saribiturk aga haturk
Of that jungle the road they took there they went

100. Aga malurk tamork hurku manda
There the four brothers they remained

101. Aske bagane Koitor balle Parbatin chinta lagtee
Then anywhere Gonds were not to Parwati care become

102. Tapshya mandi kitu
Devotion she did

103. Sarung mahinang atung
Six months became

104. Párbatáná tapu nintu Bhagawantáná dolhara hale matu
Parwati's devotion fulfilled Bhagawán in a swing to swing began

105. Borbhaktajan nawa kalite bor tap kitur hon tandat
What devotee my resting time who devotion did who (it is) see
hukum Narayantun kitur
order to Narayan he made

106. Veru hudale positur wasi Dhoulagiri parbatne
He to see went out having come to Dhawalagiri mountain

107. Wasi Parbatanige nila latur ime badi jiwate tapshyá kiti
Coming near Parwati to stand began thou in the mind devotion did
náwáng paring kodang Koid pink disong
my threshingfloor Gond god appear not

108. Itke ana tapshya kitang ihun indál hanu ime malsikun
Therefore I devotion did so she said go thou back again
veha Bhagawán veru mata latur vichike taksike hatur
tell Bhagawán he to return began running walking he went
hanjikun nila latur veru Narayan Bhagawantige ehata
having gone to stand he began that Narayan to god to tell
latur
began

109. Purbatal tapu kitu idu paran kadang Koitang tanwor
Parwati devotion did these twelve threshingfloors Gonds where
pusi kinta sabe dongude hudtur halle bagane disork
are asking in all jungle seen (they are) not anywhere not seen

110. Hanu pajane ime veha amot niwak Koitorkun hudsi sikom
Go back thou say we thy Gonds will make visible
ihun indur boru Bhagawano
so said who Bhagawán

PART II.

The Birth, Life, and Death of Lingo.

1. Hadu usade Bhagawantun chinta lagtu pahindi mada manda
To that god care fell of Puhandi a tree there was

2. Tan pungar waial tan garbhá mandál pungatun dinkumandana
To it flower will come to it featus will be to flower days will remain

3. Usade kimár pentun ankár dhukar chute matu chidor abhar
Then by god's doing clouds winds were loosened small cloud

4. Seta ichor watu garjan atu bijli chamke mata
(Like) a fan so big came thunder roared lightning flashed

5. Pungár khule matu abhar khule mata andhárártur din jake matu
The flower opened clouds opened darkness fell day hid was

6. Kamkata gundo aral
Of turmeric the powder will fall

7. Nalung pahark din posital sakada pahara abhar karke matu ahune pungar ukale
(At the) four watches of night day will arise in the morning clouds resounded therefore flower opened

8. Phakane pungar peitu ahune Lingal peida atur hanjikun mirtur khamka gundak artur
With a crack flower burst so born was having gone sprang into powder (of) the turmeric he fell

9. Abhar phake matu yadita jaku lagtu Lingal ade latur
Clouds cleaved (at) the light (of) the dawn to weep began

10. Pentun chinta lagtu aga toddi wati latu gundat akbhame
(To) God care fell them face to dry began amidst the powder

11. Penta kinni kechal toga madu mata tanparo phuki mata
(By) God's doing near a Ficus glomerate tree was on it honey was

12. Phuki warsi hatu chidur mando arta toddite
The honey burst a small drop fell in his mouth

13. Rasu tana phukita aré latu ihun toddi chaple kiyalatu
The juice of that honey to fall began so his mouth to suck he began

14. Dupar atu wadi lagtu Lingal poindi latur
It was noon wind blew to grow began

15. Agatal deisi ukade hanji atur aga jhule
Thence having leapt into a swing having gone he fell in a swing

maia latur ahun kinake din mulet
to swing began so doing day set

16. Lingal parkane techi hatur ukade kadangi latur
with haste arose and sat in a swing to swing began

17. Her Lingal yetun dag malke lingandag halle
That (was such that) to water might be a stain but to Lingo there was no stain

18. Bomli hira kapadi tira pen pariyor
On his navel was a diamond on his forehead a sandle-wood mark a divine saint

Lingal salmetor atur rand salknor atur
of a year's full became of two years became

19. Gundate khumká garsawa ukade narmana ihun bange
In turmeric powder he played in the swing he slept so some

diyang atung
days (passed)

20. Puro naw warshang atung her toddati bange tinwa
Full nine years became in his mouth anything must not eat

donguda mada guta tang
of the jungle tree (or) of thickets

21. Linga aske tanwa dilte itur ige bore disor manyalk
then in his mind said here no one is seen man

disor bade janwar diso
appears not some animal appears not

22. Naleha batiyo diso naleha bagamatke aga hankan
Me like some appear not me like somewhere will be there will I go

23. Ihun itur agatal undi diya pasitur munne sigar hatta
So said thence one day he rose before straight he went

24. Suyalmata tan paro tarktur aga Mundita kumbita madak
(Like a needle) hill on ascended there Mundita kumbita trees

matang
were

25. Tan khalwa Kirsadita mada mata tan pungak wasi adena
Below them Kirsadita tree was to it flower had come

26. Hike hatur pungakun hudsi kusi tanwa jiwate atur
Thither he went flowers having seen (in his) mind came

pungakana wasu yetur
of the flower the smell to take

27. Agatal habade hatur sugal matate mundi
Hence beyond he went on a precipitous like a needle hill up a tree

mada tarktur
he climbed

28. Agatal hudi latur hona bajute Kachikopa Lahugadta dhua
Thence to look began on the side (of) smoke

ata dhua hudsi
arose having seen

29. Id bati andu itke itur aga hanji hundana itur
This what is so said he there having gone must see

30. Agatal raktur dhua hudsi handi latur herku nalurk
Thence he ascended smoke having seen to go began these four

tamurk matark verk matkise sikar tachi matuk tan
brothers were they quickly prey brought had it

borsandurk bange vetal bange pahana tindurk
they were roasting some cooked some raw they were eating

31. Achlate her hatur boru Lingal hen hudsa horku
Meanwhile (at that time) he went who him having seen they

neturk herku neturk herkun hudsa her nitur warona
stood up seeing them he stood them having seen he stood still with each

waror
other

32. Wadkork nalurk aske aga tamwa dilte inda laturk
They did not speak the four then there in their minds to say began

33. Aplo nalurk manda dada ahun boru seiwark tamark
We four are O brothers this is he five brothers

aikat rodada hon keyat
we will be O brothers call him

34. Handakat hon talkat aske handa laturk
We will go him we will bring then to go (they) began

35. Honige haturk ima bor andi ihun iturk bon Lingan
Where he was they went thou who art so said to whom Lingo

36. Lingal inda latur ana satodhar Lingana andu matate
to say began I am a saint (named) Lingo I have on head

kupar ihun itu borkun
the knot of hair so said to whom

37. Nalurk tamurkun herku inda laturk mawa ronu da dada
Four brothers they to say began (to) our house come O brother

38. Hon ari waturk aske jagate sikar arsi mata
Him having taken (they came) then in that place game had fallen

39. Lingal inda latur idu bati andu herk indalaturk amot
to say began this what is they to say began we

sikar tatorm dada
game brought O brother

40. Batê andu inda latur Lingal padi andu
What (kind of sikar) is it to say began Lingo a pig it is

41. Tena tadaki nakun simtu aga tadaki halwake aske inda laturk
Its liver to me give there liver was not then to say began

42. Kenja dada bintadakita amot janwar jitorom
Hear O brother without liver we animal have killed

43. Aske inda latur bintadakita janwar baduro ando
Then Lingo to say began without liver animal what is

madun had simt
to me see allow

44. Aske herkun artu sankat veninga bagata hudurskom
Then them fell the thought to him now of what place we shall show

bintadakita
without liver

45. Janwar ihun iturk waror bang intor nawa bat kenja
An animal so said one what says my word hear

her mandachi alpo manda pedhork hen dongude
this one is a little we are great him in jungle

warkat padhang tonginrapo
we shall carry large (among) stones

46. Sakunrapo sanding walukat aske daranar udanur
Among thorns in thickets we shall roam then he will be tired he will sit down

47. Yer watkanur harosanur aske tanaiye malada indanur
For water he will thirst he will be hungry then back turn he will say

48. Lingan donguda sare tanturk tirkamtang keide bitur
(With) Lingo jungles road selected bow and arrow he hand held

49. Munne kurs dist tan jaka itur
Onward antelope appeared it kill said Lingo

50. Tan tadake manta munne maw disal tan jaka
To it liver is before a sambur will be seen it kill ye

51. Aden tadaki manda munne malol disal tan jakat
To it liver is before a hare will appear it kill ye

52. Tan tadaki manda
To it liver is

53. Lingal daror hirk nalurk tamurk darturk
tires not these four brothers were tired

54. Yer watkturk paro mata sareg hata tan paro
For water they thirsted above the hill steep was it on

tarkturk yeta kojhudi laturk
they ascended for water to search began

55. Usade ron handana nauran wadade khagora tanparo
Then (to) house go on bridegroom a ring put on him

akari dastana
56. chain put

Kieda paryaknang danang siana
(In) hand of rice grains give

Undi ask munne aiyal pajaye walle asku nitanang
57. One woman before become behind many women shall stand

nauran
of the bridegroom

Gamade muchustanung mitustale
Blanket cause to wear apply tika (sacred mark)

58. Bat pata waranung
Then song sing

Dada kowsi paryak mitusa hori aiyanur tamu dada
Brother with smile rice apply he will be father O brother

59. Kowsi paryak mitusa ade aiyale awwale dada
Laughing rice apply that will be mother O brother

Kowsi paryak mitusa adi aiyale selade dada
Laughing rice apply that will be sister O brother

60. Kowsi paryak mitusa hore aiyanur akoye dada
Laughing rice apply that will be grandfather O brother

Kowsi paryak mitusa dada ade aiyale kakoye
61. Laughing rice apply O brother that will be grandmother

dada
O brother

62. Kowsi Paryak mitusa selak tangek
Laughing rice apply to sister bhowajai

63. Rontatana nouran kuttulwatana honang kalknorana
Home bring bridegroom (make) seat spread his feet wash

64. Hike hake pichi sitadekiana nauran pichi sakana
Here there saffron sprinkling do bridegroom saffron apply

65. Bati pata warana hona bidhita kotkator pattadin
What song we will sing our household priest O Pardhan

66. Kayat babare bidhi chawadi vehtanur
Tell O father household story tell

67. Yer kineke bad pata warana
At bathing what song will sing

Kere gaba mendul dadana kumakore masori dadana
(Like) plantain pith (is) body (of) brother elegant (is) nose of brother

68. Usade verku marsu neli madturk wadsi siturk hanjikun
Then they the hatchet down threw (having) thrown away gone
Linga
to Lingo

69. Mawang keikun phodk watung verk marsk wadu siturk
To our hands blisters come they hatchet have thrown down
undikuk
one said

70. Haturk hanji watur usade Lingal tetur mars
They went (aside) having gone they sat down then rose the hatchet
keide bitur
in hand he took

71. Natka latur madakun paro neadak aruta tanag sirk kata
To cut began trees the trees fell then roots to dig
latu
began

72. Netematur ihun dongan natka undi gatkate baloparka itur
He applied himself thus jungle to cut (in) one hour a good field made
verku
he

73. Mawang keikun phodk watung undi mada mawa wastne
To our hands blisters came one tree by us
halle iwata halle ver
not (is) cut down that

74. Lingal undi gatkate bachole madak warktur
Lingo (in) one hour several trees has cut down

75. Cariyal todi kitur tanrapo wanjing yatur bheke nake
Black soil he has made on it rice (dhan) he has sown here and there
walum kitur
a hedge he has made

76. Undiye darwaja irtur tantati dohotur aske
One only door he has kept to it a tatty (shutter) he has bouud

77. Verku agatal teturk anwa natena sariye handa laturk
They thence arose to their own village by the road to go began
tamwa ron waturk
to their own house they came

78. Pabilo mirag lagtu chidore abhadun kariyal disa latu
First day (of) rainy season began a little cloud black to seem began

79. Hainal wade sute matu abhar sabbe din yake matu
With great force the wind was loosed sky all day cloudy was
piru barse matu
rain to fall began

80. Sawan jagate tongron handa nete matu sabbe gardorang
In open place up to knees rills to go began all the holes
buje matung
to fill began

81. Pir sute kio mund diyang aneke pir ugade bagane
Rain ceased not for three days having became (rain) fair all
wanjing parsiya latung
rice to spring began

82. Sabbe nel hirwal disa latu undi diyak nalung botang
All field green to appear began (in) one day four fingers breadth [high (rose)

83. Undi mahina atu tongron wanjing
(In) one month became up to knee rice

84. Sola kandiyang mawk mandung havenrapo mamal
Sixteen scores of deer were among them uncle
bhasiyal karbhari
nephew (were) chief

85. Id wanjing wás sute mata aven kare mata aske menake
This rice smell spread was to them known it became then to graze
hake banda
thither went

86. Paraing selate mamal padtur kalwa selate bhasiyal padtur
On the upper end uncle sat on lower end nephew sat

87. Bhasiyal katkut tetur deitur paro
Nephew with cracking his joints arose leaped upwards

88. Randok kauk nilutung phedate kushite watur deisike
Two ears upright it made greatly into pleasure it came leaped
mamanige
near uncle

89. Nel manda eiwaka wanjing hérwalk distang kowaro charo
Field is beautiful (of) rice green appears tender fodder
manda ihun itur
it is so said he

90. Makun chidor hukum siani amot sola kandiang mauk
To us the little one please give it we sixteen scores (of) rohis
hanerom
will go

91. Wanjing tanji waeron nawa bat kenja bhasa
The rice having eaten we will come my word hear O nephew

92. Sabbeta paror mata Lingana padkata parur yenma ihun
Of all the names take Lingo's field's name take not so
itur boruhoru imate sola kanding mauk mantrit mikun
said though you sixteen scores (of) deer are to you
vijatun 'undi irnal halle
for seed one keep will not

93. Usade bhasiyal intor ima mantani sedal mantorom riyark
Then nephew said thou art old we are young

94. Amot hanjikun tindokom bore hudanurte deikom
We having gone will eat any one will see then we will leap away

95. Teik kutang deikom ima seda mamyal sapade
Five cubits we will leap thou art an old man will be caught

96. Maiki itke warintantori niwa kenjom ima wanma
To go thus thou art afraid thy word I hear not you come not

97. Bor bhasiyal ihun itur sarke tokar kitur kasuk kauk
Who nephew so said straight tail did erect its
kitur paja maltur
ears did back turned

98. Maman lagtu doka usade tetur pajaya handalatur
Uncle felt grief then rose after them to go began

99. Maman wale laku watsi siturk mawku padkat
Uncle very far thrown they gave (left behind) rohis the field
kacbul hatu
near went

100. Bhasiyal mawkan paja kitu agatal sari hudi latur sari
Nephew (the) rohis behind put thence way to look began a way
bagane puto
any where was not obtained

101. Mawk intang marapo mamal shahanal mator amot bon
The rohis said among us uncle wise was we whom
puse kikom
shall we ask

102. Honpaja irtit makun ima karbhari matini
Him behind (you) left to us you chief are

103. Vehatur bhasiyal ana karbhar kintone nawa hudsekun imat kinit
Said nephew I work do my having seen you do

104. Tana munne atur bang inta undi maw
He in front became when says one deer

105. Munne mama vehandur Lingal padki andu ima kenchta
At first uncle has said Lingo field it is you did not hear

106. Paja munne huda ihun itur
Behind before look so he said (be prudent)

107. Sedanas sug kimal ihun itur boru bhasiyal
Old man's company keep not so said who nephew

108. Munne atur timme deitur bhasiyal nadum wanjing
In front became (went) a spring he leaped nephew in the midst of the
rapo nitur
rice stood

109. Mawku paja deisi honige handa latur
Rohis behind leaping near him to go began

110. Pajadal veru mamal watur walamonige wasi niltur
Behind him uncle came the hedge near having (come) stood

111. Sabbe mawk wanjing tinda latung maman sari puto
All rohis rice to eat began uncle way find did not

112. Seda manyal deia paror sabbe mawk padkutun tinji
Old man leap could not all rohis the field ate
wadtung nadum jagite
up (of) centre place

113. Hagatal pasitang walum deisikun bahera pasitung usade
Thence they went the hedge having leaped out went then
bang wadka latur boru mamal
what to speak began who uncle

114. Kenjatro sola kanding mawkanil id padkatun titi
Hear O sixteen scores (of) rohis this field you have eaten
beskitit miwor babo hudit wantor
well you have done your father to see will come

115. Miwa batal upaw kintor usade paja mator boru horu
Your how method does then behind he was who he
bhasiyal munne watur
nephew in front came

116. Kenjatro gadialknit kenjatro dadalknit imet igedal sodisidat
Hear O friend hear O brothers you hence fleeing go
undi nawa palo kenjat
one my word hear

117. Tongitparo kalk irsike hantu akin paro kalkan irsike
On stones feel placing go on leaves feet leeping
hanto kakadan paro jadit paro kalkan irsike hantu
go boughs on on grass feet leeping go
toditparo kalk irmate ihun itur boru bhasiyal
on the soil feet keep not so said who nephew

118. Bahun vehatur ahune kenshtung sola kanding mawku
How (as) he told so only they heard sixteen scorce (of) rohis
sodita latung
to run began

119. Halle bagane kojing disong ivena bagane mohojba lago
No where marks of feet appeared their no where traces appeared

120. Bade padte bide nilta bade narumta
Some sat down some stood some slept

121. Pungak muskundur narumsi Lingo mandur adho ratne
(Of) flowers in the smelling sleeping Lingo was (at) half of the night

122. Horu kanchktur hadu padka mawku titung newang
He was dreaming saw a field by rohis eaten they have
ushto wanjing
spoilt rice

123. Lingal agatal positur Kachikopa Lahungadota sari bitur
Lingo thence departed Kachikopa Lahugad's road to look

124. Agatal pasitur horkunige watur dada itur rotal
Thence went to them come brother he said of the house
bahero pasiyat
outside come ye

125. Undi batu kenjat apalota padka tang wanjing mawku titang
One word hear our field of rice rohis ate

126. Nawo apalo bapi watkat halle ihun iturk borku
Firstfruit to us to offer is not so said who
nalurkte tamurk
four brothers

127. Usade Lingal intor kenjatro dada apalotang wanjing
Then Lingo said hear O brother our rice
titung
they ate

128. Ushto atung avena nawo halle mawkna tadakita nawo
Spoilt have they firstfruit we have not of the rohis liver a firstfruit
watkan
I will offer

129. Lingoban pariyona aikan hallete nawa sato handa
Lingo a devotee I will be otherwise my power will go

130. Anà pugàk muskintona nawa pir pajinla
I with the flower of smell my stomach I fill

131. Koitork mantork horknà pàrbàpi nindàl horkna tindànà
Gonds are their bellies with what will they fill their eating

132. Wanjing ushto kitung bawu mawku ihun itur boru Lingal
Rice (spoil) did what rohis so said who Lingo

133. Ahun itur nalurk tamurk hatiyar biturk tirkamtang
So said four brother's weapons held bow and arrow

134. Tachikun ron woyana usikun upustana upusikon. madming
After rising home take having taken make sit after sitting wedding

gawanang talana
cakes bring.

135. Have gawanang sabbe tintang pata badaro warintang
Those cakes all eat and song with loud voice sing

136. Sarutan waktne babina gawanatun jim dada.
(At) turning time to Bhowajayi's garment beat O brother

137. Tanpaja bate anta tindana undana mora bang manda
Thereafter what happens (of) eating drinking custom what is

Ghagadi mond kal tatana raehade irana manyalkun keyana
138. Pitcher full liquor bring in compound keep (to) men call

wartalkun keyana rachade upusikna upusikun sabbe askun
(to) guests call in compound make sit after sitting all women
139.

chiduk padhanung keyana sabbe rachade upustana.
small great call all in compound make sit

140.
Ghagaditun tika paryakna mitustana ghatyan
To pitcher tika of rice apply to pitcherman

141.
Mitustana usada sabbotun mitustana
Apply then to all apply

Mitusikun kada uklekim chaka tirutana
142. After applying to (the) lid of the cover open it cup distribute

Jawadi kudingporo wade tan paro kusari watana tanparo
143. Soji of jawari plates on serve it on dal put it on

undi mircha watana
144. one chilly put

Nuka sawor irana kudinparo watsikun bahun pensita
145. Little salt keep plates on after serving how god give

acho wade
so serve

146.
Tinjikun atu usade keikun dhatiyate norustana ihun
After eating (is) ended then hands in a brass plate (cause to) wash so
147.

kiana mandita mora
do eating custom

148.
Techikun bang kiana nawranige rator handana manyalk
After rising what do bridegroom house to go (let) men

149. sawari kiana
preparation make

150. Nalung kongtane aturk tirk jhodekiturk avanjia
(On) four corners having become arrow applied to them to beat

laturk parodal Lingal jia latur
began from on high Lingo to strike began

151. Mamal pistur undi mawa pistu tansistu bitur tir khalwa artu
Uncle seemed one rohi seemed at it aim he took arrow below (fell)

152. Lingal tanwa dilti itur nawa keida tiru airtu id batal sat
Lingo in his mind said out of my hand arrow fell that how omen

distu
appears

153. Tanwa bhaktal japo matur honu mamal distur apalota
Thy servant worships thee that uncle appears of mine

bange tita halle
anything has not eaten

154. Madee sodita latu tan toda mamal sodite latur nalurk
Female (rohe) to run began with it uncle to run began four

tamurk tan paja lagturk ige biyakat aya jihat
brother them behind pursued here we will catch there we will catch

155. Ihun iturk sapade mata halle bawu mawku paja masi
So said found they were not who rohis (behind) turning

hudturk
looked

156. Pador kenjatro dado mawku hatung disong halle mawar
Eldest said here O brother rohis have gone appear not our

Lingal paja manda
Lingo behind is

157. Tak rehe mat aploto malsidat ihun itur bora
At the distance remained let us return so said who

pedhartamu itur
eldest brother said

158. Harkun puse kitur imat baga hanji ihun itur boru Lingal
To them asked you where gone so said who Lingo

159. Amat hanji matoram dada mawun paja matorom maw
We gone had O brethren rohis after had rohis

sodisihatu diso halle amot maltom nihiga
fled appear not we returned near you

160. Mikun vehatantona begane hudat miwa
To you I will show anywhere see in your

161. Nadide chakmak matang avan tandat kis aduyat ihun
Waists steels may be them bring out fire cause to fall so
itur boru Lingal
said who Lingo

162. Verku nadidal chakmak tanturk kisu aduṭa laturk
Their waists steels brought out fire to fall began

163. Tdatun tundo balle ihun kinake undi pahar (dinu
The matches ignited not so doing one watch of night passed (day
tarktu)
ascended)

164. Chakmakun pheki kiturk Lingoban pariyoni mantoñi
The matches they throw did Lingo saints thou art

165. Kis naḳun veba mawang kis halle arta
Fire (where is) tell us show (why) our fire not falls

166. Lingal intor igetal mund koskunpara manta Ṛikad Gawadi
Lingo said hence three coss (on) is Rikad Gawadi

167. Hona parkate kis mandá dhuá pasintá agá hantu ihun itur
In his field fire is smoke will appear there go so said
boru Lingal
who Lingo

168. Kis muchuk waymát mane ihun itur Lingal
Fire without come not so said Lingo

169. Hanji Lingan pusi kiturk amot hudtá halle ihun iturk
Having gone to Lingo asked we have seen not so said
beke hankom
where we shall go

170. Makun diso halle bati kisu usade Lingal intor
We (see) not where fire (is) then Lingo said

171. Ana tir jintona aga
I arrow will discharge there

172. Bagark handal agark imat handakit usade kis
In what direction it will go in that direction you go then fire
putal
you will get

173. Ihun itur bor Lingal tir jode kitur umsi yetur undi
So said who Lingo arrow applied having drawn he took one
tir jitur
arrow (and) discharged

174. Sari sawari atu banji dakaṛang narku
A way it made smooth some twigs it broke

175.

Bange	jhaḍi	koiṭur	sari	artu	hanjikun	tiru	arṭu	agaṭal	sedana
Some	grass	It cut	a road	fell	after going	arrow	fell	thence	at the old man's

176.

Kisunparoḍal	tir teṭu	hanji	yedung	sedanang	miyak
From off the fire	arrow arose	having gone	(to) seven	(of) the old man's	daughters

177.

Haveṇa	darwajaṭe	artu	tiru	hawa	huḍtung	vichike	watung	hadu	tiru	pehaksi	watung
In their	door	fell	arrow	they	saw	having run	they came	having	lifted	they took	away

178.

Tirtun	irtung	babon	puse	kindung	ḍawa	mawang	madming	baske	indung
They	kept (it)	their father	they	asked	O father	us	in marriage	when	will you give

179.

Haun	yedung	selak	sedal	indur
(Thus) who	seven	sisters	of old man's	said

180.

Nawa	diltor	putanur	honku	sikun	mikun	halllete
According	to my mihd	will be	to him	I will	give you	(or) no

181.

Ahune	mandakit	ihun	indur	sedal	boru	Rikad	Gawdi
As you are	you will remain	so	said	old man	who	Rikad	Gawadi

182.

Kenja	ro	dada	nawa	palo	ana	jitona	tir
Hear	O	brethren	my	word	I	discharged	arrow

183.

Ad	sariya	bantu	munne	kisu	disal	agatal	kisu	talkit
By	this road	go	before	fire	will appear	thence	fire	bring

184.

Hor	intor	home	ima	hanu	intor	ana	hanor	chidor	tamu	hatur
(Thus) he	said	to them	they	to (one to another)	said	I	will not go	youngest	brother	went

185.

Kisu	distu	kisu	kachut	hatur	agatal	hudtur	phedaye	kodt	leha	sedal
Fire	he saw	fire	near	went	thence	saw	a large	trunk	like	the old man

186.

Lakanal	hudtur	sedana	padka	bhowatal	walum	kisi
From afar	he saw	old man's	field	around it	hedge	was made

187.

Undi	sari	irshi	tan	tate	dohachi	nadum	padkate	kis	kisi
One	road	he kept	to it	a shutter	he had tied	in the middle	of the field	fire	was made

188.

Irukna	kodku	mangita	yachi	maṭor	mad	sajnang
Of a Mohwa	the trunks	of Anjun	were	put in	trees	of Saj

189.

Tekatang	katyang	jama	kisi	kisu	patusi	mator
Teak	faggots	where gathered	on fire	fire	was	kindled

190. Kisnirusi mata kisna shekane Rikad Gawadi sedal
Fire was blazed at the fire by the heat Rikad Gawadi the old man

hainake narumsi mator
(in) deep (sleep) slept was

191. Rakasun leka disandur ver narumsi ver Ahkesaral walsike
Giant like he appeared he was sleeping the Ahkesaral stealthily

kachum hatur sedan hudtur sedan kodaneke
near went the old man saw the old man (while) beholding

mendodun pinakatang watung
to (his) body cold bustles came

192. Tadake deia latur jiwate waditur manda ihun itur
His liver to leap began in his mind much afraid he was then he said

193. Veru sedal sedanur nakun hudsi tindanur nana arkate
If the old man rises me he will see (and) eaten I will be

194. Kisu kalsikun woyaka aske nawa jiwa pisar
Fire having stolen I will carry then my life will survive (safe)

195. Ver watsike kisunige hatur undi viskur bitur hadu viskur
He secretly near fire went one brand took that brand

tamadita andu
of Tembhur was

196. Tahuneke tana sidange mirtu sedana kulatun hanjikun
When having lifted it a spark leaped away on old man's hip it having gone

tuuatu
fell on him

197. Thaliatsor venu phoda watu veru sedal daske masi
As large as a lota the blister had come that old man alarmed became

tetur ven
he arose

198. Nakun karoo wasta bagane tindale puta khankna
To me hunger is felt anywhere to eat I get not of flesh

nawhari asi mata
the desire is felt

199. Kowan kakade leka bhalo wati ihun inake
(A) tender cucumber like well (hast thou) come so said

veru Ahkesaral
to that Ahkesaral

200. Sadita latur pajaye sedal vita latur kis wadsi
To run he began behind old man to run began fire (brand) he threw

situr mupneta
away in front

201. Munne sodita latur pajaye sedal vita latur ige bika naga
Onward to run he began behind old man to run began here I will seize

utonk
said he

202.	Hagatal	maltur	tanwa	padkate	watur	kisunige	hanjikutur	bang
	Thence	turned	to his	field	came	near fire	going	sat	what
	rande							
	nonsense (is this)							

203.	Kawaro	ina	sikar	wasi	mata
	Tender	like	prey	was	come

204.	Tinka	itan	pasisi hutur	nawa	keide
	I would have eaten it	he said	it is escaped	from my	hand

205.	Hatte	hami	baskane	wayar	itkhepne	hatu
	(It is) gone	let it go	sometime	I will get it	this time	it has gone

206.	Munne	bang	atu	Ahkesaral	hatur	malsikun	aga
	Before	what	happened	Ahkesaral	went	having returned	from thence
	tamurkun						
	to his brothers						

207.	Itur	kenjatro	dada	ana	kismun	hatan	imat	rohtit	aga
	Said	hear	O brethren	I	to fire	was gone	you	sent	there
	padkate	padhoree	mautor	sedal					
	in field	a giant only	was	old man					

208.	Keik	wadseke	kalk	tacheke	vitur	ana	pissi	wator
	Hands	throwing	feet	lifting	ran	I	having	survived
	watan							
	I came							

209.	Amot	hanom	ihun	iturk	borku	nalurk	tamurk	Lingal	iturk
	We	will not go	so	said	who	four	brothers	Lingo	said
	igene	udat	ro						
	here	sit	ye						

210.	Dadalknit	bator	sedal	mantor	ana	budsi	wayaka
	O brothers	what sort	of person	he is	I	having seen	will come

211.	Agatal	pasitur	munne	taktur	jhodi	lagtu	aga
	Thence	he went	onward	he walked	river	happened to be	there

212.	Mund	tumang	distung	munne	hutur
	Three	bottle gourds	appeared	in front	he saw them

213.	Waduda	kati	distu	aden	tahtur
	Bamboo	stick	appeared	he	lifted it

214.	Jhoditun	usa	aga
	The river	was flooded	there

215.	Paras	pade	tana	arsi	veli	velitun	tumang
	(It washed away) the bottle gourd	tree	its seed	fell	to each	twinner	bottle gourd
	lagsi						
	were						

216.	Waduta	kati	pongsi	wasi	adena	kitur	jantur
	A bamboo	stick	in its hollow	he pushed	its	made	guitar

217. Watatang chuting randu tartur adena tar kitur
Of head hairs two he plucked its string made

218. Kuji bitur akra naddang kitur tan upustur adene
A bow he held eleven keys he made (to) it and fixed it
nekustur bakone nektu
played on it well it played

219. Lingal tanwa dilte bakone kusi
Lingo in his mind (was) much pleased

220. Aden bitur sari lagtur sedana padkata disunige handa
It he held his way took to old man's field near fire to go
latur
began

221. Sedal narumdi mator boru Kikad Gawadi kisunige
Old man sleeping was the Rikad Gawadi near fire

222. Kodtleka kudsi mator palku kisi mantar burtai
Like a trunk fallen he was his teeth made were bad

223. Todi dakane kitor jhopane mator Lingal nehanage hoodtur
(His) mouth gaping he kept in sleep he was Lingo well beheld
sedan
the old man

224. Kan lagta ihun itur Lingal ingatae woikan sedal
(His) eyes were shut thus said Lingo now (is not time) to carry away the old man
narumtor
while slept

225. Lingal munne kal wadtur paja malsi hudtur kachule mada
Lingo before his foot threw behind turned and saw near a tree

226. Alita sarko mata aden khanding Nehanage hudtor
Of Peepul erect was to its branches Surprisingly he looked
udanlaik
(it is) fit for sitting on

227. Bakota distu adenparo tarktur paro sendata hatur
Very good it appears on it he climbed on the top he went
udanjogto
to sit

228. Udnakene gogote kustu munne Lingal inda latur din
As he was sitting cock crew before Lingo to speak began of day)
pasitana wakhtu
rising (it is) time

229. Ichalate sedan tehtana itke jantur tahtur Linga
In the meanwhile the old man will rise therefore the guitar lifted Lingo
keide
in hands

230. Bitur tana tokar jitur bekone nektu tanrapodal waja
He held it a stroke he gave well sounded from the midst of it music

tantur nurakting
he drew of hundred tunes

231. Bakota neki latu tana leng Todde wartap
Well to sound began its (sound) (Was) with mouth as if sung

pata kenjile wanta
a song can be heard

232. Tana agajne mada mata kamekene atang
At its sound tree hill silent became

233. Sedala nehanage konde saran sodita harkane tichi
(In) old man's loudly ears the sound entered in haste having risen

utur jakane sedal kanku tahata latur
he sat up quickly old man his eyes to lift began

234. Nehahnaye kenji latur hake hakehudi bagane diso
He desired to hear began here there to look anywhere appeared

halle
not

235. Pite bagatal wata nendu wadki lata bakota kogadleka
A bird whence hast come to-day to sing began good maina like

236. Madak hudi latur bagane bange diso khalwa hudsi mator
Tree to see began anywhere nothing appeared below looked

237. Paro halle hudta sandi gondi hudtur
Up did not look in thickets ravine he looked

238. Halle bange diso sedal waya latur sardige wator
Not anything appeared old man to come began near road he came

rapo soditor kisunige hanji niltur
into midst of field he entered near fire having gone stood

239. uchi uchi techi techi deisi deisi kuds
(Sometimes sitting sitting standing standing jumping jumping rolling

kudsi yendi latur
rolling to dance he began

240. Pata wari latur din pasit hona sedo sakad ene
A song to sing began day dawned his old woman in the morning

kenji latur
to hear began

241 Kenstu mawa padkat heke eiwake waja nekinta
She heard her towards fields a fine music played

242. Tanwa padkata walumunige hanji niltu tanwa kowde waja
Of her fields near the hedge having come with her ears music

kensta
she heard

243. Idu sedo bang kita tanwar šedan hike muedon nike
That old woman what did to her old man her husband at her

vehachi
she called

244. Keik sahachi yenda latur kalk tahachi yenda latur wadel
Hands stretching out to dance began feet lifting to dance began neck

wadsi yenda latur
having thrown down to dance began

245. Sedan hike sedo huda latu nawar sedal nawar
The old man towards the old woman to see began my old man my

muede
husband

246. Venku idu waja bakota lagta venleka ana yendaka idna
To him that music melodious was like him I will dance (said) that

sedo
old man

247. Kuskane soga tandta dhangunkita
Quickly the folded end of her dress drew out (and) having made free

walumunigetal yenda latu
near the hedge to dance began

248. Veru Lingal tanwa pite bang wadkintor ana satodhari
That Lingo in his belly what speaks (as) I am devout

Lingal aika penpariyor Lingana aika
Lingo I will be God's servant Lingo will be

249. Dakate dhangun matate kupan nikun mandu
I wear down to heel the fold of dhote on head a knot to me is

bomali hira kupade tira yetun dag mandan
on the navel diamond on forehead tika water stain has

250. Nakun dag halle ana Lingana aika sedal sedon diwadita
To me stain not I Lingo will be old man to old woman Diwalis

dandhar
dance in dandar

251. Koitona sar bisuka pata waruska verkun yenchuska
Of Gonds in rows will held song I will cause to sing them I will cause to dance

ana Lingana aika
I Lingo will be

252. Weru Lingal sewakintor tanwa pendun Budhal pentas paror
That Lingo worshipped his god Budhal god's name

mudtur Adal pentas paror mudtur
he invoked Adal god's name he invoked

253. Sola satikna paror mudtur attara khaukna paror madtur
Sixteen satis name invoked eighteen flags name invoked

Manko Rayetal Jungo Rayetal Pharsipenda paror mudtur
Manko Rayetal Jungo Rayetal Pharsipenda's name invoked

254. Sewa sewa itur idu janturta parin paharana keide bitur
Salutation said that guitar (of) various tunes in hands held

255. Nawu jantarta iven mohani artu ihun indur boru
My guitar this is an allurement that has fallen so said who

Lingal bade jantartun kameke kiya latur
Lingo that guitar silent to make began

256. Laknal parodal mama sewa itur veru Rikad Gawadi
From afar from on high uncle salutation said to that Rikad Gawadi

sedal
the old man

257. Madata sendatparo huda latur sewa bhasa
(Of) trees (on) top to see began salutation nephew

258. Ihun itur bhalo makun ime darusti bhasha yendusti
So said well me thou hast deceived O nephew thou hast caused to dance

bhasha bendal beke wati
O nephew whence to whither hast thou come

259. Bhasha ime wada bheting yetkat horu Lingal madital
O nephew thou hast come (let us) embrace each other that Lingo from the tree

ragi lator
to descend began

260. Sedana hanjikun keiye bitur mama sewa utur horkna
Old man's after going hand caught O uncle salutation said their

bheting atung
meeting took place

261. Bhashal werke matur maman mamal warke matur
Nephew known become (to) uncle uncle known became

bhashan
(to) nephew

262. Verkna randate jankna bheting atung mamana kie bhashal
Those two persons meeting took place uncle's hand nephew

bitur
caught

263. Hanjikun kisunige utturk ver mamal pusi kindur ime bhasha
Having gone near fire sat that uncle asked you nephew
bendal beke watin
from whence to what place hast come

264. Nikun mama malum halle sola khandyang mawakin jāktona
To you uncle known not sixteen scores of rohis have killed
havena tadakitun rodsi tindakom
their livers having roasted we will eat

265. Itke itom chakmakne kisu adundom kisu aro
Thus we said from chakmak fire we were causing to fall fire fell not

266. Mater niwa padkatige kis manda itke agatalte jitan niva
But your in field fire is therefore thence arrow I discharged

267. Kisunige tira watu igetal tettu hike munne niwang
Near (your) fire arrow came thence it rose here before thy
miyakna darwajate hanji artu
daughters door having gone (it) fell

268. Niwa miyak pehaksi watung bhalo manda mama nikun
Thy daughters having lifted carried it away well done uncle to you
budhi halle
sense not

269. Nawor tamu kisunsati rohachi matona bonku Ahkesaral imet
My brothers for fire sent I had whom Ahkesaral you
tindale vitlinmawa
to eat ran

270. Ime begeni beyeni ime tinene ana baga hudena
(If) you would have caught you would have eaten I where would have seen him

271. Ihun itur sedal anate chukton bhasaha nawa bang
So said old man I then have erred nephew I what
kiyana mata hadu atu
I done have this is past

272. Usuade bangu wadki lator boru Lingal ye mama anate kenja
Then what to speak began who Lingo O uncle me hear
mama sola khandyang mawku jaktona davi mama khandk
uncle sixteen scores of deer I have killed go uncle flesh
tara mama hainake tinvi
bring uncle much eat

273. Ihun itur boru Lingal usade munne bangu wadkanur boru ver
So said who Lingo then before what did he say who that
sedal nawa palo kenja bhasha yedung miyak mandang
old man my word hear O nephew seven daughters have
nawang
I

274. Haven wom havenige kandku dohachi Sike veru
Them take away their eyes having tied thou shalt give them

madming
(in) marriage

275. Lingal itur agatal lattur munne niltur hantorom mama
Lingo said thence arose before stood I am going uncle

276. Ihun nawa sewa yena mama itur agatal Lingal pasitar
So my salutation receive thou uncle said he thence Lingo went

sedanang miyakna rota sariye handa latur
old man's daughters house way to go began

277. Hanjikun havena darwajate niltur veru Lingal bara warshana
Having gone in their door stood that Lingo of twelve years

jani disi latu
a youth to seem began

278. Sola warshana umbar dista munnetal hudneke maratha
Sixteen years (of) age he appeared in front when seen foppish

riyon leka distor
young man like appeared

279. Pajatal hudneke bamna riyon leka eiwake riyor distor
Behind having seen Brahmin devout like good servant appeared

280. Rot rapodal selak yedung bahero pasitung venku mani
The house from within sisters seven out came those regarded

kiturk
him

281. Riyanleha awu watung baharo Lingal munne nitung
As a young man they came out Lingo before stood

282. Makun veha ihun indung selak yedung
Us tell so said sisters the seven

selak puse kindung ime boni andi
sisters to ask began thou who art

283. Horu bangu wadka latur niwor babo nawor mamal
He what to say began thy father (is) my uncle

miwa awal mawa ato
thy mother my aunt

284. Ana satodhari Lingana andan pen pariyor Lingana andan
I am devout Lingo am God's servant Lingo I

285. Nawang palong kenjat ho bai nawa tiru miwa rotige
My words hear O sister my arrow to your house

wasi arta ana nanegatal hudintona
came and fell I am from a long time searching it

286. Nawork nalurk tamurk dongude attork ana sola
My four brothers in jungle sat I sixteen
khanding mawaku jaktonah
scores of rohis have killed

287. Aunde dongude artang havenege nawor tamurk uttork
They also in jungle fell near them my brothers are sat

288. Ana kisunsate watona hikene nakun walle ushir atu
I for fire have come here to me much delay became

289. Hake nawork tamurk sari hudseke mandanurk horkun
There my brothers way expecting may be to them
karu wasi mandal
hunger felt may be

290. Yer watksi bagada yer bagoda sodi horkun
For water they may be thirsty of what place water where bread they will
putal
get

291. Ihun wadki lator Lingal venku bangu wadki latang
So to speak began Lingo to him what to speak began
yedung selak
seven sisters

292. Kenja mawa palo dada ime maman marine amot
Hear our word O brother thou to uncle son thou art and we
atin miyaknem andom
to aunt daughters we are

293. Niwa mawa eiwake nato manda niku baga sutikikom
Your and our good relationship is you how will leave (us)

294. Amot niwatoda naiakom imet wateke ana badtun halle
We along with you will come you come thou wherefore not
indaka
sayest

295. Payana matkete lakon saware mamtu munne amtu
Come (if) you come (then) quickly ready be forward be
saribimtu ihun itur boru Lingal
way take so said who Lingo

296. Iwu tamwa toranang gindang muchanang dikring
These of their beds the clothes for covering heads (and) garments
bitung Lingana tir hona honkun sisi
took Lingo's arrow they to him gave

297. Munne munne Lingal pajaye pajaye riyang handa latung
Before before Lingo behind behind young women to go began

298. Tamurk matork uchimatork hakene hudundurk baske wanur
Where brothers were seated there they were looking when will he come

299. Lingan waneke laknal hudturk kenjatro dada mawor
Lingo coming from afar they beheld hear O brother our
Lingan leka distor
Lingo like appears

300. Techi nilturk huda laturk munne Lingal pajaye yedung janik
Having risen to see began before Lingo behind seven persons

301. Kenjatro dada bonangte miyak bonangte kodiyak mawor
Hear O brother whose daughters whose daughters-in-law our
Lingal arti
Lingo haviug taken

302. Wantor hudat dada eiwake distang riyang mandang
Is coming look O brothers of good appearance young women are

303. Siyur Lingal amot baikok kiyerat dada ihun
(If) Lingo would give (then) we wives would make of them O brothers so
indur borku nalurk tamurk
said who four brothers

304. Ver Lingal kachul watur yiltur mawa palo kenjatro dada
That Lingo near came stood my word hear O brother

305. Yedung janik mamana miyak iwu watang
Seven persons uncles daughters these have come

306. Iwinsati suring tandat iwu mawkna tadaking simt
To them knives bring out of these rohis livers give

307. Verku suring tandturk mawknang pir wobaturk tadaking
They knives took out of rohis belly ripped (split) livers
tanturk bore tatur kachara kisu patusturk
took out some brought faggots fire enkindled

308. Kiturk tana ubara khandk haven bodsturk tanturk neli
On its blaze flesh they roasted took out (and) down
irturk
laid it

309. Idu tadaki perta parode idurkate
This liver in God's name offer

310. Ihun iturk borku nalurk tamurk Lingal tettur
So said who four brothers Lingo arose

311. Tinda laturk sabe tintork Lingal tinor
To eat they began all ate Lingo did not eat

312. Lektor handa simt haven baven yedung selakun avenor babo
Quickly to go allow them the seven sisters their father
ranganur wallene
an abuse will give

313. Kenjatho bai imet lokor hantu miwa awal rang sike
Hear O sisters you quickly go your mother abuse may be
mandal
giving

314. Kenjtung kenchikun indur kenja ro Linga ime bhalo
They heard having heard said hear O Lingo thou who art
indana bhurain
called good bad called (may be)

315. Amot hanom igene mankom niwatoda waikom handakit
We will not go here will stay along with thee we will come where you go
hakene amot waikom
there we will go

316. Nalurk tamurk wadkintor kenja ro dada kenja ro Linga iwu
Fourth brother said hear O brother hear O Lingo these
yedung selak eiwake
seven sisters well say

317. Inge in dada iwekun woikat madming
Yes say thou O brother these we will carry (in) marriage

318. Kikat baikok kenja Linga nawang palong itang
We will make wives hear Lingo our word (ie) such

319. Lingal kenchikun ida latur imet iven woikit madming
Lingo having heard to speak began you to these take (in) marriage
baikok nakun pedha kushi wayar
wives (make) to me (then) great pleasure will come

320. Hagane woneke igene miwang madming kisiya
Whither will you take away here only you marriage make
miwang baikokun arikun hantu
I will give leave wives to take away

321. Herku hona palo kenchikun baugu wadki laturk kenja ro
They his word having heard what to say began hear O
dada mawang palong niwa mata riya eiwake disal
brother my word if thou wish young good looking that you see
aden ima kimu
to her you marry

322. Batang puting makun sim aven amot kikom
Whosoever (is) bad looking give to us we will marry

323. Lingal bang wadki laturk kenjat ro dada nakun halle
Lingo what to say began hear O brothers to me it do not
lago
want

324. Mikun kisikun nawa kamma halle
You having married I will go they are of no use to me

325. Ihun itur boru Lingal imet kikite nawa kamno
So said who Lingo (if) you marry then to my use they
wayanung
will come

326. Badeka nawang tangek aianung imet padhork manturit ana
Who to me a sister-in-law will be you eldest are I am
chidur
younger

327. Nakun yer sianung yetkan sade nakun tarsi sianung.
Me water they will give I will take bread for me bed they will spread

328. Ana narmika nakun yer mihatanungkikan dhadotang sukanung
I will sleep me water they will give to bathe clothes they will wash

329. Nakun tangek wanung awakunleka disanung
To me sisters-in-law they will be like mother they will appear

330. Ihun itur Lingal ahun awak inake nalurkna tamurkna
So said Lingo when mother he called them from four brothers
dilta pappasisi hatu
mind sin departed

331. Honige handa laturk hon pusi kiyalaturk kenja ro Lingal
To him to go they began to him ask began hear O Lingo
lokor mawang madming
quickly our marriage do

332. Kintoni sim yedung janik mantang amot nalurk mantoram
(If) thou wish (then) give seven persons they are we four are

333. Apalo apalo baikokki sim Lingal
(To) each one their wives distribute O Lingo

334. Lingal bang iutor imat padhork rehall rehaku kimtu chidur
Lingo what says you are elder-one two two marry (he who) youngest
manton hon unde simtu
is him one give

335. Iturk Lingal unde nawa palo kejat ro dada ige
Said Lingo the my word hear O brother in this
dongude
jungle

336. Chipadite baga kintirit apalota Kachikopa Lahugad
In the plain how can you do it our Kachikopa Lahugad

337. Nar manda aga iven wokat aga madming kikal ige
Town is there to them we will take there marriage will do here
halle kiwa
not do

338. Ihun itur Lingal hona kenchikun ahune kiturk agatal positurk
So said Lingo they having heard so did thence departed

339. Borku seiurkte tamurk awa yedungte selak agatal pasitung
Those the five brothers those seven sisters thence departed

waya latung herk unde munne takintork pajaye
to go began they and in front they walked (the women) behind

awuwantang
followed

340. Ahune tanwa nate waturk Kachikopa Lahugad rapo
So to their village they came Kachikopa Lahugad of

madmina sama kiya laturk
marriage preparation to make began

341. Ige halle manyalk halle baikok Lingal yer
Here there are no men no women Lingo water

342. Tatintor hore yerkasu sintor hore pichi watiekintor
Brings he bathes having boiled he turmeric pounded

343. Manda dasintor toren dohtinton
Bower he erected leaf garland he tied

344. Nalurk tamurkun keitur hike hake pichi wadtur
The four brothers he called here there turmeric powder sprinkled

345. Nalurk tamurkun yedungte selakun pichi soktung
To four brothers to seven sisters turmeric he applied

346. Madming latung nawa palo kenjat ro dada warsan
Marriage cannot be my word hear O brothers all at once

347. Undi madming kikat waye janik mandnung dhando
One marriage we will do the rest remaining work

kiyanung
will do

348. Usade avenang madming ayanung tehawn dhando kiyanung
Then their marriage will be those (remaining) work will do

349. Barenang munene madming ayanang awu usade dhando
(Those) whose at first marriages shall be they then work

kiyanung
will do

350. Ihun itur boru Lingal usade nalurkte tamurk iturk inge
So said who Lingo then four brothers said yes

dada ahune kikat
O brother so do

351. Ahun kinake madming atung bange diyang atung padhor
So doing marriage finished some days passed eldest

tamu intor nawa palo kenjat dada
brother says my word hear O brother

352. Apalotor Lingal apalotor eiwake kitor madming kisitur
Our Lingo our good did marriage did
apalotang baikok apalotige watung
our wives to our place brought

353. Lingal bin baikonor Lingal ven baiko balle kenjat ro
Lingo without a wife (is) Lingo to him wife not hear O
dada apalota bhalo kitur tanwa halle kita
brother our good did his not did

354. Tenka bagane watawa apalotor babon leka veru atur boru
Him anywhere throw not our father like he became who
. Lingal
Lingo

355. Dongude daikat sikar jikat pungak tatakat Lingal ukade
(To) jungle we will go game will kill flowers we will bring Lingo in a swing
udar dada
will sit O brother

356. Ihun indurk nalurk tamurk
So said four brothers

357. Ukade uttur Lingal yedung selak ukad uhtinta
In a swing sat Lingo seven sisters the swing swung

358. Nalurk tamurk tawang tir kamtang bisikun dongude
Four brothers their arrow and bows having held in jungle
haturk
went

359. Paja banguata yedung selak tamwa pite bang wadkintang
After what happened seven sisters in their belly what said
kinjat hobai ver Lingal
hear O sisters this Lingo

360. Mawor sherandu andur vena amot tangek andom
Our husband's young brother is to him we sisterinlaws. are
venu kawale awjinta
with him sport can be

361. Kei bise imale awjinta masi wadkale awjinta
His hand by holding pull we can with us to speak he can

362. Ver Lingal matoda kawor matoda wadkor mahake hudor
That Lingo with us does not laugh does not speak toward us look not
kank pehachi sitor
eyes he has closed

363. Kawanur mawatoda garsanur ihun ita
(But) he must laugh with us must play so said they

364. Bade bita kei bade bita kal bisikun nmalatang ver Lingal
Some held hand some held feet having caught pulled him that Lingo
adike kanka pihachisitor
more eyes closed

365. Halle wadkor halle hudor halle kawor usade
Not spoke not looked not laughed then

366. Lingal bangu wadki lator kenjat ho bai imet nawa kei bisi
Lingo what to say began hear O sister you my hands held

367. Umi kalk bisi umi imette nawang selakaik
(And) pulled feet caught and pulled you are my sisters

368. Imette nawang auhaknik ihun badi kintorit anate pen pariyor
You are my mothers so why do this I am god's servant

379. Nawa jewa handal bale mari anate mihake hudsi halle
(though) my life will go never mind I will at you see . not
kawanar halle ihun indur boru Lingal hona kenchik
laugh will not so said who Lingo these (words) having heard

370. Pedha selad hadu bangu wadkinta kinjat ro bai verte Lingal
Eldest sister she what says hear O sisters that Lingo
wadkor halle hudor halle imet
speak not look not at you

371. Hanjikun bilange matang Lingana ris wata dakata
Having gone to embrace they began to Lingo anger came from heel
risa matate tadkta
anger to head ascended

372. Matate risu kadkne reita kadku kalk itang Lingal
From head anger to eyes descended from eyes to feet came Lingo
munne hudtor
in front looked

373. Bangete dista halle wanjing usana uskulam aden hudtur
Anything appeared not rice for cleaning the pestle that he beheld

374. Ukadal nele raktur uskulam keide beitur
Out of the swing down he descended the pestle in hand held

375. Bainake tanwa taugekun jia latur jineke
Much to his sisterinlaws to beat began as he was beating

376. Yedung selak munne sodita latung mudanleke jhodpang
Seven sisters in front to flee began like a cow bellowing

377. Lingal bagatal paja maltur tanwa ukadige wasikun
Lingo thence behind turned to his swing having come

378. Ukatparo narumtur iwa yedungte janik hamake
In a swing he slept these seven persons much
uskulamtang mar tinji matang
pestle beating had received

379. Hagatal paja maltung tanwa ron watung apaloapalo
Thence behind returned to their houses came to their own
kontane hanjikun
rooms having gone

380. Yedung janike yedung jagangneh hanjikun narumtang
Seven sisters in seven places having gone slept
Lingal ukade narumtor
Lingo in a swing slept

381. Ihun kinake dupardin tarkta wayana velo aita nalurk
So doing it was noon the coming time it was (of) four
tamurkna
brothers

382. Bore jaktor kursu bore jaktor malor bore jaktor
Some killed she antelope some killed a boar some killed
malu
a peafowl

383. Bore beitor urum bore pungar kweitor
Some held quail some flower had plucked

384. Hagatal handa laturk rota sari biturk tamwa rachade
Thence to go began house road took to their compound
waturk talanang wajenk rehachi irturk davitro dada
came of head burdens down kept let us go O brothers
Lingan intork
to Lingo said they

385. Pungak sikat sari hudsike mandanur verku nalurkte
Flower we will give way he expecting may be those four
tamurk rotrapo soditurk
brothers in the house entered

386. Ukadige hangi nilturk Lingaa hudturk Lingal narumtor
Near a swing going stood to Lingo saw Lingo was sleeping

387. Bade diso kenjatro dada Lingal mantor narumtor apalotang
None appears hear O brother Lingal is slept our
baikok halle disong
wives do not appear

388. Havekun hundakat usade Lingal tehakat agatal pojpa·
Them we will search then Lingo we will awake thence they returned

389. Apalo apalo kontana handa laturk hanjikun hada
To their own rooms to go began having gone to see
laturk
began

390. Iwaw narumtang yadki watap kuthe mantang yerku
These are slept as if fear had come panting they
pusikiya laturk
to ask began

391. Badi narumtorit Lingana ukad uhavit mawa palo kenjat
Why hast thou slept Lingo are not swinging our word hear

392. Hor Lingal miwor tamu bachojel amot makuskom
That Lingo your brother's (acts) how long we may hide

393. Imet dongude sirkartum hantorit paja Lingal mawang yat yetintor
You to jungle for hunting to go (allows) behind Lingo our shame takes

394. Bachajel pite daskom ital buddhi vena Lingana manta nerdom daskom
How long in belly shall we keep such the conduct of this Lingo is till to-day we have kept

395. Inga amot halle kenjanal amot mawor babona nate handakom
Now we will not hear we to our fathers' town will go

396. Amot halle rehemayom undi baikon rehall muedork baitun pahiji
We not will remain for one wife two husbands why should be

397. Tamurk wadki latork ver Lingan munnene indal
Brethren to speak began that Lingo formerly told us

398. Aga yedung selak manda evenrapodal achikun ime munnene baiko kim
There seven sisters are amongst them having chosen one you before us wife make

399. Pissanung hon haven amot kikom ver Lingal indur
Those who shall remain them we will marry that Lingo said

400. Nawang selak andung nawang awak andung
Our sisters they are our mothers they are

401. Indur papi Lingal dushte Lingal karam chandali Lingall
Said sinner Lingo wicked Lingo of bad conduct Lingo

402. Sikarita parode nade kikat
Of hunting in the name deceived us

403. Dongude woikal venku jaksi watkat venang kadku tandakat
In jungle we will take away him having killed we will throw his eyes will pull out

404. Nend dom kursana sikar jindom maloda sikar jindom
To-day till antelope we have killed of hare a prey killed

405. Lingana sikar jikom honang kadku tansikum
Lingo's hunting will do his eyes having taken out

406. Goling garsakom aske sodi tinkom yeru undakom
As marble will play then bread will eat water we will drink

407. Hanjikun Lingamige nilturk tendaro Lingaitedaro dada
Having gone to Lingo they stood rise O Lingo brother
chidore
the youngest

408. Badi dada tata halevit punga malsi watit
Why brother you have not brought flower why have you come back
achorte dinu banda
so great a part of the day is set

409. Bate janwar andu hadenk hainake jintorom hadu aro
Whatever animal it might be to it however we strike it does not fall

410. Halle sodigo hagane nilta amot jineke dorsi hatom
Not flee there it stands we by striking tired

411. Lingal ukadal tettur uttur tamurkun hike hudtur
Lingo from a swing arose (and) sat brothers there look

412. Hadu janwartun jiakan ihun itur Lingal
That animal I will kill so said Lingo

413. Agatal titturk rotal pasiturk davitro dada baga manta
Thence arose from home went come O brothers where is it

414. Munne Lingal pajaye nalurk dongude laturk dongude
Before Lingo behind four to jungle to go began the jungle
sari biturk
away they took

415. Pedha jat mata korite haturk mada hudintork
Large kind was it (*viz.* the animal) as they went trees they searched
jadi hudintork
grass searched

416. Lingal bangu wadkintor kenjatro dada nawang palong
Lingo what says hear O brothers my word
hatute hani hatte
if it has gone let it go

417. Lingal sarekata madat sid hanjikun utur verku
Lingo the Char tree below having gone sat those
nalurkte dada iturk
four brothers said

418. Uda Lingo yer tatinterom habadi aturk
Sit O Lingo water we will bring yonder went

419. Madakun adam aturk Ukesaral bangu wadki lator kenjatro
Of tree to the side came what to say began hear
dada eiwake Lingal dhadmite utor
O brother good Lingo in shade sat

420. Ide wakht manta nalurkte tamurk nalung tirk tandat suti
This the time is four brothers four arrows took and
kiturk
discharged

421. Bore jitur talladun worshi

Some hit to the head (it) split open

422. Bore jitur gudangatun gudanga hata bore jitur tadakitun tadaki

Some hit the neck neck fell some hit to the liver (it) cleft

423. Abune Lingana jiwa pasisi hatu

So Lingo's life went away

424. Nalurte tamurk waya laturk wasikun Lingan kachul nilturk

Four brothers to come began having come Lingo near stood

425. Suring tandat kadku tandat suri tantur

A knife let us draw out eyes we will draw out knife (they) drew out

426. Lingal kachul hatur randute kadku tantur bangu wadki

Lingo near went two eyes drew out what to say

latur simtu

began we will bury him

427. Kakadang ari Linganparo mucha latur

Twigs having taken on Lingo to cover began

428. Bangu wadki latork Lingan jaktat Lingal dusht

What to say began Lingo we have killed (that) Lingo wicked

429. Pandta mada tanang aking koitork hadena dona kiturk

Ripe tree its leaves they plucked its cup made

430. Hadurupo randute Linganang kadku irturk nadide

In it two of Lingo's eyes placed in their waist

dohaturk

they tied them

431. Handa laturk Rota sariye waya laturk ronu waturk

To go began house way to come began to house came

432. Bangu wadkintor undi kenjatro baikoknit lakore kisu patusat

What says one hear O wives quickly fire kindle

433. Diveng dasat iwu munguda huradi umtung kisu

Lamps light they of the leaves the flax stalks drew out fire

paturtang

enkindled

434. Bangu wadkintor undi kenjatro dada eiwake vedachi

What says one near O brother good light

ata ingane goling gursakat

has become now marbles we will play

435. Verku hadinropodal kadku tanturk usade undi bangu

They from waists eyes took out then one what

wadkintor yedungte selaknit imet wadat goling

says O seven sisters you come marbles

garsintorom

we will play

436. Verku	kadk	tanturk	undi	kad	khalwa	irturk	undi
Those	eyes	brought out	one	eye	side	kept	on one

kad	paring
one eye	on another (side)

437. Tamurk	uchi	horkonigi	situr	keida	botate	goltleka
The brothers	sat down	near them	gave (in)	hands	finger	marble like

biturk
they held

438. Hagatal	golitleka	jitur	jineke	verkun	hikekhalwa
Thence	marble like (will)	strike	while striking	to their	side

watu	golina	garsmud	verkna	lagtu	undi	gatka
came	the marble	game	their	lasted	one	hour

PART III.

The revival of Lingo, and his delivery of the Gonds from bondage.

1. Bang pendun kimad
What god did (now)

2. Rayetan kimad Pharsipentun kimad bang atu parodipne
did did what happened in the upper worlds

3. Sabbe penkna uchu kacheri Sri Israna
All minor divinities having sat in the court of god's

4. Horu bangu wadki lator kenjatro gadyalknit kenjatro badu
They what began to say hear O friends hear in what
Dipne murda arta
world (has this) dead body fallen

5. Hona koju kimtu bor andur
His trace will do who may he be

6. Seiyung akina vida kitur rishirk munne wadtur
Five leaves bida he made of rushis in front he threw

7. Hudatu hudi ikun nahaga wadatu nahaga veha ihun itur
Having seen him near me come (and) me tell so said he

8. Vida rishi halle tahatork
Bida the rishis not lifted

9. Usade siri isral hainake risne wator ranga lator
Then to god much anger came to reproach began

10. Siri Isral tettur thalite yer keyustur kei kal nortu
God arose in a pot water called hands and feet washed

11. Mendoda machu tantur tana kawal kitur tanrapo amrit
(From his) body dirt he took (of) it crow he made on him ambrosia
wadtur
sprinkled

12. Sajjiv kitur Kagesur paror irtur keide bitur tanku
Made it alive the name of Kagesur he kept in hand he held it

13. Wadkintor Siri Isral handuki dongude matan rupo karitrapo
Says God go in jungle between hills glens
samtinrapo joditrupo yetrapo hududi
valleys in rivers in water shalt thou look

14. Agatal kawal handu latu parodipne walita latu
Thence crow to go began in the upper world to roam began

15. Halle bagane diso hagatal sidtadipne watu haga huda latu
Did not any where see thence in the lower world came there to look began

16. Kachikopa Lohugad adena dongude wasikum hudu latu
of its jungle having come to look began
matane korite
in the hilly valleys

17. Najur batu kakadang distu agatal kawal tettu
Sight fell twigs appeared thence crow arose
hanjikun kakadanige uttu kakadanrapo hudu lattu
having gone near twigs sat under twigs to search began

18. Lingal artor burotaye distur honku kadk halle honu
Lingo was fallen bad he appeared to him eyes were not his
talla worta distu piru worta distu paduk pasitang
head burst appeared belly burst appeared intestines come out
distu
appeared

19. Kawal hudtu agatal kawal tettu tuda latu waya latu
Crow looked thence crow went to fly began to come began
parodipne
in the upper world

20. Siri Israna keitparo wasikun uttu veru Siri Isral pusi kitur
God's on hands having come sat that God to ask began
baga manta kharone veha
where (and) what is truly tell

21. Usade Kachikopa Lahugad hadena dongude watan haga
Then in its jungle I came there
hudtan waror manyal koritrapo artor
I searched one man in a cave is fallen

22. Siri Isral tanwa pite kemekena atur samje matur
God in his belly became silent (and) understood

23. Hade dongude pahindi pungar mada mata Lingal
In that jungle Pahindi flower's tree was (where) Lingal
Jonme masi
was born

24. Askedal wata halle
Since then came not

25. Botutal amrit tantur keitur Kurtao Subal honku vehatur
Out of his finger ambrosia took out he called to him said

26. Ime idu honu amrit womu todakeparo pitparo watakin
You this to him ambrosia take on his liver on the belly sprinkle
tallatparo watakin
on the head sprinkle

27. Munne kawal paja Kurtao Subal handa laturk Kachikopa
In front crow behind to go began to
Lahugadta

28. Kenja ho kawade mawor Lingal andur ihun itur
Hear O crow my Lingo is thus said
Kurtaoa Subal

29. Amrit tantur hona todde wadtur hona tallat puro
Ambrosia brought in his mouth put and his head on
wadtur hona pit paro wadtur usade Lingana talla
put his belly on put then Lingo's head
jude maya latu
join to began

30. Mendol kastu
(His) body became warm

31. Linga techikun
Linga arose

32. Uda latur kawalhike huda latur bangu wadki latur Linga
To sit began crow to see began what to say began Lingo
nana hainake matona
I in deep (sleep) was

33. Nawork tamurk beke haturk
My brothers where have gone

34. Undi kawal waror manyal distor nawork tamurk disork
One crow one man is seen my brothers are not seen
ihun ineke
so said

35. Wadkintor Kurtao Subal bagatork niwork tamurk
So he said Kurtao Subal where are your brothers

36. Ime te sasi matoni arse matoni amot watom nihun tehatom
You dead were lying you were we came you raised

37. Tamurkna paror matintom horke nikun jakturk horku
Of brothers name take they you killed they
haturk
went away

38. Indur Kurtao Subal veru Linga bangu intor kenja
(Then) said to Kurtao Subal that Linga what says hear
kaku
O crow

39. Ana handakan nawung sola kadang koiturk
I will go to my sixteen scores (of Gonds)

40. Handakan horkun hudakan aske wayakan
I will go them I will see with them I will speak

41. Kawal Kurtao Subal verku andu laturk
Crow and Kurtao Subal both to go began

42.

Linga	handá	laturk	dusara	sarye
Linga	to go	began	another	way

43.

Linga	hatur	undi	mata	waiintu	undi	mata	turginton
Linga	went	one	mountain	passing	one	mountain	ascending

dongude	handu	lator	haneke	din	mulitu
in jungle	to go	began	then	day	was set

44.

Veru	Lingo	bangu	wadktur	inga	dinu	hatu	ige	rehe
That	Lingo	what	said	now	day	is set	here	stay

mayka	waronaye
I will	alone

45.

Benke	chital	wayah	nakun	tindal	benke
From somewhere	tiger	will come	me	will eat	from somewhere

yadjal	wayal	nak	tindal
bear	will come	me	will eat

46.

Veru	pedhajat	nirura	mada	aden	hudtur
That	large	niroor	tree	to it	he went

47.

Tanparo	turktur	shendute	aga	din	mulit
Thereupon	he climbed	to the top	then	day	set

48.

Dongur	gogoting	kusintang	mulk	tahosintang	kursk
Wild	cocks	crowed	peacocks	cried	antelope

chamrke	mantang
afraid	were

49.

Yedsku	gume	mantang	kolyalk	kolla	kintang	dongur
Bears	wagged	their heads	jackals	a yell	made	jungle

gajbaje
resounded

50.

Ardho	rat	ata	Lingo	bangu	wadkintor	eiwake
Half	night	passed	Lingo	what	was saying	good

jango mamal	pasitor
moon	is up

51.

Yedachi	atu	sukkuk	pasitang	verkun	pusi	kiku	nawa
The light	coming	stars	appearing	to them	ask	I will	about

koiturk
my Gonds

52.

Mund	pahark atu	gogoti	kustee
At the third	watch of night	cock	crowed

53.

Via	sukkum	pasitor	lal	abhar	atu	din	pasitu
Morning	star	appeared	red	sky	became	day	appeared

54.

Veru	Lingo	madatal	rutur	vichike	handu	latur
That	Lingo	from tree	came down	running	to go	began

dintunige	hunjikun	sewa	kitur
towards the sun	having gone	salutation	made

55. Vehatu nawa sola kadang koitork baga mantork
Tell my sixteen scores of Gonds where are

56. Kenja Linga nanate siri israna chakari kiritona nalung
Hear Lingo I of god's service I do four
pahark takintona
watches I travel on

57. Distu halle
I saw (them) not

58. Agatal Lingo jango maman ige watwi
Thence Lingo moon uncle to came

59. Sewa kitur han pusi kitur mama nawang
Salutation made him asked O uncle my

60. Sola kadang koitorkun hudsi kenja jango mandaki
Sixteen scores of Gonds seen hear O moon if you have
nakun vehata
to me tell

61. Kenja Lingo anate narkapoding takintona din
Hear Lingo I night all walk day light
pasinta aske udintona siri israna chakari
Until then I sit (in) god's service

62. Nakun malum halle
To me known not

63. Agatal handa lator ver Lingo karyal kumaitunige
From then to go began that Lingo to black kumait

64. Hanjikun sewa itor pusikitor nawang sola kadang koitork
After going salutation made asked my sixteen scores of Gonds
baga mantork
where are

65. Kenja Linga sabbena paror muta koitorkna paror mutma
Hear Lingo of all the names mention of Gonds names do not mentio

66. Gadhana jat koitona barabar manda
To asses' caste Gonds equal are

67. Bilal unde tintork yalli unde tintork ghusi unde tintork
Cats also they eat mice also they eat handicoots also they eat

68. Padi unde tintork mudatang khandk yedmitang tintork ital
Pigs also they eat cow's flesh buffaloes they eat such
buratai mantork
bad they are

69. Horkunigerk nakun barkur pusi kiya
About them me why you ask

70. Dhawalagiri Parwat Jumnagiri tirith
Dhawalagiri mountain Jumna place of worship

71. Haga Mahadewa manda hom sabbe kottorkun bisikun
There Mahadeo is he all Gonds caught (having)

72. Yaditrapo muchi sitor sola kutang tongi tana todtparo
In a cave shut did sixteen cubits stone on its mouth
darwajate muchi situ
door covered

73. Basmasur Deituna pahara irtu deitur kepintar
Basmasur giant as a guard kept the giant watching (the place)

74. Lingo agatal positur taka latur amte unde takintu narka
Lingo from there started to walk began day and he walked night

75. Tap kitur bara mahinang atung vena tapu nintu
Devotion made twelve months passed when devotion was completed

76. Mahadewa undana sonota chowrang dagmage muta
Mahadeo's sitting golden stool to shake began

77. Mahadewa indur nawa Dhawalagirat paro boru Ristu wator
Mahadeo said my Dhawalagiri on what Devotee has come
ige tap kitu nawa paro
here devotion made me upon

78. Waje kitu ihun itur Mahadewa
Load he put thus said Mahadeo

79. Handa latur huda latur maka latur
To go began to see began to wonder began

80. Lingan kachul haturk lake nilturk hagatal hudturk
Lingo towards went after stood from there saw
verte Linga
he was Lingo

81. Halle kei maluyor halle kal tahator kadkne hudor
Do not hand shake do not feet lift up with eye do not see

82. Sabbe savi watta padekaye pista ihun Lingal sahakun paro
All flesh was dry bones remaining thus Lingo thorns upon
nasumtu
was asleep

83. Mahadewa bangu wadkilatur
Mahadeo what began to say

84. Ime taluka bang talukiya bang indaki hade sika
You ask what ask what you wish that I will give

85. Ver Linga bang intor
This Lingo what say

86.

Nakun	badandaye	kamti	halle	nawang	sola	kadang	koitork	nakun	sima
For me	any thing	less	is not	my	sixteen	scores	of Gonds	me	give

87.

Mahadewa	intor
Mahadeo	said

88.

Paror	mutma	baga	daye	rajye	tuluka	bange	rupyang	tuluka	uchi	tendake
Name	dont take	of any	place	kingdom	ask	any amount of	money	ask	which	you will enjoy

89.

Mawa	puror	mutaki	ihun	itur	Mahadewa	Lingal	kenjta	halle
My	name	take	thus	said	Mahadeo	Lingo	agree	did not

90.

Koitorkun	taluktur	Mahadewa	jaba hare	koiturkun	situr
Gonds	on asking	Mahadeo	disappeared	the Gonds	gave

91.

Kenja	Linga	bhuyartrapo	niwork	koitork	mantork	horkun	wom
Hear	Lingo	below the earth	your	Gonds	are	them	take away

92.

Lingal	tettur	sewa	itur	handu	latur
Lingo	arose	salutation	made	to go	began

93.

Veru	Narayan	bang	intor	kenja	Mahadewa	sabbetinne	koitork	verku
This	Narayan	what	said	hear	Mahadewa	all	Gonds	these

94.

Besh	makstu	paror	marse	mata	sasi	manerk	mukun	bukota	mata
(Were) well	concealed	(their) name	forgotten	is	(if they)	were dead	to me	good	would have been

95.

Unde	verku	koitork	jitoaturk	bhuyatal	positurk	ahune	kinurk
Again	said	(if) Gonds	living	from below the earth	came out	as usual	they will eat

96.

Yedming	tendanurk	pileng	purhuk	tendanurk	kawal	giduk	dhokuk
Buffalo	they will eat	birds and	pigeons	they will eat	crows	eagles	and vultures

97.

Ruaming	beke hake	was	wayal	padekang	arunang	burotai	disal
Will alight	here and there	stink	will arise	bones	will fall	bad	look

98. Mawa Dhawalagirita satwo bude mayal
My Dhawalagiri's purity lost will be

99. Hona kenjtur Mahadewa kenja Narayân undi palote
His (word) heard Mahadeo hear O Narayan my word
ana sisi
I have given

100. Chuktan nawaipe dusaro halle
I erred near me another here is not

101. Narayan bang intor
Narayan what said

102. Kenja Linga mawa punjatun karyal Bindo pitetang
Hear Lingo for my offering black Bindo birds
chiwak ime arikun
young ones for me bring

103. Usade nawork koitorkun womu
After that from me the Gonds take away

104. Lingo yontur daryawun kachul hatur aga hudintor beke
Lingo reached the sea near went there he saw here
heke yer dista
and there water was visible

105. Ina kudkate karyal Bindo pitetung chiwaku ma nda
Of that sea-shore black Bindo the birds young ones were
admanasalk
male and female

106. Randute dongude hatung
Both to jungle had gone

107. Aada pite batal mandu yenin jakund tanang
That bird how was elephant killing of that (elephant)
kadnu tindu talla wohtund tana maddur
the eyes they ate the head breaking of that brain

108. Chiwakun tatund piteta yedung khopka yetrapoda
For young ones they brought of this bird seven broods aquatic

109. Bhowarnag manda tarasu idu tinji mata ver Linga
Bhowarnag was snake he eaten had this Lingo
kachul hatur
near went

110. Chiwakun hudtur bang wedkintor
The young ones seeing what (he) said

111. Paja woyakan nakun kalle indanurk
In absence if I take (the young ones away) me a thief they will call

112. Horkun munne woyakan ana Lingana aikan
In their presence if I take them away I Linga will be

113. Chiwakun kachul narumtur hainaki
The young ones near he slept with comfort

114. Itumna kodtleka tarasa tosuro distu
Name trunk like snake thick appeared

115. Setitichor tana phadi kitu idu Bhowarnag
Like basket (for winnowing corn) his hood was this Bhowarnag
tarasu yetropodal chiwak tendale waya latur
snake from water the young ones to eat to come began

116. Iwu chiwak torasun hudtung hainake wuritung ada
These young ones the snake seeing much were terrified to cry
latung
began

117 Lingobhan parekatal tir tantur kamtatun jodi kutur
Lingo from his back arrow took (in) bow fixed
tiru
the arrow

118. Jitur turasna yedung khandang kitur nake vitur
Shot the snake seven pieces he made fast ran
yedungte khandang
all seven pieces

119. Mahachi tuttur talla wada vitur aden para
Carried and brought (of) his head on the side he kept at
muchi situr
covered

120. Usade dongudal kuryal Bindo radute admunsaolk
Then from the jungle black Bindo both male and female

121. Bade jakta hutum bange jaktork yening badena konku
Some they killed camels some they killed elephant some eyes
bitork yenotang
got of elephant

122. Ihun chiwakan sati charo arikan waya latung
These young ones for food taking coming began

123. Iwu chiwaku charo tinong
These young ones food will not eat

124. Usade bangu wadku latung bodu kuriyal Bindo pitte tanwor
Then what to say began female black Bindo's bird to her
muedon bangu inta
he ones what said

125. Yedung velku atung asikun
Seven times I got notwithstanding

126. Ana tongu wangu yedmileka mantona iwu teri
I am now without (young ones) buffalo like I am these if
pisanung
can be spared

127. Ana chawa wale disuka ihun itan usade nawang chiwang
I like mother of child will look thus said again (on) my young ones
batita diti lagta
what evil eye has fallen

128. Iwu tinung halle
These eat do not

129. Tanor munsur neli hudtur pandri distu Linga narnmsi
Her he one alighted (and) looked white appeared Lingo sleeping
hon
this

130. Hudtu kenja ho mawang chiwak tenal halle neli huda
Saw hear these our young ones eat do not below see
manyal
a man

131. Mantor hontu jaksi wata hona tullada madur tansi
There is him kill of his head brain take out

132. mawang chiwaka charo tindanung
Our young ones food for eating (will be)

133. Chiwaku kenchikun bangu wadkintang
The young ones hearing what they said

134. Makun ime charo tatan amot bahun tindakom imet babo
For us you food have brought we how eat O you father
ime awal mawor andit
you mother of us are

135. Makun wadsikun dongude handit ige mahaga
Us leaving to jungle you go here near us
boru rehe mandur
who remains

136. Makun boru kepandur
Us who will guard

137. Idu yetrapodal Bhowarnag makun tindale wandu
This aquatic Bhowarnag us to eat was coming

138. Horu manwal mator mawa jiva pistu met hudtit
That man was here our life was saved you saw

139. Ponko tindale dosat horu tindanur usade amot tindakom
Him to eat give he eats after we will eat

140. Usade chiwakna kenjtu
After (of) the young ones hearing

141. Awal neli Lingan kuchal wasikun utto hona tullawadutat
The mother below Lingo near coming sat his head from

142. Dupta tuhustu hudtu hagu yedung khandang Bhowarnag
Cover having lifted saw these seven pieces of Bhowarnag

143. Hudsikun tanwa pite bangu wadki latu
Seeing in her belly what to say began

144. Ide taras sabbe nawang chiwak titu nakun wanjulal kitu
This snake all my young ones ate me childless made

145. Veru manyal halle idunde kepne tinji mamwal usade
If this man was not (there) the young ones eaten would have again
karyal Bindo
the black Bindo

146. Pitte bangu wadki lata tedu ro dada tedura baba ime bonu
Bird what to say began rise O brother rise father you who
andi beke wati
are whence you have come

147. Nawang chawanu jiwa pisusti mawor pedhor baba ati
Of my young ones the life you saved our grand father you became

148. Ime bangu indaki hadu amot kenja kan
You whatever say that we hear will

149. Linga bangu wadkintor kenja
Lingo what said hear

150. Ho karyal Bindo pitteti anate satwadhari Linga penparyor
O black Bindo bird I am a devotee Lingo worshipper of deity

151. Ime bartun wati Linga makun veha ihun itu badu
You why came Lingo us tell thus said who
pitte
the bird

152. Kenja pitteti niwang rundute chiwakun nakun simu
Hear bird your both young ones me give
ihun itur boru Lingal
thus said who Lingo

153. Usade chiwakna paror mutaneke kuryal Bindo pitte
Then of young ones the name on taking black Bindo bird
hainake adu latu
much to cry began

154. Kudhek tantu bangu wadki latu
Her eyes lifting up what to say began

155. Kenja Linga unde bange talukem ana seyena
Hear Lingo any other thing if you (would have asked) I would have given

156. Nawang chiwakna paror halle matni
My young ones name do not mention

157. Usade bangu wadki latur Lingal
Then what to say began Lingo

158. Haga Mahadewa mantor hona najude hudansati niwang chiwakun wontona
There Mahadeo is for him with eyes to look your young ones I will take

159. Usade bangu wadkinta kuryal Bindo pitte
Then what said black Bindo bird

160. Kenja Linga Mahadewa keitor amot wayakom
Hear Linga (if) Mahadeo calls we will go

161. Unde khato pakal paro tanwa randute chiwakun upusta undi khaku Linga upusta
One side of wing on their both young ones made to sit on one side Lingo made to sit

162. Usade karyal Bindo pittetor mansur bangu wadkintor kenja Linga
Then black Bindo bird's male what said hear Lingo

163. Ana bartun mandaka mikun hainake yaddi lagal
I for what will remain you much sun will feel

164. Ihun itur neli modi tudintu paro
Thus said from below the female flew up

165. Tanor mansur dhadim kitur daryawan igetal tuda latur
Her male shelter making towards the sea thence to fly began

166. Sarung mehinana sari mata iwu pitteng sakadene pasitang
Six months' road was this bird early in the morning started

167. Dupar ayo te wasikun Mahadewata rachede reitung
Mid-day till they flew of Mahadeo in the court they alighted

168. Duadal hudtur Narayan vichike hanjikun Mahadewatige vehata latur
From door seeing Narain ran and going Mahadeo to show began

169. Kenja Mahadewa ver Lingo karyal Bindo petten ari
Hear Mahadeo this Lingo black Bindo bird has brought

170. Usade Mahadewa bangu wadki lator kenja Narayan
Then Mahadeo what to say began hear Narain

171. Anate wadkandan anate vehandan ime halle verhorte Lingo
I told I understood you hear did not Lingo

172. **Tatanur suti kiuar halle**
Will bring leave will not

173. **Usade mahadewa wadktur kenja Lingo niwang sola kadang koitorkun**
Then mahadeo said hear Lingo your sixteen scores of Gonds

174. **Womu sitan hanu Lingal**
Take I have given and go Lingo

175. **Mahadewatun sewa kitur yadit karun hatur Phursipenda paror**
To mahadeo salutation he made cave near the he went great god's name

176. **Mutatur Rayetana paror mutatur basmasur deituro habadi kitur**
He took of Rayetan god's name he took basmasur giant in front made to go

177. **Sola katang tangi chira tachikun hahadi irtur tamvang**
Sixteen cubits of stone piece lifting up aside kept his

178. **Koiturkuro bahers tantur horku koiturkun hudtur verku koitork bango wadkintor**
Gonds out brought those Gonds saw him these Gonds what said

179. **Kenja Lingo mawor bore halle makun veru mahadewa**
Hear Lingo we have one no to us this mahadeo

180. **Gahokna pindi bone situr janana pindi**
Of wheat flour to some gave of millet flour

181. **Boue situr paryok**
To some he gave rice

182. **Yadite aturk atu laturk honake intork**
To river went to cook began some were saying

183. **Kondi kusi mator muwa jiwata hotal solu kitur**
What he had kept them our lives how punish he did

184. **Usade Linga bangu wadkintor**
Then Linga what said

185. **Imet yadite datu imet atatu tintu usade wadkakel**
You in river come you cook and eat then you speak

PART IV.

The subdivision of the Gonds into tribes, and the institution of the worship of the Gond gods.

1. Lingo pistur rotang kitur kusari atatur sabbe koitorkna atmad atu
Lingo (havіng) kneeded thick cake made pulse cooked all Gond's souls satisfied

2. Ihun abhal tettu piru ara latu
Then clouds arose rain to fall began

3. Joditun usa waya lata sabbe koitork bangu wadki
To a river flood to come began all Gonds what (began) to speak

4. Linga hainake pir tetta palang pirurinta
O Lingo much rain rose up rain is falling

5. Verku koitork handa laturk sabbe koitork joditrapo handa laturk
Those Gonds to go began all Gonds in middle of river to go began

6. Horkun rapadork nalung koitork Lingan toda rahe maturk
Them amongst four Gonds Lingo with remained

7. Hotu Lingal hudtur bangu wadki lator kinjat dada
That Lingo saw what to speak began hear O brother

8. Joditur usa wata apalo had khak bahur handakat
To river flood came we that side how we shall go

9. Adhike abhal watu andhar atu
More clouds came darkness became

10. Verku nalurkte jank Lingal bang wadkintor
(To) those four persons Lingo what speaks

11. Kinjat dada bahun kikat bahun handakat din hanta
Hear brother how we will do how we will go day is going

12. Dame kasuwal Puse magral yetrupo garsiki
Dame the tortoise Puse the aligator in water were playing

13. Waya latung virkunkachul yetropodal wadka latung
To come they began to them out of water to speak began

14. Kinjatro dada imet badi kamekene atorit adintorit
Hear O brother you why silent became (and) cry

15. Mawang sola kadang koitork achorte haturk amot rahematam
Our sixteen scores (of) Gonds all went we remained

16. Bahun handakom kinjat dada mawang palong amot mikun rehachi sikom
How we shall go hear O brothers our word we you a crossing will give

17. Makun imet pari kikot te amot rehachi siya
With us you oath keep then we a crossing will give

18. Wadki lator kenja bai imet te Puse magrani imette Dame kaswane
(They) to speak began hear sisters you then Puse the aligator you Dame the tortoise

19. Undi verku nalurk jank mantork nikun munne pari kinurk
First those four persons (who) are you first oath keep

20. Nikun bora jianur jiasmar halli bori biamur biasenar halle
(If) you any will beat to beat we will not allow any apprehend (to) catch we will not (allow)

21. Imette verkna nulurkte jankna pedha turad aiki ihun itur
You to those four persons eldest sister will become thus spoke

22. Dame kaswal Puse magral todit kachul waturk verkmal urkte jank Puse magranporo parekate warore Lingal Dame kuswana parekate
Dame the tortoise Puse the aligator face near came those sat persons Puse the aligator's on back alone Lingo Dame the tortoise on back

23. Dame kaswal paja atu Puse magra munne atu usatrapo sodita
Dame the tortoise behind became Puse the aligator in front became in flood entered

24. Bangu kiya latu nalurkunte arikun opoadhike muduta
What to do began to the four having taken in deep water to drown began

25. Verku ada laturk usade kaswal bangu wadkinta kinja Linga
They to cry began then tortoise what spoke hear O Lingo

26. Ime kai simu horkun nawa parikat paro umsi yena
You hand give to them my back on drag

27. Lingal kei situr nalurkunte bitur umsi yetur kaswana parikate upustur
Lingo hand gave to the four caught dragged from water tortoise on back caused to sit

28. Idu kaso rechachi situ tana parekate nulurkte jank
This tortoise a crossing gave on his back to four persons

29. Kal kara laturk kenjtin kaswa amot nikun halle beimaw anal
On feet to fall they began hear O tortoise we have to you not faithless become

30. Usade verku handa laturk donguda sariye undi mata Torgentork
Then those to go began by jungly way one hill ascended

31. Undi mata runtork handa latork munni
One hill descended to go began forward

32. Verku madak nadktur rohk dohaturk munda laturk bekebake
Those trees cut house built to remain began here there

33. Netku kiturk achorte rohku koitorkna kiturk pedhojat naru atu
Fields made all house for Gonds made large city became

34. Agane hatum nehaturk pedha nar Bhumi atu
There a bazaar held large Bhumi became

35. Wadki lator dada imet netku yadakit janang anung
To say they began O brother you fields sow jawari will spring

36. Usade verkun bara mahinang atung aiwake Bhumi sahar disa latu
Then to them twelve months became a good Bhumi city to appear began

37. Bone kondang halveke honku kondang atung
Who bullocks have not those bullocks became (received)

38. Bon godang halveki hon gadang atung sabbe wadang naru nande matu
Those who carts have not to them carts became all enclosures (of) city prosperous became

39. Lingal achorte koitork waturk manditel woriya
To Lingo all Gonds came close to thigh in rows

40. Utturk nadum Lingal niltur usade Lingal wadka latur
Sat in midst Lingo stood then Lingo to speak began

41. Kenjatro koitork
Hear O Gonds

42. Achorte koiturk nit imet bange samje mavit nit bon
All you Gonds to you anything understanding not to whom
indana dada bon indana baba
to call brother whom to call father

43. Bon indana pari bona myad talukana bon siana
Whom to call a relative whom a daughter to ask whom to give

44. Bontoda kawana usade verku koitork bangu wadkintork
With whom to laugh then those Gonds what said

45. Lingo imete pedhar buddhitone eiwake wadkte
To you great understanding (is) good spoke

46. Bahun wadkte ahun Linga niwa keide khamk kimu
How spoke so Lingo you with hands that do

47. Lingal sola kodang koitork miatork korkun ropodal
Lingo sixteen companies (of) Gonds that were of them from amidst
nalung kodang undi khak tehatur
four bands one side raised

48. Warona kei bitur bon intor ime ro gadiga manawajia
One's hand caught whom said he you O friend manawajia
atung
become

49. Aske horu manawajia atur usade dusarona kei bitur
Then he manawajia became Then another's hand caught
kenja ro gadiya mete dahakiwali ojal aike
hear O friend you dahakwale bard be

50. Horu dahakiwale ojal atur
That dahakiwale bards became

51. Unde dusroni kei bitur hon itur ime gadiya
And another's hand caught him said you friend
koilabutal aiyaki horu koilabutal atur
koilabutal be he koilabutal became

52. Usade dusrona kei bitur honku bang itur ime
Then other's hand caught to him what said you
gadiya koikopal aiyake
wild koikopal be

53. Horu koikopal atur ihun kineke nalung kodang martung
he koikopal became thus he made them four scores became

54. Bara kodang pistung usade Lingal nalung kodang tantur
Twelve bands remained then Lingo four bands separated

55. Muneta kadutun korku kitur dusaro kadatun bhil kitur
(Of) first band korku became (of) another band bhil became

56. Tisaro kadatun kolami kitur choutotun kotoleyal kitur at kodang
(Of) third band kolami made (of) fourth kotolegal made eight bands

57. Mortung at rehe matung usade bangu atu tiju weishakna mahina
(Finished) ended eight remained then what became third of weishak month

58. Watu usade Lingal wadkintor davitro dada makun halle
(Came) arrived then Lingo said come O brothers to us not

59. Pen bagane diso apalo penu kikat punja
God anywhere appears we god will make and worship

60. Achonti jank undiya palo
All persons one word

61. Kiturk seiyung warshana bakral
Spoke five years' old goat

62 Salmeta kusana ghogoti mund worshana kuwarik padnag
A year old crowing cock three years virgin calf

63. Gai randu taratu
Cow two, bring

64. Manaojan keyat pen ghagarang
Manaojan call god chain

65. Dongur mudana tokada gangawan chawur tarat ihun itur Lingal
Wild cow tailed cow tailed fan bring thus said Lingo.

66. Dukan mandekimtu poladna Pharsi pot banekimtu
Shop spread (keep) of steel Pharsi pot make.

67. Dongude hantu waduda kate norksi taratu iehor
To jungle go bamboo stick cut (and) bring it

68. Dhanegaon penman dana satik mandana Anegaon
(In) Dhanegaon god keep goddesses keep (in) Anegaon

69. Sakade lettur jodite hatur yer kitur usade dhote
(In the) morning arose (to a) river went water took then garment
pondtur
wore

70. Kapade tira metatur veru hang wadkintor kenjtro
(On) forehead tika applied he what said hear
ojal kun
oja to

71. Keyat joda dahaking keyatu penkate torata ver Lingal
Call two drummers they call god stick brought he Lingo
katitun
to the stick

72. Ghagarang dohatur Pharsipot paro dastur gangawan chawar
Gangara (bell god) bound Pharsipot in shoved cow tailed fan
paro tuduta latur tuna kei jodikitur sewa sewa Pharspendi
on to wave began his hand joined hail hail O Pharsipen

73. Kati tahatur tahaneke Manko Rayetal, Jango Rayetal
Stick (lifted) took when lifting Manko Rayetal, Jango Rayetal

74. Pharsipen wase niltu vena mendode rummematu
Parsapen (having) come stood in his body played

75. Lingal pen kotedal atur hainake ghume matur deiya latur
Lingo god devotee became much to turn he began to jump began

76. Munne munne Lingal pajayk bakralk ghoghotin kuwaring
In front Lingo behind goats cocks virgin
padang
calf

77. Undi jagpaniaturk bhumi sutikiturk
(In) one place assembled the place left

78. Waturk inda laturk pedha
Came to speak began loudly

79. Wadki laturk borku koitorku kenjatro dada imet nilat penti
To speak began who Gonds hear O brother you stand O god

80. Kal kurat pusi kimtu baga pen kada koda
(On) feet fell asking made where O gods (for) each band
marana chun indur
shall we prepare place so said

81. Usade sabbe koitork munne aturk keik jodikiturk nilturk
Then all Gonds in front became hands joined (and) stood

82. Usade	pus	kiturk	Pharsipen	bang	wadkinta	kenjatro	dada
Then	to ask	began	Pharsipen	what	says	hear	O father

83. Parin	matan	gondite	yedung	sandite	imet	datu	higa
Between twelve	hills	in caves	in seven	hilly	dales	you	go
higa	nawa	pen	kada	kimta			
there	my	gods	place	make			

84. Munne	pen	kate	pajaye	sabbete	koitork	handa	laturk
In front	god	stick	behind	all	Gonds	to go	began

85. Imet	datu	higa	reiturk	jadi	tora	laturk	tonging	worsi
They	went	there	alighted	grass	to pick	began	stones	threw

86. Bangu	wadkintor	Lingal
Then	spoke	Lingo

87. Kenjatro	dada	munne	dista	biwalata	mada	tan	narkat
Hear	O brother	yonder	appears	bijesal	tree	that	cut

88. Tana	dhole	kintu	mars	biturk	medetige	haturk	mada
Its	(drum) dhol	make	axe	caught	near tree	went	tree
nad turk							
did cut							

89. Bone	sola	biturk	soramend	yer	tatturk	todi	katurk
Some	pitcher	held	pitcherful	water	brought	earth	dug

90. Tana	wadata	kiturk	adenparo	penkate	irturk	
Its	chabutra	made	on it	god stick	placed	
kinjatro	dada	niwa	dhol	atu	halle	atu
Hear	O brother	your	dhol	became	not	ready

91. Munne	kis	patusturk	diyeng	dosturk
In front	fire	burn	lamp	light

92. Seyung	torang	palnide	shendur	nahalork	seiyung	torang
Five	tolas	in ghi	vermilion	wet	five	tolas
raru	tanturk	kisun	paro	wadturk		
ral (resin),	take	fire	on	threw		

93. Munne	Lingal	uttur	keide	pen	Ghagarang
Before	Lingo	sat	hand joined	god	Ghagara

94. Ghagarang	nekusta	latur	vena	mendode	pen	Rayetal	watu
Gangara (bell god)	play	began	that	(in) his body	god	Rayetal	came
Pharsipen	garsa	latur					
Parsapen	to play	began					

95. Jorat	badakmend	phul
Bring	goglet full	of daru

96. Kathi	paro	wadtur	sewa	Pharsipen	itur
The stick	on	sprinkled it	salam	Pharsipen	spoke

97. Randute keik joda kiturk kal kara laturk kal karaneke
Two hands joined did at feet to fall began feet falling time

98. Pen Rayetal mendode watu veru Lingal deiya latur
God Rayetal in body came he Lingo to jump began

hainake hale matur yenda latur
much to move began dance (to) began

99. Usade bangu wadki latu Pharsipen ari nawa seijarang
Then what to speak began Pharsipen bring to me victims

100. Verku seiyung salkna bakral munne tachikun niluturk
Those five years goats before having brought made to stand

101. Adenang kalk norturk tona taladun sandur sokturh
Their feet washed his head vemilion applied

tanang kowdrapo phul wadturk
(in) his ears daru poured

102. Bakranku bisikun kal kara laturk
Goat having caught feet to threw began

103. Bakrana mindody Rayetal watu hoinuke kasunga latu
(In) goats body Rayetal came much to shake began

tala hale kitu kowku gode kitur mendodum jadte
head to move began ear to shake began to the body shake

situ
gave

104. Verku ran nalungcha jank viturk bakran betur tan
Then two four persons ran goat caught it

aru turk
threw (down)

105. Pentparo aske laturk achorte natur beke hake watu
God before to cut began all blood here and there sprinkled

106. Aturk taladun munne iturk bakranku taha chikun
Began the head before to keep to the goat having lifted

undi khak irturk
one side kept

107. Usade sal meta pandu gogute tan laturk haden aske
Then a year old white cock brought to it (they) cut

108. Jantur nekusta laturk dhohi nekusta laturk eiwake
Kingri to play began dhol to play began good

pendawaja nekusta laturk
god music to play began

109. Eiwake penu kusite watu garsa lata
Good god in pleasure came to play began

110. Usade randute padana kalk norturk toddi worturk
Then two (of) calf's feet washed mouth washed
avena talade sendur sokturk
their head vermilion applied

111. Aven neli aruturk aska laturk
Then down threw to cut began

112. Randu padanang talang munne irturk usade Lingal bangu
(Of) two the calves heads before kept then Lingo what
wadke latur kenjatro dada
to say began hear O brother

113. Lakore ireina padana tolk tandat bore tadaking bursat
Quickly these calves skins flay some liver roast

114. Boun tongmg taturk sodek kiturk sodekun puro atkang
Some stones brought, an oven made on oven on pitcher (for cooking)
iturk
kept

115. Atkan rapo yer wadturk yetraro khandk wadturk
Picther in water put in water flesh put

116. Mardnang akung kweisikun taturk hadenang kuding kiturk
Yen (tree) leaf having cut brought their plates made

117. Dhadiate ghato biturku toda kitang khandku biturk
In brass plate cooked rice took liver took flesh took
nalung diveng patusturk pent munne ari
four lamps lighted god before placed

118. Puja kinturk bore irintor rupya pahud pendun
An offering made some were keeping (as) rupee present (before) god

119. Ihun pendun munne rupyana tongronmend rasi artu
So god before of rupees up to knee a heap fell

120. Lingo wadki laturk kenjatro dada eiwake mawa pengada
Lingo to speak began hear O brother good (in) my god's court
atu
became

121. Hanku sikat ihun
Whom shall we give this

122. Kinjatro dada ichorkun rapodal bore waror Padal amtu
Hear O brothers (of) all from midst some one Pardhan (shall) become

123. Horku amot sikun
To him we will give

124. Usade Lingal eiwake hudtur sabbenropoo sedal pantang
Then Lingo good looked in the company old hoary
chuting wale nudtur
haired man saw

125. Paksi sedan hudtur hanjikun hona kei bitur
First old man he looked having gone his hand held

126. Ime Padani amu amot ikun wallenaye rasyud sikom
You Pardhan he we to you much wealth will give
dhadotang sikom
clothes will give

127. Nikun kongang sikom band talukaki sikom halle inar
You a horse we will give whatever (will) you ask will give not speak
halie
no

128. Bhalote dada ana seda maniwana uchikun tendaka
Well brother I am (an) old man I will sit and eat

129. Niltur sabbekun sewa itur bore situr dhadotang bore
Stood all salam said some gave clothes some
siturk rupyang
gave rupees

130. Hadu kikri venku siturk
That pipe to him gave

131. Bangu wadki latur Lingal kenjatro gidiya
What to speak began Lingo hear O friends

132. Usade bahun kiana dada veru tettuu
Then what shall we do O brother he arose

133. Yedung jankun tehatur horku undi khak nilutur imet
Seven persons made to rise to them one side made to stand you
ro dada wadkal velta yedung sagang aming
O brother kindred (one) be seven family become

134. Usade sarung jankun undi khak nilutur
Then six persons one side made to stand

135. Horkun itur sarung sagang aming seiyun jankun
To them said (of) six a family become five persons

136. Unde khak nilutur seiru saga aiakat
Also (one)side to stand (made) fifth family formed

137. Pisturk nalurk horkun bangu wadktur imet tusmartusta
Remained four to them what said you be divided
nalung sayung sagang
(into) four and five families

138. Ihun itur imet kason pari kikit
Thus said you tortoise promise keep

139. Sabburkun sewa kitur habadi hudut ro dada maw penti
All salam made yonder looked O brother my near gods
han
I go

140. Achonte jank paja malsi hudturk hike Lingal mayad latur
All persons behind turned and looked here Lingo to hide began
Lingal turtur seri Israna saba ti hanji niltur
Lingo quickly go (to) gods courts in going stood

141. Achonte koitork mahaka laturk beke hatur mawor Lingal
All Gonds to look began where (is) gone our Lingo

PART V.

The institution by Lingo of the rites of Marriage among the Gonds.

1\.

Munne	Padal	atur	joda	hudile	handaka	ihun	itur	Padal
Before	Pardhan	became	spouse	to look	I will go	thus	said	Pardhan

2\.

Ihun	itur	Lingal	nalurkte	upalotork	chidurk	padork
Thus	said	Lingo	to four	your	small and	great (ones)

mandauork	temile	mamt	undi	jaga	unat	undi	palo
remaining	join (gather)	become	(in) one	place	sit	one	council

kimt
make

3\.

Achode	koitork	usadi	Lingal	intor	mawa	palo	kenjatro
(To) all	Gonds	then	Lingo	says	our	word	hear

dada	Padan	rohkat	adena	bichar	kikat
O brother	Pardhan	I will send	his	consideration	take (do)

4\.

Aske	rohkat	paryak	yet	rapo	watkat	paryatun
Then	they sent	for rice	water	in	put	rice

5\.

Parya	tundal	usade	rohkat	te	halle	rohanal
(If) rice	sticks	then	we will send	if	not	we will not send

6\.

Koitork	usade	walork	Lingan	paja	munne	nilturk
Gonds	then	came	Lingo's	behind	before	stood

7\.

Paryak	yetrapo	watat	rand	paryat	usade	yetrapo	waturk
Rice	in water	cast	two	rice	then	in water	they cast

8\.

Paryaku	unditun	undi	judematung
Rice	to one	to one	joined

9\.

Usade	Lingal	hudtur	tanwa	kankne	hudtur	tanwa	mante
Then	Lingo	looked	with his own	eyes	looked	his (in)	mind

intor	bahun	itan	ahune	atu	mawa	madmina	sagun
said	how	said	so	become	our	marriages	omen

bakota	distu	kenjatro	dada
good	seems	hear	O brother

10\.

Apalotor	Padan	misati	velak	hudile	handa
Our	Pardhan	for you	wives	to see	let go

11\.

Usade	Padan	saware	kitur
Then	Pardhan	ready	made (himself)

12. Lingal intor Padan kinja nawa palo ima handaki
Lingo says O Pardhan hear my words you go
Kachikopa Lahugad
Kachikopa Lahugad

13. Aga koitork mantork horkunige handaki
There Gonds are to them go

14. Hanjikun ima nitki sewa dharnirknit
After going you stand salam (make) to the head man

15. Nawa jahar mikun yavvi ihun indaki iun vehtur
My salutation to you may reach this tell thus say

16. Hona palo kinjtur bor Padal agatal pasitur Kachikopa
His word heard that Pardhan thence departed Kachikopa
Lahugadta sariya handa latur
Lahugad way to go began

17. Bor Padal horkna hatur rachadi niltur bor Padal
That Pardhan their went in compound stood that Pardhan
sewa dhanirknit
salam (made) to the landlord

18. Ana miwar Padana andan dada nakun Padal kitur
I your Pardhan am brother I Pardhan was made
mawor Lingal mikun nhanirk kitur
our Lingo you lord made

19. Lingal mihigi rohtor miwang tudik bade mantang
Lingo me sent you daughters possess therefore
mawor Lingan rohtor miwang tudikun talkana
our Lingo sent your daughters to ask
madming
in marriage

20. War hudsikun amot kikom
Bride having seen we will join them

21. Nalurkte tamurk inda laturk Lingan mawa sewajahar
The four brothers to tell began (to) Lingo our salutation
vehakun sikom
tell we will give

22. Padal sewa kitur tanara natenda sari bitur Linganiga
Pardhan salutation made to (his) town way took to Lingo
hatur
went

23. Ihun itur bor Padal Linganige mawor Lingal kintorte
Thus said that Pardhan to Lingo our Lingo (what) does
kia sim
(let him) do

24. Mawang tudik sikom ihun iturk bork nalurk tamurk
Our daughters we will give so said those four brothers

25. Bor Padal tudik talkite haturk bork koitork
That Pardhan daughter to ask went (of) those Gonds

26. Padal munne hanjikun palong vehatur bor Padal sewa
Pardhan before having gone word told that Pardhan salutation

dhanirknit tatur talite yer arikun
to landlord gave a pot (of) water having taken

27. Sewa saderknit ihun iturk
Salutation son-in-law thus said

28. Kalk norturk rachade utturk
Feet washed in compound sat

29. Padal palo tantur aga palo lave kitur kaladi
Pardhan word brought out there word establish did kalal's (liquor)

godite haturk
shop went

30. Bachomanda acho Lingal vehatur sabbe Koitork kiana
Whatever that Linge said all the Gonds do

kintork ahune munne ahun inga anta kenjat dada
are doing as before so now (it) happens hear O brothers

madminang
about marriage

31. Seiyung tudik kesikun pichi kohkustane
Five daughters assemble turmeric grind

32. Rota penjanan wet siana
(To) domestic gods offering give

33. Avena paroda rota pen pichi watan
By their names (to) house gods turmeric offer

34. Kaluhtale kalk norana sewa jahar kiana keik jodekim
Drink feet wash salutation do hands joining do

35. Gamading tarana sabbe Koitork chidur padhork udana
Blanket spread all Gonds small great make sit

kudang ghagading tatana nawran hinda nawarin
(of) liquor pitcher bring (on) bridegroom's side (on) bride's

hinda adho ghagadita tatana
side half a pitcher bring

36. Ayimaikun chiduk padang tapana aven apustana
To the women small great bring to them make sit

37. Tindana keide ghagadi koda irana dawa kiede adute
On right hand pitcher of liquor keep (to) left hand half

kada irana
(pitcher) of liquor keep

38. Ghagading indana kaluhtana mora

Pitcherful (of liquor) call give to drink (according to) custom

39. Dadiyate diwa paryaknang danang irana rand peisang

In brassplate a lamp rice grains keep two pice

irana akita vida kukuta dabba irana gulyada pudi

keep betel rolls kuku box keep gulal powder

irana ghagaditun munne tika metustana

keep (of) pitcher to the front tika (sacred mark) apply

40. Ghatiyan mitustana tanpâja sabbetun mitustana

(Then) to pitcherman apply after (it) to all apply

41. Tanpaja ghat wahatana usade ask pata tandana nawarin hindang

After it pitcher break then women song sing on bride's side

42. Joda gamoding tartil babare bain hare matil surwan parematit

Pair of blankets spread O father daughther is lost (in) promise dearest who was brought up

43. Babare chaka lobhi bainor surwanor hare

O father (for) liquor's love daughter dearest is lost

44. Kada chaka ghatiyan siana

(Of) liquor drinking cup pitcherman give

45. Tanpaja ghatiyal chaka undana paja sabbe pangetun siana

After this (let) pitcherman the cup drink after all to company give

46. Usade sewa kiana ihun kaluhtana

Then salutation do thus custom

47. Jawayer undana

Eating drinking

48. Sakade sari boroni nowran hindorkna kisiana sewa jahar kiana

(In) the morning way sending (or despatching time) bridegroom's side do follow salutation do

49. Mela bheting yestana apalo ron handana nawran hindork hanjikun nawaran ron

Embracing take to your house go bridegroom's side having gone (at) oridegroom's house

50. Kalk norana nawaranork wartalk knlbhtun

Feet wash bridegroom side guests may drink

51. Munne bang auta ask pichi nawrintang aga bat pata
Before what happens women saffron grinding when what song
warinsang
may sing

52. Ange indanur angewo kural indanur
(Bhowjai) elder brother's wife will speak O Bhowjaee bridegroom will speak
angeowona pata ask waranung
Bhowjai's song women will sing

53. Tanpaja sabbe patang warana pichi nor sikum
After this all songs may sing (of) saffron ground having
kamkang kohkana
saffron make powder

54. Bawajai indanur dadal ihun pata
Bhowajai will say brother so sing

55. Saffron kahksikun arti kiana dadiyati irana akina
Saffron having ground wave lamp in brass plate saffron keep
vida irana seigo supari irana
bida (roll) keep whole nut keep

56. Kukuta dabba irana paryaknang danang irana
Kuku's (red powder) box keep rice grains keep

57. Thalite yer trana Laguyal badukne kel biana
In a pot water bring (in) Laguyal bottle liquor keep

58. Rotal pasitana lagnal munne aiana hon munne
House from depart one who marries in front may become him before
dholta
musicians (follow)

59. Pata warana bada pichi walutuna pahile pichi
Songs sing loudly saffron (in) procession (take) first saffron
natebhiman
(to) town Bhimsen (give)

60. Dusaro pichi nate marain tisaro mitawan chouto
Second saffron (to) town Mata (god) third to matewan fourth
pichi Siwarya boharyakun
saffron to boundary and surrounding gods

61. Pachawo pichi nate Hanumantun sahawo pichi
Fifthly saffron (to) town Hanuman sixthly saffron
Panderitang penkun satwo pichi sana dumalkun tenpaja
(to) Pandhari god seventh saffron (to) (departed manes) after this
id pata warana bhimanige
this song sing to Bhimsen

62. Nil tarutana pata warana
Oil offering song sing

63. Usade ron handana nauran wadade khagora tanparo
Then (to) house go on bridegroom a ring put on him

akari dastana
chain put

64. Kieda paryaknang danang siana
(In) hand of rice grains give

65. Undi ask munne aiyal pajaye walle asku nitanang
One woman before become behind many women shall stand

nauran
of the bridegroom

66. Gamade muchustanung mitustale
Blanket cause to wear apply tika (sacred mark)

67. Bat pata waranung
Then song sing

68. Dada kowsi paryak mitusa hori aiyanur tamu dada
Brother with smile rice apply he will be father O brother

69. Kowsi paryak mitusa ade aiyale awwale dada
Laughing rice apply that will be mother O brother

70. Kowsi paryak mitusa adi aiyale selade dada
Laughing rice apply that will be sister O brother

71. Kowsi paryak mitusa hore aiyanur akoye dada
Laughing rice apply that will be grandfather O brother

72. Kowsi paryak mitusa dada ade aiyale kakoye
Laughing rice apply O brother that will be grandmother

dada
O brother

73. Kowsi Paryak mitusa selak tangek
Laughing rice apply to sister bhowajai

74. Rontatana nouran kuttulwatana honang kalknorana
Home bring bridegroom (make) seat spread his feet wash

75. Hike hake pichi sitadekiana nauran pichi sakana
Here there saffron sprinkling do bridegroom saffron apply

76. Bati pata warana hona bidhita kotkator pattadin
What song we will sing our household priest O Pardhan

77. Kayat babare bidhi chawadi vehtanur
Tell O father household story tell

78. Yer kineke bad pata warana
At bathing what song will sing

79. Kere gaba mendul dadana kumakore masori dadana
(Like) plantain pith (is) body (of) brother elegant (is) nose of brother

80. Ite yerkiana pata warat tanpaja walli patang manda
So bathe do song sing after it many songs sing

81. Nauaran nalung asku kutudun nawaran uttal
(To) bridegroom four women (on) seat of bridegroom make sit

82. Hon tahatana bon nauaran rachade woyana aga
(Make) him to rise that bridegroom in compound take there

upustana
make (him) sit

83. Hon bhawatal nalung thaling irana aven thalining nul
Him round four pots keep those pots thread

gundi
bind

84. Sirmut kiana
Surround (it) make

85. Usade nawarana talat paro kache sukud kotana
Then bridegroom head on (in) iron spoon push

kopasaditun biana
cakes hold

86. Tankhalwa seiyung janik asku kiek irana talat
Under it five individual women hands (may) keep head

paro kieku irana
on hands keep

87. Paro ni watana
On it oil pour

88. Sikim yer kopasadet paro hona talat nawrana yer
Pour water cakes on of his head bridegroom (with) wat r

mihatana
bathe

89. Aga bad mura kiana naurana tange gangal paro
Then what custom do bridegroom of Bhowajaye's bathing vessel on

sewmuchal undi piesa watintor
the cover one pice (cast) will put

90. Yer jokekintor tana sew puhtantor mendul purnal
Water sprinkle (till) her lap will wet (till) body is wetted

91. Yer watintor tanggen paro usade nauran yermihitana
Water throw Bhowajai on then bridegroom will bathe

92. Yer michikun bati mura kiaha kuku mitustana kuku
Water after bathing what custom do kuku apply kuku

mitusnake bad pata warintang asku
having applied what song will sing women

93.

Todde	vida	kapade	kuku	bore	Rajanar	kuwaral	ihun	waringtang
In mouth	bida	on forehead	kuku	what	Raja's	son is	thus	sing

94.

Usade	bad	mura	anta	paryak	mitustantang	usade	pata	warintang
Then	what	custom	happens	rice	apply	then	song	sing

95.

Indanure	dadal	angede	tawrite	walleni	dosima	angede
Will say	brother	O bhawjaai	in lamp	much (oil)	is not put	bhawajai

indanure	dadal	munneye	tawri	pajaye	nowri
will say	brother	(in front)	bridegroom (is) lamp	after (behind)	(is) bride

96.

Dholi	nekusta
Drum	beat

97.

Usade	surnaite	dhobrk	nehanaye
Then	in pipes	musicians	gladly (sing)

98.

Riyang	asku	sedo	sadoku	tanwa	jiwateni	phurke
Young	women	old	old (women)	in their	minds	glad

maiyanung	undi	jani	padkne	techikan	nawran	tahtanta
will be	one	person	forcibly	having risen	the bridegroom	make rise

99.

Podi	paro	upastanta	nouran	yedinta	nehanaye
Dung hill	on	make sit	bridegroom	and dance	gladly

100.

Tanpaja	undi	jani	kuttul	ari	naurana	yerkital	yedinta
Thereafter	one	person	seat (wooden)	having taken of	bridegroom's	bathing	may dance

101.

Tanpaja	arti	bisi	undi	jani	yedinta
Thereafter	a waving lamp	having taken	one	person	may dance

102.

Aven	paja	baren	kushi	aw	yedintang	aven	paja	subbe
Then	after	who	wish	those	may dance	then	after	all

patang	waristing
songs	sing

103.

Morang	nawrana	mantang	yerkiana	atu
Custom	bridegroom's	is	bathing	ended

104.

Aske	bang kiana	unde	nauran	kuttudi	upustana	nalung
Then	what do	and the	bridegroom	on the seat	make sit	four

aski	tahtana	nawran
women	make to rise	the bridegroom

105. Tachikun ron woyana usikun upustana upusikon madming
After rising home take having taken make sit after sitting wedding

gawanang talana
cakes bring

106. Have gawanang sabbe tintang pata badaro warintang
Those cakes all eat and song with loud voice sing

107. Sarutan waktne babina gawanatun jim dada
(At) turning time to Bhowajayi's garment beat O brother

108. Tanpaja bate anta tindana undana mora bang manda
Thereafter what happens (of) eating drinking custom what is

109. Ghagadi mond kal tatana raehade irana manyalkun keyana
Pitcher full liquor bring in compound keep (to) men call

wartalkun keyana rachade upusikna upusikun sabbe askun
(to) guests call in conpound make sit after sitting all women

chiduk padhanung keyana sabbe rachade upustana.
small great call all in compound make sit

110. Ghagaditun tika paryakna mitustana ghatyan
To pitcher tika of rice apply to pitcherman

111. Mitustana usada sabbotun mitustana
Apply then to all apply

112. Mitusikun kada uklekim chaka tirutana
After applying to (the) lid of the cover open it cup distribute

113. Jawadi kudingporo wade tan paro kusari watana tanparo
Soji of jawari plates on serve it on dal put it on

undi mircha watana
one chilly put

114. Nuka sawor irana kudinparo watsikun bahun pensita
Little salt keep plates on after serving how god give

acho wade
so serve

115. Tinjikun atu usade keikun dhatiyate norustana ihun
After eating (is) ended then hands in a brass plate (cause to) wash so

kiana mandita mora
do eating custom

116. Techikun bang kiana nawranige rator handana manyalk
After rising what do bridegroom house to go (let) men

sawari kiana
preparation make

117. Keyana undi asun talada ghatu thalita siana
Call one woman (on) her head ghat (with a lamp) of pot give

tanparo patal tawari irana thautparo tansirmul aking
on it a burning lamp keep on the pot around it betel of

nagweltang dohaehikun
naguel be fastened

118. Sabbe manditork ane asku handana
All in company those women let go

119. Sabbe saware mayana nawran toda paring dostale rotal
(Every) preparation being made bridegroom with his friends from home

pasitana
may depart

120. Apalota penta paror yetana yechikun rotal pusital
Of their god name taken having from house let them depart

121. Pasisikun Marotin vida chade nawral kal karana
After departure to Maroti bida offer bridegroom (or) feet fall

122. Nawrina rota sari biana munne dholik dhol
Brides house way take before (in front) musicians drum

nekustana
beat

NOTE.—The word vida, or bida, occurs frequently in the above song. It means an offering of betel-nut made to the gods.

FINIS.

PART IV.—APPENDICES, CONSISTING OF MISCELLANEOUS MEMORANDA.

Note by the Editor.

The following seven appendices have been selected or extracted from a common-place book kept by Mr. Hislop, and relating to a great variety of subjects in connexion with the natives of the Nagpore country. These selections, or extracts, relate, of course, to the aboriginal tribes described in the foregoing Essay. Though doubtless all the points which the author regarded as of the most importance have been given in that Essay, yet these appendices may be of use by way of corroboration or of illustration, and, therefore, have been included in this publication.

It was Mr. Hislop's practice not only to take down in writing the statements which he obtained from individual members of the tribes whom he met with on his tours, or from persons specially acquainted therewith; but also he used to employ catechists, and others connected with the Mission, to collect information regarding the customs, the feelings, and the faith of the wild people among whom their ministrations lay. From their reports or verbal accounts he would record notes. And it is from notes recorded from one or other of the above named sources that these appendices have been taken.

These appendices will be found to relate to the Gonds of each of several districts, namely Nagpore, Chindwara, Seonee, Bundara, Chanda, and also two other aboriginal tribes, namely the Mádias and the Koorkus.

R. T.

APPENDIX I.

The following Note is ascertained to have been taken by Mr. Hislop at Nagpore.

Three Gondi women, named respectively Mangali, Tami, and Mohani, came to me to-day (25th July 1861) with Paharsingh. They are natives of this district (Nagpur). Mangali worshipped six gods, and the two others seven. All say that there is one Creator, whom the Hindus call Bhagawán, and they call simply Pen, *i. e.* god. Among the six gods the greatest is Pharsi Pen, so called from Pharsi, a battleaxe, in the form of a Barchi, eight inches long, because he is said to have been born in the house of a Lohar. 2.—Khode, or Khodial, so named from being made of the trunk of a tree, called in their language *mundi*, but in Marathi, Karam, of this form I/O; the spherical part being about three inches in diameter, and the projecting head, which is made of the same piece, about 3½ inches. When it is worshipped on Akhádi, Jiwati, Shimga, and Diwali, it is placed, as above, on a chabutra; at other times it is kept in a *ghagar*, or earthen pot. 3.—Sánálk, from Sátur, to die, or a dead man; in the Marathi expressed as Utranche dewa, *i. e.* the god or gods who descend (utarane) to the earth again after they have left it by death. On a day devoted to the worship of the manes, for which no time is fixed, the relatives of the deceased assemble and go through the prescribed ceremonies at the house; after which they go to an open place, where into the hands of the Pujári come down, as is imagined, two or three morsels of a white thing like quartz, of the size of a rice grain. The ceremonies include the sacrifice of a goat, when they make a chabutra, and place on it four or five pebbles, and at the four corners new *ghagars* encircled with thread; and rice, poli, and wada, according to the number of the deceased's gods, are placed around the chabutra. They throw a little of each on the pebbles with daru; the relatives saying, "Accept it and willingly descend." The women sing,* the musicians make a noise, and into the hands of the Pujári comes Sánálk. 4.—Munjal, which means an unmarried man (kuwará). It rises like a protuberance, about one and a half inches high, of shendur (red lead), spontaneously on a chabutra in the house at night, when no person can see. This is to commemorate dead unmarried men; and the supposed miracle does not take place so often as in the case of the Sánálk. 5.—Durga (is a god, and not to be confounded with the Hindu goddess). His form is like Khodial, and is made of the same wood, and is kept in a earthen pot, except when he is worshipped on Akhádi, Jiwati, Shimga, or Holi and Diwali. When sick they make vows to him, and if they get better they fulfil their vows on the days mentioned. Khodial they worship also, on Jiwati, Holi, &c., but not in consequence of a vow; they simply remember him when they are feasting, and pay him the attention of a finger full of vermilion and a hen. Pharsi Pen is worshipped at full moon of Weishák, every third year. He was worshipped last in 1860. To him they offer a white cock, a white he-goat, and a white young cow. 6.—Chuda Pen, *chuda* being the Hindi for the Marathi *yer, or kada*,—a man's bracelet. He is worshipped under the form of a bracelet of iron, along with Khodial and Durga, on the four feasts. The two worshippers of seven gods said that the above-named were theirs also, and they added a seventh, *i. e.* Sakali Pen, equal to the chain god, which is spread out on the household chabutra in the form of a circle, above one foot in diameter, worshipped along with the others that are adored on the four feasts. Pharsi Pen is not worshipped with these, though a little honor is paid him on Akhádi; when, going out into their compound, the men offer him there a few Mohwa fruits, throw a little rice, which they allow a chicken to eat; after which, the chicken is killed, cooked outside, and eaten, women not being allowed to be present. So when Pharsi Pen's great feast takes place every third, fourth, or fifth year, and people assemble from a distance, the ceremonies are conducted with great secrecy; no Hindu, or even Gond women being allowed to be present. On that day, if a Gond woman in black comes to the door of a Gond house, she is not admitted. No fire is given from the house.

The Sat-dewala can intermarry with the Saha-dewala, or five and four-god worshippers; but the six, five, and four-god worshippers might not intermarry, they being reckoned one. The Kúls (sects) among Sat-dewala are—Maskola (to which my two informants belonged), Madavi Bhalávi, Masaram, Dhurwal, Irpochi, Kursangal, Kouratti, Sarotal, Sariyam, Gajyam, Seryam,

---

* Dondera madá dolka nike látá.
(under) Bauhinia tree (when) the drum to beat has begun.
Nago endi látor.
O Nago (any dead man's name) to dance thou hast begun.

Kandatal, Buransha, Karpatirk, Kokodyal or Kokotta, Jugnakal, Yunati, Pandaram, with one or two others. These Kûls are the Adnaw of the Sat-dewala, as Sirkia, &c. are among the Mahrattas. Maskola must not marry a Maskola woman, they must look out beyond the seven to the six Dewala. The Kûls among the six Dewala, are Kumral (informant), Wikal, Watti, Marapal, Ghodam, Kodapal, Pendam, Malgam, Mandhari, Narpachi, Salanik, Sedam, Gadam, Namurtal, Puranik, Tedanganik, Warkadalk, Adalk, Neitamk, Kowalk, Markamk, Tekamk. The Kûls of the five or four-god worshippers are reckoned among those. The seven and four are the most numerous. Khusram, Tadam, Koriam, and Kotlam are six Dewallas; others, mentioned by Colonel Balmain, as at Raepore, are not known here, *e. g.* Seduram, Pandoti, Jagret, Sakkam, and south of Wurdah, Surpam—five, and Atram, Kulmutta, Yerma—six.

My informants, whether seven or six-god worshippers, call themselves Koitors, and say that although the Pardháns* follow the same religion, and are sub-divided, according to the number of their gods, yet the caste is different, and they neither eat nor intermarry with them. The Pardháns will eat from the hands of the Koitors, and are reckoned inferior. Mohani, one of the seven-god worshippers, is a Pardhán, and goes to the house of Tami, where she may eat; but if Tami goes to Mohani's house, she may not eat. The Pardháns, like Mohani's husband, who, however, is employed in secular service, discharge the functions of Bhats, *i. e.* sing songs and give information on genealogical matters. But these are few. They also think it no indignity to play on stringed instruments; they call themselves Raj-Pardhán, as Tami is a Ráj Gond. Beneath them there is a sub-division whose women tattoo Gonds and Hindus. Beneath them again is a sub-division who play on wind instruments of wood, while there is still a lower class who speak more Marathi than Gondi, and play on wind instruments of brass, and spin thread like the Mhars. All these, however, worship the same gods, and are sub-divided accordingly. The Bhumuks in the villages are either Gonds or Pardháns. They profess to keep the boundaries of the village free from wild beasts and cholera, and are entitled, on that single account, to a field and some mango and other trees from the Patel, and to an allowance of rice and other grains from each cultivator, Hindu or Gond. Gawaris profess the Gond religion, but speak Marathi. They act as servants in keeping the cows and buffaloes of others; but in general have none of their own, except in the jungly districts, where they loosen a heifer for sacrifice.

FESTIVALS—Akhadi, Jiwati, Pola, Diwali, and Shimoa.

On Akhadi, which this year, 1861, happened on 23rd July, the men go out to their work; but the women clean the house and vessels, bring water, bathe, grind, and breakfast about noon, when the men have returned from their work. These now bathe, and, without eating, prepare for celebrating Pharsi Pen's worship, which takes place in the compound of each about 3 p.m. There the head of the house prepares a spot with cowdung, and lays on it a small heap of rice (tandul), and above that again he besmears a little dry vermilion, sets before the heap a whole supari on five betel leaves. Then he kills a young cock, and sprinkles its blood on the heap, on which he subsequently pours libations of arrack. After this he throws into the fire, which is burning before the heap, a fruit of the Mohwa tree (*Bassia-latifolia*); and then proceeds to boil the fowl for his own entertainment, which he eats, after having drunk off a bottle of arrack. There is no image or representation of Pharsi Pen, except the rice; and at the time of offering the vermilion and young cock, he simply says, "I am a poor man, and give you this vermilion and fowl; accept it at my hand. Keep us safe; bless our fields; and if I survive, I shall worship thee next year." Then about four o'clock he enters the house, and all the family join in drinking daru. The male members then go out and drink more at the liquor-shop, and don't return till about eight. At 10 the household feast commences, which consists of small cakes of *udid*, and of wheat fried in Mohwa oil, (which is forbidden to be eaten new from the tree till that date), rice, pulse, fowl, and vegetable. Before the company commences to eat there is a copious allowance of arrack drank. Then when the women have served up the eatables to the males, they themselves sit down at a short distance to partake, though sometimes they wait till the others have finished. About 11 at night all go to sleep.

Jiwati, which is in the month of Shravan.—In the morning, having attended to household duties, as before, the mother about 12 gives the children their breakfast. About 3 p.m. she begins the cooking for the feast. About 8 p.m. the ceremonies commence, till which time both the parents have been fasting. The wife brings forward the articles, and the husband places them in order. On each side of the chabutra in the house are placed small cakes (as above)—two of udid, two of wheat flour covered with *gul* (sugar). On the chabutra are placed 3, 4, 5, 6 small heaps of rice, according to the number of gods professedly worshipped by the family, wanting one for Pharsi Pen. On the rice heaps is poured dry vermilion. After which on the chabutra in front of the heaps is laid a cock or a young pig, which may be bought at 4 annas. Then joining hands, and pronouncing the names of his gods, with the exception of Pharsi Pen, *e. g.*, Khodial, Sánálk, Munja, Durga, Chuda Pen, and Sakali Pen, he asks them to receive the offerings to keep the hands and feet of the family safe, to bless

---

*Hindu name equal to Pradhán (Prime Minister), but among themselves, Pathádi.

them in their labours, and to grant children, if in that respect there be a deficiency. Then arrack is poured on the heaps, the head of the victim lying before these. If on the liquor going into the ear of the pig it shakes its head, or if the fowl on becoming wet shakes its body, it is held that the offering is accepted. Till this sign is given they wait. Then the victim is killed, while resin (ral) is burning on the fire. Plates of leaves covered with dál, bhát, and cakes, are placed before the heaps, and arrack poured on the provisions. Three or four bottles of daru are now consumed in the family; and dinner is at 9, like that on Akhádi.

Polá.—Having cleaned the house and bathed, &c., from 8 or 9 they begin to cook for the bullocks and themselves. At 2 the cooking is over. Then the bullocks are adorned with tinfoil and hemp, and sprinkled all over the body with round spots of red ochre, and led outside of the village to be marshalled with the rest, where the owners boast with one another about the superiority of their own bullocks. Then at an appointed signal from the Patêl of the village all start off as fast as they can towards their respective homes. Here the pair of bullocks have their feet reverently washed; then on a brass plate an offering of rice, kuku, (woman's powder for marking the forehead, which is made chiefly of saffron with something to turn it red,) and a lamp is presented,—rice and kuku are stuck on their foreheads and on that of their driver. Then in a new basket part of the dinner which had been cooked is given to the bullocks to eat, consisting of rice, pulse, bread, small cakes fried in oil, vegetables of cucurbitaceæ, &c. Then the bullocks are led round to various houses, the owners of which are expected to give a pice to the driver. At 10 supper commences. These are very much the ceremonies that prevail among the Hindus. No worship is paid on the Polá to Gond deities.

Diwali.—On this day the same rites as on Jiwati, and so on Shimga (which falls between February and March). If on any feast the worship of their gods is neglected, and disease enters the family, the doctor tells them that the gods are angry, and that they must be careful by vows to propitiate them and to perform these vows on the next feast.

Pharsi Pen's great worship takes place every 3rd, 4th, or 5th year in Mágh, or also at the end of Waishák. Early in the morning the women quite overturn the house, spread new clay on the floor, and whitewash the walls, and buy new earthen vessels for water and cooking, a new *sup* for winnowing, new baskets, brooms, wooden spoons. The parents dress in new white cloths, and a new white *dhotra* is carried by the father as a gift to the Pardhán. The father and his boys start about 7 a.m. for the scene of the day's ceremonial. There about twenty or forty, including relatives from a distance, assemble, and take down from among the branches of a Saj (*Terminalia tomentosa*) or Mohwa (*Bassia latifolia*) tree a small javelin, cased in a bamboo and covered with grass. After they have spent sometime in preparing the spot and collecting wood, they bring out the god, and with two bells (ghángará) on the fore and third finger of each hand the Pujári clasps the iron dart, which they then carry to a tank or river and bathe, and set upon a chabutra under the tree with the four bullock's bells (ghángará dewa) in front. They apply vermilion to him; and when the cow is offered they slaughter it by striking it on the head with the back of a hatchet. There they remain all night feasting and drinking, and return to their village about 3 p.m. next day. When they approach the village the women meet them, and stretch a bamboo across their path, singing that they are the daughters or the wives of their priests, and that they must not pass after they have been away engaged in worship until they have given a present in money. Perhaps 10 annas will be collected. Arrived at the house, they throw more pice into a chatty, and about Rs. 1 is spent on the women that wash the men's feet; then all drink and all dine together. Besides the seven there are* village deities, whom all, whether 4, 5, 6, 7, worship together; *e.g.* Koda Pen, horse god,—a stone which is worshipped on the outskirts of the village at the commencement of the rains in the Mirg Nakshatra. The women do not go out to its worship, only men. A Bhumuk acts for the village on the occasion, and he may be either a Gond or Pardhán; whereas Pharsi Pen's worship being that of a family, it would seem that a Pardhán generally officiates. First of all, the Bhumuk besmears the stone with red lead, presents a horse of pottery, then a heifer, on the head of which he pours *daru*, and says to the deity,—"Thou art the guardian of the village; we have come and offered to thee according to our ability. If in anything we have failed to please thee, forgive us. Protect our oxen and cows; keep us in safety; let there be no fear in the jungles." After this, with a blow from the back of an axe on the animal's forehead, they prostrate the victim; the flesh is then boiled, and part of it is laid along with suji, made of jhondale flour, on a leafy plate before Koda Pen, and the company, assembled, dine on the remainder of the beef, suji, and daru. The Bhumuk for his trouble receives from each man 2 or 4 pailies of jhondale.

Bhiwasen's worship takes place two or three days before Akhádi.

Birth.—After a child, whether male or female, is born, the family bring into the house a chatty of daru (pitcher full of spirits), and then neighbouring women, being assembled, divide it among them. On the 5th or 6th day, when the dried part of the umbilical cord

*A god named Kolasur is worshipped with offering of earthen horses on the top of a hill near great Ambora.

falls off the child, they shave its head, and clean the floor and walls of the house. Then the child, who had been washed daily from the day of birth, with the mother, are bathed for the last time, and the women of the neighbourhood are called in, to whom is distributed a brass plate full of turmeric flour to apply to their bodies. Then these women baths and receive a portion of a dish composed of fried sesamum seeds, gul, and cocoanut. Arrack is brought in a pot and poured over the now filled pit dug in the floor for the water used in bathing the baby and mother; the nurse worships Chhati, who is supposed by Hindus on that day to write on the skull of each child its future destiny. The worship consists in offering pan-supari, and one pice, and kuku, and a little lamp black, which is applied with the finger to the ground, and a little tooth powder. After this, they lay down on the same spot a portion of the sesamum, gul (sugar) and cocoanut mixed together; then daru is sprinkled; then an unboiled fish named tepari (small), like minim, which is sometimes living, sometimes dead, kichari, and dal bhat. After this, all the women dine and drink together: from that day the family are free from ceremonial defilement. On 7th day is Bársá, so called by Hindus because it is observed on 12th day among them. On this day the family invite friends and relatives from a distance, who come with presents of cloth for the mother and child, and bangles for the latter. After all the women, both of the village and other villages, are assembled in the house, and the men in the compound, a chatty full of arrack is brought to the latter, the women sing—

Hóroré boro deurál bainór
Tedaro shendukókó jhelá nadi dohá
Phulkátá chhakáwálhnyá
Targnáké chidung chadung
Reináke ghátung te jhelá peiyaka deurmoré.

Of this lady, who (is) the brother-in-law (husband's younger brother)?
O brother-in-law dada, rise O! with dupata bind (your) waist.
The arrack dividing go round.
To ascend I am pregnant.
To descend over the hills (without) cloth a child will be born, O my brother-in-law.

And after having partaken liberally of the liquor, all dine. On 9th day the name is given. They first distribute boiled wheat and gram; and women in a cloth rock the child to sleep, at which time the name is given by all the women present.

Marriage.—The betrothal takes place generally about two years before the marriage. The father of the young man goes to the house of the young woman and asks her father if he is willing to give. Before giving his consent omens must be consulted. Into a brass plate they pour water, and put one grain of rice for the lad, and another for the lass. If they adhere, then the betrothal proceeds. The father of the former promises to give the father of the latter Rs. 16 (apparently a constant amount Rs. 14, to which other 2 are added on the plate, see below) and two lugade. The rupees are given about one month before the marriage; and the young man, having his body anointed with oily turmeric, with a retinue goes to his future father-in-law's village, outside of which he is met by the father-in-law, with a number of friends also, and he is lodged in the house of a neighbour (wánosa of Mahrattas). There all remain during the night, receiving from the father-in-law something to eat. Next day the bridegroom's father, &c., go to the bride's house, where they are seated outside of the threshhold, the father-in-law being in the inside. The bridegroom's father presents to the bride's father on a brass plate kuku, rice, a lamp, and Rs. 2, and the latter presents to the former in a brass plate kuku, rice, a lamp, 2 pice, and red powder, which is thrown by each father on the other and the rest of the company. Then they give each other daru to drink in a brass cup. Then the bridegroom's father brings two chatties of daru, and the bride's father one, when all join in drinking. The bride's relatives take the bridegroom's father, &c. to a river or tank, cover them with turmeric, and bathe them, when they return to the house. The bride's father provides a pig (with the 2 rupees) for the entertainment of the company. He also brings one chatty of daru, and the other father two chatties. Meanwhile, the bride has left her own house and hid herself among the rafters of some neighbouring tenement; and the women, taking a kamli (blanket), go in search of her, singing—

Teda kamlo awar aia látá
Sai awar ai teri kamlo tedon.

Rise lady, delay is happening.
Go: delay is, still, O ladies, I rise not.

Then they climb up towards her; she leaps down; they seize her, and covering her up with the kamli, she all the time struggling in vain, they bring her to the house, where she grasps her parents and all her relatives, and hangs on their necks weeping. Then the entertainment proceeds. This is the great Sagai in Marathi (in Gondi, páring) or betrothal. Next morning the bridegroom and his relatives leave for their homes. At parting, the bride's female relatives, having made a garland of the pig's feet, a small cake of udid, onion, and red pepper, the bride's father throws it over the neck of the other father, and on his moustache and face, the seed of some plant (called, in Marathi, ashta) like tulsi, whose seeds are at first black, but by steeping in water become white. The bridegroom's relatives contribute among themselves pice, cowries, red thread, pieces of cocoanut; and give the bride—and so depart. On that same day the bridegroom's relatives, after reaching their home, commence to build the marriage bower. (From the day that the Rs. 14 were given, the bride had begun to go weeping, along with other two, also weeping, to neighbouring villages, and they are entertained by relatives for a day here and there, and receive a cow, goat, pice cloth, &c., according to the ability of the givers). That evening in the house a lota is filled with water and a pice thrown into it, and a cover is placed on the top of it and set before the bridegroom, who is seated, arrayed in a new cloth; and in this position he is obliged to remain till the bride and her party arrive—about 2 o'clock next morning. At their arrival they salute the bridegroom's relatives with opprobrious songs and beat wooden cymbals; friends are received in the same manner by the latter. Quarters are appointed to them in a neighbouring house. Then about 5 o'clock they return to the house; but before entering, the bridegroom goes out and meets the bride in the plain. The friends of both hold up between them two dupattas as veils, with a slight interval between them. A woman who had taken up the lota attends the bridegroom with it on her head, and so a woman, similarly furnished, attends the bride. And now the bridegroom creeps under the veil into the intermediate space, and so does the bride. Then, when both are met, the veil is withdrawn, and they are left facing each other; when the bridegroom puts his foot on that of the bride to prevent any resistance, and an iron ring on the little finger of the bride's right hand, and fixes his left little finger in her right little finger. Then an old man, not necessarily a relative, knocks their foreheads together; and while they are remaining in this position he kills a chicken, and places its body under the compressed foot of the bride, adding in a whisper an exhortation to them to be faithful to each other. Lifting two balls, one of rice and another of cowdung, he waves them round their heads and throws them away. Again, taking a fowl he wrings its neck and waves its body round them and throws it away, and so with a cup of daru. Then from one side and the other women throw on the two jhondale colored with saffron. If the bridegroom is six or seven Dewala, then, according to the number of his gods, cakes of wheat, and udid fried in oil (poli and wada), along with rice, are brought in a new basket and given by him, together with the fowl and any daru that remains, to the old man, who had remained about two days fasting, *i.e.* from the time of erecting the bower. Then the bridegroom leads the bride to the bower. Here in the centre a pole has been erected, round which, holding still her finger, they walk five times, the bridegroom's female attendant being before him all the time with the lota on her head and pouring water on the ground by a spout out of an earthen pot like a teapot; the bride's female attendant following her with the lota on her head, but pouring no water. The bridegroom is not only linked to the bride behind him, but to the attendant before him. Then under the shade of the bower a chabutra is constructed, on which the two young people sit in a line, the bridegroom with his lota at his side, and the bride with hers, and have the skirts of their respective garments knotted together by the bridegroom's elder brother's wife or by his sister. After this the bride anoints her spouse with saffron and bathes him. Then both having filled their mouths with water squirt it on each other, and holding each other by the little finger they go to his house, at the door of which they are met by his sister, who asks something before she will permit them to enter. The bridegroom gives a bracelet, and promises a cow, whereupon they are permitted to enter. Here they sit on a kamli side by side, with the bridegroom's thigh resting on that of the bride. Then the bridegoom gives a handful of rice into the hand of the bride, who puts it into a small earthen vessel, and her eyes being covered by the bridegroom's sister she spills it on the floor, and *vice versa* she gives him, the bride's sister blindfolding the bridegroom, and he spilling the rice. Then before each of the two, 2 leafy plates of rice, poli, and wada are set, which they snatch from each other; these remaining with the stronger party; but ultimately all are divided among the company. Instead of their dal bhat, some rice cakes are placed before them, when the bridegroom endeavours to feed the bride by force. After which, about 8 a.m., the wife leaves him and goes with some girls to the separate house appointed for her reception. There two opposite rows of women strike up abusive songs, responding to each other, and drinking an abundance of daru, which continues till 2 p.m. Then a pig is prepared for the coming entertainment, which takes place at 10 p.m., and consists of the pork, rice, poli-wadi, and daru. At the end the bride returns to the separate house as before, but next morning she is brought to her husband's house and left with him, when her relatives take their departure; the bride's father being now the wearer of the pig's foot garland; the bride crying, and all throwing red powder on each other. In nine days after the bride's father pays them a visit, and takes away the bride to the home of her youth, and returns her to her husband on Jiwati. There is no specified month for marriages among the Gonds, but she must return on Jiwati. In some places a marriage necklace (in Marathi,—garsoli; in Hindi, pot;) is bound; but this is learned from Hindus.

Death.—If the deceased had been rich, they purchase a new cloth; if poor, an old one is used for the purpose. They first bring the body out of the house, bathe it, and anoint it with turmeric, and then with ghee, and cover the loins with a langoti. Then they lay it on a bamboo bier, and cover it with the cloth, and tie it with cords. Then the men carry it to the place of interment, on a river's bank or in the jungle, and bury it, after having stripped it of every piece of cloth and laid a leaf of Palas or Rui (*Calotropis gigantea*). The face is kept upwards, head to south, the feet to north. Then they go to the river, bathe, and repair to a liquor shop and drink. The women have meanwhile cleaned the house; the neighbouring women bring bread, rice, &c. to it; and all the men who had gone to the funeral sit down to eat. On the spot where the deceased expired a basket is placed with rice, two roots of huldi, and one chicken, and a little flour is scattered on the ground, and all is covered up with a large basket all night. Next morning they open it up, and place the contents in an earthen vessel, along with butter, turmeric, and red lead, and one carries the whole over his shoulder with a hatchet. All the men of the village form the procession, and at the river anoint themselves with the turmeric and butter, and under a tree make a *thàpnà*, and on it offer a little heap of rice and red lead, asking the dead man, now deemed a god, to accept them. They then sacrifice a chicken. There the men remain, cook and eat. Men bring daru; and the women who had been cooking at home carry some of the victuals toward the same spot, and on the way, on a branch of Calotropis placed for the purpose, they throw some dal bhat and daru and water, and ask the dead man to receive them; after which they return home. A messenger from the thàpnà now comes and carries off the provisions and daru, and the men feast at the tree; while the women do the same at the house. When the men return, they dine again. Then the co-religionists of the deceased bring daru, and dipping in it a branch of Nim tree, sprinkle the heads of the members of the family, and serve the whole male and female present with as many cups of daru as the deceased worshipped gods.

This Note is ascertained to have been taken by Mr. Hislop at Nagpore.

GONDS: 27TH SEPTEMBER, 1862.

Mánge Pardhán Sedam (4-god-worshipper) and Dubali Dholi, Maskola (7-god), from the Motibag. The Gawali dynasty ruled over this country. At Deogad and Nandbesur, near Girad, Chimnaji and Goudaji, two brothers, were the representatives when Bade (great) Row, originally of the Kangali tribe, and afterwards, for the reason afterwards given, made the head of a new tribe, was his Bhumuk. His great god Pharsi Pen was set up at Jamb, 3½ koss above Deogad, on the Dewa River. In Mirgeshwar (*i. e.* beginning of the monsoon) this river was flooded and brought down many Kheir trees; all the inhabitants of Deogad went out to secure the spoils, and among others went the Bhumuk. Others took the small trunks, but not so he. A large one came, and immediately he leaped upon it, but it eluded his grasp and floated up the river, he swimming after it. It stopped not till it came to Jamb, and there he brought it out to the bank, when it appeared very beautiful. At the sight the captor was overjoyed, saying, in his mind, that I will make out of it a splendid baton. At last, with a promise of Rs. 5 to a carpenter, he had made out of it a wooden sword (khanda). Going to a Jingar he made a similar promise for a scabbard, but fulfilled neither, as he was but a poor man. Then off he went with the weapon under his arm to the Kachari of the Gawali king, and, after making salaam, stated that he came for service. On being asked how much salary he wanted, he replied 16 Kudus of rupees a month (1 Kudu=10 seers, or 8 pailies). "What will you do for such a large salary? stay at home, and come when occasion requires." The Raja consented, and the rupees were duly given for six months, during which Bade Row built for himself a house. But one of the Rajah's servants, who professed great friendship, discovered, on one occasion, when the sword was inadvertently laid on the ground out of its accustomed armpit, that it was of wood, and communicated his discovery to His Highness. The Raja said we will soon see; in 10 days is the Dusara. Let a five year old male buffaloe be provided for the occasion, and let the Gond be appointed to cut off its head with his khanda. The poor man was sorely perplexed. How could he with his wooden sword accomplish such a feat. He could neither eat nor drink. The god Pharsi Pen, and Manko Rayetál his wife, appeared to him in a dream, told him to be of good cheer, to take his weapon at the same time with the others to the river, but to go higher up the stream to wash it, then to carry it home and worship it. The preliminaries over, he smeared a spot in his house with cowdung—set up on the chabutra the khanda. While engaged in the worship a shout from two men at the door of the angan reached him, calling him to come, as the buffalo was ready. He told them to tell the Raja he was in the middle of the ceremonies, and would come when they were finished. The Raja sent three more. The same reply. Then four, who were ordered to bring him by force. Now he called on his gods not to allow him to be dishonored: "O Adhalpen, Budhal Pen! O Pharsi Pen, Manko Rayetal! O 16 Satis! (who offered themselves on the funeral pile, when Pharsi Pen killed his three brothers, Subhadra, Kubhadra, and Lingobhan Pariyor,—the 16 being the mother of all, three wives of three, and the 12 daughters of Subhadra) be favorable to me." The answer was, "Why do you fear." "But what sign do you give of your favor?" "Draw your sword and you will see." He drew the sword and it flashed like lightning, at which he was blinded and prostrated on the ground. The gods, moreover, told him to inform the Raja that when he should lift his sword to kill the buffalo, the King should set 750 men with their matchlocks ready turned on him and discharge their bullets, otherwise Pharsi Pen would render all the women of the city barren.

APPENDIX II.

Note made by Mr. Hislop from information obtained from Captain Chapman.

GONDS OF THE CHINDWARA DISTRICT: 1ST NOVEMBER 1861.

Jawahir, a worshipper of five gods, stated to Captain Chapman that his divinities are,—Pharsi Pen, or Dula dewa; 2, Nurma; 3, Ghangrah (according to Captain Chapman), or Gangara; 4, Rayetal; and 5, Badialtal. Dula dewa is the god of the battleaxe, and superior to all the rest. He is worshipped once a year, about a month before the Holi. His worship continues fifteen days, or a month, according to the leisure or devotion of the worshipper, and is as follows. The head of the family leaves his house with an offering of flowers, fruit, or animals—*i. e.* sheep or fowls—to lay at the foot of the Saj tree, which is supposed to be inhabited by the god. If on their way they find the road miry, they return home without making the offering; if otherwise, they proceed. On arriving at the tree, the fruit is cut in half, or the animal slaughtered, and a part offered with daru (spirits) to the god. The whole is then cooked, during which the officiating priest addresses the audience; and then he and the other Pardháns eat what they want of the part that was offered with the daru; and if any remain, it is buried in the earth. The people, in like manner, eat and drink of what was not offered. The officiating priest never gets drunk on these occasions; but the non-officiating and the people are under less restraint. Nurma appears to be one of the Penates; his form is ó, made of a piece of Hardua or Mundi wood. Four of such pieces of wood (to represent the minor gods) are fastened to a flat piece of iron, and suspended in a chatty (earthen pot) from the roof of the house. The worship of Nurma is celebrated four times in a year, and is as follows. The four pieces of wood are taken out of the chatty (earthen pot) and carried to any convenient tree: there the ground is plastered with cowdung, in the form of a square, of about four feet. The four pieces of wood are then laid upon the ground and covered with a new cloth, and two sucking pigs are brought, which are laid, with their feet tied, in front of the god; and the priest or Pardhán is sent for. On his arrival he opens the Shastras, and having read a portion, some ghee, or butter, and coarse sugar are burnt together in front of the idol. Then all the worshippers stand up, both male and female, and name the various gifts which they intend to present to the Pardhán,—cows, sheep, rupees, cloth, &c. They then take up the pigs and idols, and return to the house, outside of which they remain till one, who had been purposely left behind to plaster the floor and walls of the house with cowdung, comes out with a brass vessel containing water and 1¼ rupees, and sprinkles the pigs, idols, and worshippers. As the people are sprinkled they pass into the house: last of all comes the Pardhán, who receives the remaining water; and in order that none may be wasted, turns the vessel upside down, and the 1¼ rupees fall into the priests hands, and soon find their way into his pocket. In the centre of the house is a raised altar (chabutra), upon which five eggs are now broken, one cock, and the two sucking pigs slain, one cocoanut broken, one bottle of daru (spirits) poured, and five loaves cooked in oil, and a small quantity of rice placed. The four idols are now put in the middle, and covered with the blood of the victims. The priest breaks the besmeared bread, and hands it soaked in blood and liquor to each of the worshippers. He then repeats certain words, and removes the idols from the altar to the chatty (earthen pot) again, when they are suspended as before. All the company now take off the clothes they have worshipped in, and putting on other clothes, cook the offerings,—cocoanut, sucking pigs, fowls,—and men women and children all partake of the viands with a plentiful supply of liquor. The worship of the remaining three idols is celebrated at the same time, and with the same rites, as Dula dewa.

1, Dula dewa is represented by a battleaxe fastened to a tree; 2, Nurma, by a round piece of wood like an orange; 3, Gangara, by an iron chain of four links; 4, Rayetál, by an iron tiger about 3 inches in length, which is sometimes kept in the house, and sometimes in certain appointed places in the jungle; 5, Budial-tal, also by an iron tiger, he being looked on as the brother of the last.

Digas are the bards among the Gonds. They play on a low-toned, wired instrument, called kinkree, with a horse-hair bow, and their music is accompanied by a recitation in honour of their gods; they wander about from house to house,—remaining two or three days in one place, and living on the bounty of their audience. The Pardháns occasionally imagine themselves possessed of a demon. Captain Chapman's watter-carrier, a Pardhán, a month ago, went to his house and took a handful of wheat, which he sowed in the middle of the house; in the centre of the wheat he put a new chatty of water, and over the chatty a lamp—the wick of which was so long that it burnt for nine days and nights. These nine days and nights the waterman appeared possessed—he jumped, he danced and sang; but the demon allowed him to sleep near the wheat. At the expiration of the ninth day, the demon suggested that a lime should be fixed on the end of a sword, which the man had in his hand. The women put earthen pots of water and wheat upon their heads, and, dancing and singing, all went to the river and threw in the offering of the first-fruits. Whether this was an unusual possession, or whether it always accompanies the offering of the firstfruits, I cannot exactly find out.

APPENDIX III.

Note made by Mr. Hislop, from information obtained through Serajooddeen, a Native Christian, Inspector of Police.

GONDS OF THE SEONEE DISTRICT · 26TH NOVEMBER 1861.

His informant was a seven-god worshipper—Bada dewa, Matiya, Sale, Palo. Sakal dewa, Gadawa, and Kham; Khatar Pen, and Khawariyal (Kodiyal). Three others were mentioned, as Dhanbai, Dhan-takoor, and Dhan Gopal. Khatar Pen and Khawariyal are represented by balls of wood, and Dhanbai and the other two by balls of iron. When Gonds die they are committed to Gadawa, who is the god of the dead, and takes care of them. Kham dewa is worshipped under a Saj tree. Chhota dewa, is represented by a little stool, with short legs, about 10 by 8 inches, of one piece of wood. There is offered to him a chicken, pig, shendur (red powder) and daru (spirits) but no sheep or goat; bukra (sheep) is offered only to the great god. Matiya dewa remains with the great god, and is like his Kotwal. They offer him a young pig. Sale is nearly equal with the great god, and sits with him on the same gaddi (cushion or throne). He is offered a she-goat. Gangara and Palo are offered a cow.

The Gond informant said: Our gods eat cow's flesh, and why should we not? Gadawa dwells in our houses. After performing the funeral ceremonies of the dead, in his name we commit them to his protection. He is represented by a chatty (earthen pot) with a little vermilion in it, and a lid, like a lamp, covering its mouth; it is hung up to the inside of the roof, and taken down by a man after bathing, when it is to be worshipped. Kham dewa is worshipped under a Saj tree, and similar offerings are made to Chhota dewa. Pharki Pen is not a dewa; he is pât or saint. Vows are made to him; and those who have them fulfilled, worship him: but all do not. Along with Chhota dewa there are two gods of wood, called Khawariyal and Khatar Pen, and three of iron, *i. e.* Dhanbai, Dhan-takoor, and Dan-gopal. Besides these, is a chain of iron, which is called Sakal dewa. On the day of Amawashya, I put it on after worshipping; then take it through the bazaar, which is held on Monday, with the sound of drums; and on the eleventh day, after worshipping it again, I will place it inside of Gadawa, which is suspended from the roof. Chuda Pen is the same as Sakal Pen; the symbol in some cases being a chain, in others an iron bangle. Hole Ray (Ray=King) is represented by $\overset{|}{O}$ of wood; he is worshipped only by those who have cows. Bag dewa is a person killed by a tiger, and he is worshipped under that name by his family in the jungly districts around. Sana is a dead woman, and Doma is a dead man. They are also worshipped. We worship Marimátá as well. We dont worship Munjal; we commit him, like a dead body, to Gadawa. Durga remains near Khodi dewa.

We worship the great god twice a year—when the new rice comes in, and when oil is extracted from the Moha. Till worship is performed on these two occasions, we cannot eat the rice or use the oil. On these two occasions it is usual to fall at the feet of the Pardhán. Sale-Ghangara is the sign of the great god. The great god is represented by an iron spear, and those Gonds who do not possess this sign, worship him under a Saj tree. We must especially worship the great god, for if we do not, we shall suffer great calamities. Bhumka (Bhumuk) is the person who draws a line of protection round the village with charms, shuts the mouths of tigers. He is intelligent, acts as a physician, and casts out devils. There are twelve and a half castes—Ráj Gond, Pardhán, Khotowriya, Janwaiwala, Thakur, Kurri Gond, Gondhera, Thathiya, Dubarya, Panka, Nagarchi, Ojhia, Bharya, Payam; which last is the half-caste. These do not intermarry, except the Ráj Gonds and Pardháns. In marriage we do not worship any but the great god, to whom we offer a fowl or goat. The Bhumuk officiates. Any clothes, &c., that had been worn by the dead, we do not keep in our house, but give to the Pardháns. We do not reverence Brahmins. We acknowledge the difference between sin and righteousness, and we believe that we must give an account of our sins after death.

APPENDIX IV.

Account of the Gonds of Hutta, in the Bhundara District, given to Mr. Hislop by Gajraj Sing, Zemindar.

GONDS OF THE BHUNDARA DISTRICT: DECEMBER, 1861.

In the village of Hiri, part of Gajrag's Zemindaree, there are three or four Gond houses. One Gond, named Dasaru, is of the Tekam tribe, and a worshipper of four gods; *i. e.* Budha, who is also called Gagara dewa; 2, Dula dewa; 3. Mahadewa; 4, Parbati. He says he does not know any Gonds who worship one, two, three, or eight gods, but he is acquainted with some who worship four, five, six, seven, and nine. Another Gond of Hiri, named Holee, is of the Seiyam tribe, and worships seven gods: 1, Budha, or Gagara; 2, Dula dewa; 3, Sakaliya dewa, 4, Nirrá; 5, Parbatti; 6, Mahadewa; and 7, Kalha, in whose name Hindu parents, in performance of a vow made when childless, used to precipitate their eldest son, when he was about ten years of age, from the top of the Mahadewa hills. He worships six of his gods every year, either on the Dewali in the month of Kartik, when rice is new, or if not then, on Tij or Akatij (*i. e.* the 3rd) in the month Weishák, when the crop of Moha flowers is ripe. From this latter date, they begin to extract oil from these flowers. These are used as articles of diet by Lodhees, Ahirs (*i. e.* Gowars), and Gonds, &c.; but they are not so considered by Rajpoots, who simply burn the oil in their lamps. To Mahadewa, Holee offers a he-goat—to Parbati, a she one; to Dula dewa, as to Mahadewa; to Nirra, a pig. Budha, or the great god, is worshipped once in about three years. The ceremonies, including the offering of a cow, are performed at night, while feasting goes on during the day. If, in the interval between these triennial feasts, any unmarried man dies, he is reckoned among the gods, and on that occasion Budha is worshipped. A third Gond in Hiri is Kesari Pujari, a worshipper of four gods, which were enumerated as above, and of the Kumara tribe. There are two kinds of Kumara: one, that offers goats as well as cows; the other, to whom goats are an abomination; and if one should stray into their yards or compounds they throw away every chatty (earthen water pot). They offer only fowls, pigs, and cows.

Marriage—is celebrated in any month. In a flat dish, full of water, they put two grains of rice, and, naming a day for the marriage, see whether it is suitable by their sinking or going together. Then the bride goes about crying among her relatives, attended by six to twenty women singing songs: this lasts from eight to fifteen days, according as relatives are numerous and distant. Relatives give a little to the bride; after this she is annointed with haldi, and goes to the village of the bridegroom with parents, &c. Outside of the village they stop, and one sets up a spear in the village dunghill. They are now joined by the bridegroom and his party; and the young couple, standing on the dunghill, the lad takes an iron ring off his own right little finger and puts it on the lass', and strikes her on the back with his fist three times. All then proceed to bridegroom's father's house, where the women of both sides, standing in opposite rows, address each other in abusive songs. At night they feast; in the morning, the bride's relatives return home, leaving her.

The dead are buried at a distance from the village, but thàpànas (shrines) are erected, many together; four stones forming the sides of the thàpànas.

APPENDIX V.

Note made by Mr. Hislop in October 1862, *from information obtained through Serajooddeen Native Christian.*

GONDS OF THE CHANDA DISTRICT.

Gonds bury their dead with their faces up. The head may be placed towards any quarter of the heavens, but the west. Sons equally inherit; and if there be unmarried daughters they receive a share. If without offspring the nephews succeed. They swear by Buda Dewa; by sons, &c. He repeated a part of a song taken at Moharle, about Daka Dari Kesal, Sonlat Kesal, and Katikuti Kesal. Mention is made of a Shukurwar tank.

A Bhagat is one into whose body the Buda Dewa comes; in this state of inspiration he climbs the trees and brings down Buda Dewa, who near Chanda is called Pharsapen.

At Nagbhid marriage among the Raj Gonds is celebrated, after going round in the lane 4 times, by the bridegroom taking an iron ring from a finger of his right hand and putting it on the bride's. With the great toe of his left foot, he presses her foot. At Nawargaum, 4 coss south south-west of Chimur, it was related by a Raj Gond Bhumak, that the day before marriage the relatives worship the village gods as Marai, Bhangarai or Bhangara Bai (female) &c: there is a Bhangaram (male) also. The wife comes from one side and the husband from another and they both stand together in the akada (place of assembly). The bridegroom shuts his hand firmly on an iron ring. The bride shuts her hand equally firmly. Then he opens hers by force and puts the iron ring on the little finger of her right hand, after which they go to his house and drink together.

When a person at Newergaum is killed by a tiger, he gives the relatives no rest, unless they appease him with offerings: they go to a creeper named Phasi—present to it, by a Weidh, or pujari, (priest) dheep, vermilion, and kill a chicken, male or female, according to the sex of the person that had been killed, and bury it there, after which they go round the tree 5 times: The pujari then dismisses them, telling them not to look back (does he take out the chicken ?). After all are gone, he repeats a mantra, (incantation) and with one blow of his hand breaks the creeper, and leaves, himself not looking back. For the protection of cattle Kolasur is worshipped by Marathas with vermilion only; but by Gonds who reckon him their deity, with a young cock and daru (spirits). At Nagbhid, according to Katu, a Raj Gond of 7 gods, there is a chain with 7 bells (gagari) of bell metal, according to the number of gods. This is kept in an earthen vessel and hung up by a rope round the neck or mouth to the bough of a tree. It is taken down once in one or two years, by the Bhagat, when worship is to be performed, and a goat or fowl offered. A kutha, or song, the beginning of which was taken down by Serajoodeen at Moharle, 18 miles north of Chanda, is about Chohan Raja, whose father was Jádo Malhári. Jádo Malhári's wife was Naga Moti. Chohan Raja's wife was Maia Moti. Their daughter was Padmawanti. The Mohamedan Emperor of Delhi first sent a Bhat, who took the young lady's portrait, and on showing it to the Emperor, the latter was so smitten that he sent an army of Pathans like a cloud, to take her by force.

APPENDIX VI.

Note taken by Mr. Hislop in July 1856, from information obtained through Appaya Native Christian.

THE KURKUS.

Appaya made his enquiries near Asirgad and Baitul on the noth-west of Nagpore. The Kurkus acknowledge that there is one invisible Supreme Being whom they call Bhagawánjee:—perhaps having borrowed this opinion from the Hindus. But after reaping their crops of rice they sacrifice a goat, fowl &c., to Sultan Sakada who is supposed to have been some King among them in former times. Those at Asirgad say that the Zemindars or Thakurs at the Mahadewa hills worship Shiwa for them, as well as themselves. When a man dies, his family, if in the rains, bury him, if at other seasons they burn his body and afterwards offer a goat, when they set up a rude wooden image, of the deceased near the village at a place appointed for the reception of all such representations. The image is about 2 feet above the ground of this shape :

The deceased seems to be worshipped only the first year for protection.

For marriage 2½ days are required. On the first day the relatives of the bridegroom go to the bride's house and bring her to her intended husband's house. On the 2nd day they tie together the garments of the two and cause them to join hands and to run seven times round a mohwa tree after which they are conducted to the bower (mandap) prepared at the husbands house. Then they are reminded of their having been knotted together and that henceforth they must not be separated, after which all feast and drink, and one having lifted the husband and another the wife on their backs they dance.

Their employment is to cut down the jungle; with a bamboo stick to sow Kutki (pulse) on the hills; and with a plough to sow rice on the planes; and make tatties of bamboos.

All Kurkus are of one caste. They eat from the hands of Hindus, but not from Gonds or Mahars. They pound the kernels of mangoes and rub down the flowers of the mohwa, and make a gruel of each of them. This is an important part of their food. Daru, or arrack of the mohwa as usual among jungle tribes is very much drunk. They dress like Hindus and wear fewer ornaments than Gonds. The Gonds are generally the Patels of their villages and seem to be wealtheir then they.

Names of Kurku males. Bonga, Bendu, Sukali, Rajaji, Tuta, Badagi, Ramsingh, Chhotu, Naru.

Female. Irma, Batro, Rajani, Budiya, Guji, Pandiya, Manjibakan and Bodan.

According to Buldewa the aborigines who live around Gawalgad, know Marathi better than Hindi. They have a Patel whose dress and armour are different from the rest, he wearing a wooden sword, one shoe, and a coat of rags of various colours. They will eat dead animals, and yet the Hindustanee Brahmans and Rajpoots who trade among them drink from their hands

APPENDIX VII.

Note made by Mr. Hislop in April 1857, from information obtained through Appaya Native Christian.

THE MADES AND THE MARIAS.

Appaya met none of this tribe in Weiragad but in a village named Wadgaon to the east, where they live apart from Hindus. In the village just named there may be ten houses of the jungle people and ten or twelve of Hindus. But they are apt to be migratory as they find their crops not thriving or wheu death invades their habitations. They are supposed to extend from Weiragad to Kakair and Bustar.

They have broad faces and flattish noses and of the same stature as a middle sized Hindu. Appiah considers the Gonds he met in the north west of Chindwara taller than Hindus. The men wear no turband and in general only a dhotee, (round their loins) but when they go abroad they throw on any wastra (cloth) about their shoulders. They wear a brass or iron bangle and brass collar round their necks—they carry hatchets in their hands. The women wear a great many strings of beads; from 30 to 40; and at Chamursi, they also adorn themselves with a string of pendent bells. Bangles, (4 or 5) on each hand, of zinc, a chain of the same metal is suspended from the hair and is attached at the ear to large boss that is stuck into the ear. The women are covered with a single cloth about 12 feet long which is thrown twice round their left shoulder and then covers their loins, but not bound as among the Mahratta women. In the jungles the women wear only leaves. In every village there is a bothy for young men. They acknowledge the god of the Gonds called Badà Dewa or the great god who is inferior to the Supreme Being; also Bhawani and Banga Row. They do not seem to have any worship for the Supreme Being; but in honor of the great god, they go once a year into the jungle and under any kind of tree according to Appaya, they clean a spot with cowdung on which they offer a handful of rice burn ral (a kind of resin) and sacrifice a goat or fowl. A priest (sendi mangi pujari) of the great god goes round the buildings of a tract of country and asks the people on pain of cursing to give something as an offering for the great god, when each house gives about 2 or 3 annas. They carry sick people to Bhawani's temple which is placed on a chabutra (plat form) near a wall. From a transverse beam, which rests upon two uprights, there hangs a swing with a wooden box containing kuku (powderfor women i. e., Bhawani, making the mark on her forehead). This is covered up on the exposed side by a curtain. From each side hangs a chain of iron. Near it at one end is a lampstand. In front are iron rods one of which near the lamp is high. At the other end is a morchal [fan of peacock feathers]. Near the iron rods are wooden horses and horsemen. There is no idol in the cradle. They offer Bhowani a goat once a year with turmeric and ral. When a man is brought sick to the temple they place some turmeric and burn a lamp inside of the swing, and ask the goddess to make the sick man well.

On finishing the cutting of their crops, each family has a day of rejoicing, on which better food than usual is prepared, (their crops at Weiragad are of rice and jowari (millet) for which the ground is ploughed, they cut down and burn the jungles as among other tribes).

After a birth, the mother is separated for a month and treated as unclean—no one touches her and unless there are oldish daughters, she is obliged to cook for herself. When the period is ended her clothes are washed, and she is allowed to return to the family. The house consists of a mud wall with chupper (thatch).

Before marriage a man is sent to enquire about a bride. The parents of the bridegroom give for the bride, to her parents Rs. 10 or Rs. 20. The marriage which takes place between parties of the age of 16 to 20 is consumated in a day. In the morning about 7 a bower having been erected near the house of the bridegroom the two young people are led into it and made to stand up together, and from the top of the bower, dash on their heads a chatty (pitcher) of water. After which they put on dry clothes; when having been seated all the people put rice on their heads, and the marriage is completed by an exhortation from the parents. The whole day and night, they eat, drink and dance.

After a man is dead they kill and offer to the body a fowl. The corpse is then put on a tatty and placed on the shoulders of four young strong men. All the neighbours placing on the ground a handful of rice, call to mind their own dead forefathers, and turning to the corpse place on it some rice, remarking that now he has become god and adjure him, if death had came of god's will to accuse no one, but if death had been caused by witchcraft, to point out the guilty party. Sometimes it is said, there is such a pressure exerted on the shoulders of the bearers, that they are pushed forward and guided by the corpse to some house. The inmate is not seized at once, but if other three times the corpse returns after being taken some distance back, he is apprehended and expelled from the village. The corpse is then carried to a tree to which it is tied upright and burned. (Apaya does not know about burying) Then they begin to collect money for a funeral feast which is celebrated in a year or 18 months, from the time of the cremation. Repairing to the spot where the body was burned, they and the neighbourhood surround it with a tatty, (grass screen) in which they stick wooden spears, while a flag is fixed to the tree, and at a chupper (thatched roof) built for the purpose, they sacrifice a fowl. Thereafter they return to the house of the deceased, and having killed a goat, &c., make a feast, and if the deceased was poor they continue for a day, if rich for three days with music and dancing. The dancing is performed by a string of men on one side and of women on the other, approaching and receding. On that occasion, it is no sin for a virgin to be guilty of fornication, though it is carefully forbidden at other times. Six or seven years after they carry a stone or any remaining bones of the deceased to his original village, and set up the one and bury the other. Then they offer and sacrifice, and feast the villagers; when they conclude that the deceased has been joined to or absorbed in the great god.

In making salutation the Mades say juwar; and seem to live at peace among themselves. They are hospitable to strangers, and honest, and never go into a man's house in his absence. In the hot weather they remain in villages, but at the commencement of the monsoon, they separate to their various patches of cultivation, where they live night and day. If a married woman is convicted of adultery, she is killed by her husband. Both husband and wife may marry again.

Names of men, Mangu, Bheia, Karya, Bhuriya, Lalu, Somiya, Hiriya, Kutmanji, Tengana, Lebudu, Nawalu, Dasaru, Tiya, Pakaru, Warlu, Bursu, Newaru, Sonu.

Names of women, Rukmi, Lingi, Lidi Kali, Tomi, Mangi, Sukali, Masi. Langadi, Dumi, Semi.

Names of Marias on east frontier of Bustar supplied by Captain C. Elliot, from Bustar June 1857.

Men, Odhi, Gasiya, Magadu, Wakaru, Chirke, Mugul, Ramah, Gade, Boyal, Bodka, Kutha, Chirka, Surka, Judahal, Padaru, Sumaru, Dusmi, Sunal, Kadi, Dhodi, Higal, Adharu, Jaliyal, Madhal, Badal, Kacharu, Lakhmal, Gagaru, Bakal, Pichke, Dehla, Rupu, Malal, Gedi, Bikal, Gubada, Bira, Jhitku, Masial, Dorge, Mulal, Kodal, Chatu, Miral.

Women—Hinge, Judahi, Dukari, Rame, Gagade, Kani, Beishaki, Koeli, Ratnal, Rage, Sukadi, Kado.

The following information, regarding the marriage of the same Bustar people, was furnished with the above names. When they are going to celebrate a marriage, they sprinkle (asayet) on the goddess Mata, and the god Bhima and anoint them with oil and saffron which two last are carried from their deities to anoint the bride and bridegroom, who are then dressed in the usual coarse cloth of the country, and a yellow thread is tied round their wrist. Goats are killed and arrack is drunk, until the company are intoxicated. The bride and bridegroom also share in the liquor, Gondi songs are sung, accompanied with music. Arbours are constructed at the houses of both bride and bridegroom; and out of a vessel full of water hung up in the bride's arbour, water is sprinkled on the two and their clothes are tied together; and seven times they run round a pole erected in the mandawa (bower).

Description of the customs of the Made's as obtained by Virapa Venkatachalam, January 1858 from the Patel of Waigaum 4½ coss north of Adupalli (Arpeilli) who is a Made, though his people live more to the east.

Marriage among them does not take place till the age of maturity. The bridegroom is expected to give dowry to the parents of the bride, amounting sometimes to Rupees 20. At the marriage feast which lasts for four days, four pigs, two goats, rice, jowari, and daru (spirits) are consumed. There is much dancing among the boys and girls, to the sound of the tom-tom (drum). There is no bower, but the bridegroom and bride sit in the open air, near the bride-groom's father's door, surrounded by the spectators. Females, till their marriage, wear no covering over the upper part of their body.

As soon as a person expires, his eyes are closed and his body washed, which is then carried to the jungle and fastened upright by three ropes to the trunk of a tree. Firewood is brought and the body is burned amid the weeping of the relatives and loud wailing of the others.

Some worship 7, some 6, some 5, some 4 gods. They have one great festival at the beginning of the monsoon before they sow their crops, when they repair to a hill on the top of which they set up stones in a row to represent the number of their gods,—daub them with vermilion and present to them cakes, (puria) of riceflour, ghul (sugar) and ghi (clarified butter) on teak leaves, rice pulse and daru. They then kill a pig, a goat or sheep, and a cock, whose blood they sprinkle before their deities, and their bodies they take home along with the other offerings, to make merry at their homes. They then sow millet and maize.

Worship is performed before the marriage ceremony. In the morning at the door of the cow house, they set up a row of stones, which had been carefully washed, each about 4 inches high but one in the middle, to represent the great god being somewhat larger. They pass a thread round all, and put a sectarial mark (black.) made of charcoal and oil. (Their own marks are of a white colour formed from a white stone rubbed down). A lota (brass pot) is placed in front of the big god into which each married woman drops four cowries. They offer bade (cakes of black mung, onion, ghi and salt,) rice, kill a hen, burn incense, and sprinkle water three times, when they retire to the house, the cowries being the chief property of the chief man among them and the fowl being divided. At noon the marriage commences. Charcoal is mixed with a quantity of water and poured with a brass pot on the heads and bodies of the bride and bridegroom, after which they are dried and clean clothes being put on them, and the bridegroom having received from head man a dagger (katar) which he holds in his hand all the time from day to day, they are seated at the bridegroom's door with the corner of their garments knotted to each other and each receives a white mark on the forehead. Next, turmeric and water are mixed with lime in a brass plate, which is turned red by the lime and carried to the bride's three times as a present and thrown away on the road. The elder people are seated near, and music and dancing among the unmarried youths of both sexes are kept up beyond two or three hours. In the evening at the sound of the drum the people again assemble and a similar ceremony is gone through for a like period of time. Early next morning they assemble for similar purposes and before they part they have a meal together on pigs, &c., and daru (spirits). At noon when they assemble there is no repast or present; but in the evening and during the continuance of the marriage, all the people live at the expense of the bride's and bridegroom's parents.

The Mades have good features They eat anything including beef. They reckon themselves higher than Gonds and will not allow Mahars to touch them as the Gonds do. Mades and Gonds dont eat from each others hands, the Gonds and Kolamis at Manikgad will do so.

Eight coss to north of Weiragad is a hill called Sonsari. The Zemindar of the district (January 1853 when we visited Weiragad) was Kuja Bapoo of the Halba tribe. The inhabitants are Mades, from whose hands Raj Gonds will not eat. In the Made villages east of Weiragad there are generally less than five houses one sometimes being a Gowali's. They wear cloth round the loins, and a roomal or kerchief.

APPENDIX VIII.

Addendum.

Note by Editor.

While this work was passing through the Press I have received a copy of Mr. E. G. Man's work on Sonthalia and the Sonthals At the end of this work there is a brief Vocabulary of Sonthal words. Some of these are evidently of Sanskrit or Hindi origin. Others are evidently aboriginal. These latter do not at all correspond with the Gondi words as given in the present work. But some of them do correspond with the Muâsi words as given in the foregoing Vocabulary of the present work in the following instances:—

English.	Sonthal.	Muasi.
Nose	Mu	Mu
Ear	Lutur	Lutur
Hair	Up	Op
Belly	Lai	Lai
Star	Ipil	Epal
Fire	Sengel	Singal
Water	Da	Da
House	Ora	Uru
Dog	Seta	Sita

These are important points of similarity. On the other hand there are some words of importance regarding which no coincidence is to be found.

So far as I can make out, there does not seem to be any resemblance whatever between the Sonthal language and the Gondi in this part of India. Indeed it is to be expected that if the Sonthali resembles the Muâsi to any extent, it could hardly have any affinity with the Gondi, which is a different language.

Mr. Pandurang who at my request has been good enough to examine the point further, reports as follows.

" So many of the Sonthal words resemble the Muâsi, that I should suppose that the Sonthals and the Muâsis must either have originally formed one tribe, or else must subsequently have had intercourse with each other. After comparing the Sonthal Vocabulary with the Gondi I should infer that the Gonds and the Sonthals must have been distinct and separate aboriginal tribes."

R. T.